TESTIMO1

'Chock-full of riveting facts about Britain and its varied characters, this book will leave you incredulous. A masterpiece.'
– Dr Marcia Bennett (Professor of English Literature)

'I've lived in the Thames Valley all my life and I can honestly say that until I read this book, I never knew half of what was going on.'
– Dave Dean, Thames Valley resident

'Henley is the UK's murder capital? This is shocking to the core. I have lived in Henley most of my life!'
– Aiden Mallick

ABOUT THE AUTHOR

Thomas Newport is a rambler, artist and musician who likes to get right to the bottom of things. With a talent for understanding the deeper meanings behind everyday life, he tenaciously uncovers much that is hitherto unseen or uncelebrated. He lives in the United Kingdom. Visit www.youtararmy.co.uk for all the latest updates and information from the author.

BINOCLARITY

A travel along the length of the River Thames
and into the heart of the British psyche.

Thomas Newport

Youtararmy Press,
www.youtararmy.co.uk

Copyright: Thomas Newport 2018

The right of Thomas Newport to be identified as the author of this work has been asserted by him in accordance with the Copyright, Designs and Patents Act, 1988.

All rights reserved. No part of this publication may be reproduced, stored in or introduced into a retrieval system, or transmitted in any form, or by any means (electronic, mechanical, photocopying, recording or otherwise) without the prior written permission of the publisher. Any person who does any unauthorised act in relation to this publication may be liable to criminal prosecution and civil claims for damages.

Front cover artwork by Elissa Milsome,
www.elissamilsome.co.uk

A Youtararmy Press Publication
www.youtararmy.co.uk

DEDICATION

For my beloved family who are all truly remarkable.

Contents

Preface ix

1. Observations on a People 1
2. Standing out from the Crowd 21
3. Into Eccentrica..35
4. Broken Britain? 49
5. The Source (The Journey Begins).............................65
6. Minted 81
7. Tales from the Riverbank..97
8. Dreaming Spires 119
9. Thames Valley Capital 139
10. 300 Square Miles of Murder 177
11. The Entertainers 209
12. The Vicar of Bray...249
13. Metropolis...271
14. Into The Sea 289

Preface

Crouching down in the undergrowth and watching them zoom past doesn't come naturally to me. I'm not and never have been an army type, but I guess modern man has spent much of his time crouched in the undergrowth watching something. My focus is firmly fixed on the drivers in each of these vehicles. Exactly who are these people? More to the point, who are we, the British? These thoughts clutter my mind as I haul myself up from the undergrowth. My attention is briefly redirected to my knees: I've never been a fan of crouching.

And so my journey begins. I have decided that in order to help answer that question 'who are we, the British?' I will be walking along the 184-mile length of the Thames Towpath from the river's source near Cirencester in the Cotswolds down to the Thames Barrier in East London. Including some detours along the way, my walk should be over 250 miles in total. 'Ah, but that journey only takes place in England,' I hear you protest. Do not worry, dear reader, I assure you I will be looking at Great Britain as a whole as well as the particular areas I travel through.

The British see themselves as a special people. After all, it was the British who created the largest empire the world has ever seen. In 2016 we only numbered just over 65 million, making us the world's 23rd most populous nation. Most of us inhabit little more than a small island but, as islands go, Britain isn't actually that small. In fact, Britain is the ninth largest island on a planet that contains many thousands of islands. It is our language that still, for the time being at least, remains dominant throughout the world and our heritage that is certainly one of the world's most important.

It was the British who pioneered the Industrial Revolution, leading to rapid advancement and helping to propel Britain into an almost invincible world power. Britain has been responsible for the invention of many of the modern world's most useful innovations. The reflecting telescope, seed drill, toothbrush, steam engine, tin can, electric motor, cement, passenger railway, telephone, stainless steel, jet engine, carbon fibre, world wide web, and the wind-up radio are just a few of the many and varied innovations to have been created by Britons. All this from a nation that doesn't even lay claim to one hundredth of the world's population.

There may well be an aloofness present in the British character which one could say is only inevitable when you consider our exceptionally illustrious past. The British are a proud, individual, and naturally aggressive people who frequently reflect on past glories. We are proud of our history and heritage. There still exists that much-valued spirit of 'it can be done'. They said an iron ship would never float, but on 29th December 1860, HMS Warrior was launched and became the world's first iron-hulled warship - one of many firsts in innovation that may well be expected from the world's first industrialised nation.

There are, of course, many other nations that can claim to have helped shape the modern world in profound ways. Some threatened to attain greater world domination than that of the British. Perhaps Britain just got lucky and then grasped the new opportunities presented to it with both hands. As I will discuss later in this book, the ways that luck can affect a person's life or career can be profound.

Whilst on my journey, I expect to encounter a national character that reflects the grandiosity of our past; I also know that it is counterbalanced by a sense of decline. Agriculture and then heavy industry built Britain, but both of these industries now seem to be viewed by many as being greatly diminished. Our position in the world was perhaps best summed up by the distinguished German Director of the London School of Economics, Ralf Dahrendorf. A committed Anglophile, he wrote: 'Like every other developed country, Britain is up against vexing economic and political problems. Unlike others, Britain seems to pay a price for its own, very special history: the burden of having invented the Industrial Revolution; the Empire and its loss; the conflicts of class and of race. One can understand those who fear for the country's future.' (On Britain, British Broadcasting Corporation, 1982). These words were written well over 30 years ago. They may well have been written yesterday.

The question of Britain's future became more pertinent than ever on Thursday 23rd June 2016 when the UK voted to leave the European Union. The vote, won by a narrow margin (51.9 per cent voted in favour of leaving), caused havoc amongst the main political parties, not least Labour, whom it looked like might cease to exist. Prime Minister David Cameron stepped down, and the new Prime Minister, Theresa May, was sworn into office soon after.

In 2014, a record 34.4 million visitors from overseas came to Britain, and they spent a record £21.8 billion here.

Preface

Much of what brings them here is to do with our history and heritage. Many others may be visiting to experience the power Britain still maintains as a centre for innovative cultural trends and cutting edge technology. Britain is the world's sixth largest economy. No matter what some of the media say about a 'threepenny bit' military, we have the third highest military expenditure in the world. We also maintain a hugely expensive nuclear deterrent. In global power terms, Britain is still very powerful.

One of the other issues that seems to creep into the British media with alarming regularity is the notion of a 'Broken Britain'. From rampant yob drunkenness through to a high divorce rate and an 'out of control benefits culture', it would seem Britain is being dragged down under its own weight. To what extent does this 'Broken Britain' exist? I wish to discover more. From my own experiences, I know that problems certainly do exist, but they are sometimes exaggerated by a media always clutching around for new stories with which to shock us. After all, the shock tactic seems to me to be the most effective approach any news media organisation looking to increase their profits can take.

If Britain is in terminal decline, then it is certainly not affecting everyone. Britain has over 250,000 millionaires, and the number is fast rising. We know that this towering wealth collected by the few hides an ugly truth: Britain is the most economically and socially polarised it has ever been in almost a hundred years. A higher number of people now live below the poverty line than ever before. In today's society it still holds true that who you know is potentially better than what you know. Just as in the 17th century, when Isaac Newton allegedly used his power and influence to manipulate and hold back the incredible talent of his less well-connected contemporary and adversary Robert Hooke, a coterie of influential Britons hold many others firmly in their place through a string of interconnecting networks that are as effective as a protection racket. My intrigue demands that I explore these darker elements of our society.

We often view corruption as an issue mostly associated with the developing world, but of course it exists in abundance in Western nations too. Elements of Western governments, and some of their people, know they have to deploy corruption sophisticated enough to elude the free press and the scrutiny of a media savvy general public. And elude the public it sure does. On my travels, I will uncover some corruption allegations and areas where I feel the Great British Public are being, or have been, hoodwinked. I implore you to stand up for what you feel is unjust. I truly believe that we in the much wealthier West have a duty to lead the world in the effort to stamp out corruption. We are being watched, and I fear that we are setting a bad example.

I plan a journey that will take me into the many corners of Britishness. I want to chink glasses with the movers and shakers and crash plastic cider bottles together with the tramps. I want to see the 'general public' and figure out exactly who this familiar sounding group of people are. I want to peer into the Sloane Set and see life through their rose-tinted spectacles. I want to taste the danger like Iggy Pop. Be 'The Passenger' in Pop's famous song.

I plan to uncover many of the foibles and peculiarities of the British. My travels will take me into the middle of a drunken fight, into the heart of quintessential British traditions, and into the warm hearth of that famous British humour. I will make some surprising discoveries about things that I have been told are 'best kept quiet', and my intrigue leads me to uncover the full implications of an alarming spate of murders that took place right in the central part of my travels through the Thames Valley. But for now, I've just got to brush myself down. I'm only just getting started on my journey.

The population density of Britain is very high, and England has become the most overcrowded major country in Europe. You are never very far from an urbanised area throughout most of Britain. Our roads, seas and skies are crammed full of transport vehicles. Heathrow, just outside West London, is one of the world's busiest airports. The English Channel is one of the world's busiest shipping zones, and virtually everyone will tell you how intolerably busy Britain's roads are. Housing is in short supply and has become a major issue, one that has seen rioting in East London as people are forced out of the city entirely because housing prices have shot up so rapidly. Population pressures in the south east of England mean that Britain has less drinkable water available per head of population than many Middle Eastern nations. There can be found a generally held perception among the populace that Britain can now be considered 'full'.

This book has been written through my own eyes, and it is about my own views, interactions, and experiences. I am not attempting some academic overview of the British people or our lands. Moreover, I am embarking upon a celebration of life in Britain, albeit furnished with pain as well as pleasure. There may be times when I don't like what I see. This book isn't full of praises for Britain; it is not intended as some kind of travel brochure. There will be certain individuals that I may praise, criticise, or even be ambivalent to. Whilst I have not set out to be deliberately detrimental or rude to certain people, some readers will no doubt find some of my opinions quite frank. I hope you will find this book informative as well as humorous.

Finally, I would like to thank all of the people who have helped me with this book. The people who spoke to me candidly about everything from swingers in the genteel Thames-side village of Wargrave to the changing demographics of East London. I would like to thank my long-suffering friend Toby who helped by driving me to locations some distance away from the Thames Towpath. I would like to thank all the B&B owners who put me up for the night. I would also like to extend my thanks to all the farmers who unwittingly had me sleeping for the night in their fields or woodlands, and to the great people of the Home Guard, whose fantastically strong defensive pill box I slept in on one occasion! For more information about the author, latest news, and any upcoming book releases, please visit www.youtararmy.co.uk

CHAPTER 1

Observations on a People

'The British nation is unique in this respect. They are the only people who like to be told how bad things are, who like to be told the worst.' These are the words of Winston Churchill, and they probably help us to explain why so many Britons think their nation is in terminal decline. For me, the answer can be found in perception. I think the British deliberately expect too much and love a good moan. What other reason could lie behind the fact that more convertible cars are sold in Britain than any other European nation except Germany, yet no other nation seems to talk about the changeable nature of their weather more than the British do?

Before I get started on my journey along the Thames, I want to spend a short while focusing on the British as a whole. In this chapter, I will talk about our general traits before moving on to some remarkable Britons, or those that may be perceived to be remarkable at least. I will then look at that quintessential British trait: eccentricity, before moving on to whether the notion of 'Broken Britain' has any merit.

If you listen to what the media says then it would seem the British spend more time than any other people thinking about what makes them who they are. Survey after survey has been carried out by the British press to uncover what we're all about. When the population of Britain hit 60 million in July 2005, *The Sun* newspaper asked us in a huge headline 'Who are we?' as if they were waiting for that magical number to be reached before feeling that they should ask. The main focus of the article was on ethnicity, religion, and birth rate. An article in *The Telegraph* in November 2008 focused on our apparent national attributes; 'Moaning, drinking and queuing are what makes us British' the rather depressing headline shouted out. Any reader of *The Daily Mail* would tell you that focusing on the British, or at least what lesser people we have become, could almost be the raison d'etre for the paper itself.

In 2008, the global research company OnePoll.com surveyed 5000 British adults in an attempt to find out what makes Britain unique as a nation. The top ten results in order from number one first were: talking about the weather, great at queueing, sarcasm, watching soaps, getting drunk, a love of bargains, a love of curtain twitching, a stiff upper lip, a love of all television and moaning. Despite the negativity of many of the comments, a spokesman for OnePoll.com said that 'Britons are still extremely proud of their country'. He continued, 'What this poll demonstrates really well, is how proud we are to be British; more than two-thirds of respondents said they felt honoured to be part of this country.' Other uplifting suggestions included: gossiping with neighbours over the garden fence; a soothing cup of tea to ease worries; eating meat and two veg; looking uncomfortable on the dance floor; a clever sense of humour; the ability to laugh at ourselves; being overly polite; a love of rambling through the countryside; irony, and achieving against all odds.

In conversation with others about the British, I find similar ideas are brought up: a preoccupation with the weather; a love of humour; a stiff upper lip; a reluctance to engage with one another; an obsession with queuing; not complaining about poor services; complaining about bad governments but not doing anything about it; bravery in the face of adversity, and being intensely private but extremely nosey at the same time.

The British also seem to have an obsession with giving everything a name; a well-maintained class system; a creative people; a gloomy people; a well-developed sense of one's individuality; a support for the underdog; a rudeness to foreigners; a love of alcohol; a cynicism not just of politicians but of practically anyone who has done well for themselves; eccentricity, and an ability to be contradictory.

Some traits have become world-renowned. Although the British often laugh at themselves for their preoccupation with the weather it is worth noting that, whilst Britain does not experience regular extreme weather which causes so much death and destruction in so many other parts of the world, it does have an incredibly changeable climate. It may be well worth asking about the weather as an overcast sky can give way to perfect blue skies and scorching temperatures - and vice versa - in a matter of minutes throughout so much of the British summer.

I believe talking about the weather also has a lot to do with the British reluctance to engage with each other. It is an icebreaker with a stranger that does not involve prying into anything too personal. Once the ice is broken, two strangers can go back to silence knowing that it feels a little more comfortable in each other's presence now. In terms of a naturally contradictory nature, I think it was the comedian Jack Dee who summed it up best by saying 'There's two things the British hate: Fascists and foreigners!' As for other supposed national pastimes, I find them a bit vexing;

reference is often made to a 'British love of queuing'. However, my question to this one is: how do they avoid queuing in other countries? Why does it seem like such a British speciality?

Perhaps one of the best ways to find out about Britishness is to seek out the views of the British themselves. Looking at an internet blog on the subject, I find a lively discussion: 'I'd say Britain's greatest asset has always been its adaptability,' Jimbo writes. He continues, 'its adaptability to absorb other cultures and pick out what serves us best and put it to use has led to an environment which has fostered an inventiveness.' Aurora comments, 'We have the best sense of humour in the world. We're a social people.' Other comments are not, however, so positive. 'The world famous stiff upper lip,' decries Apekool. Someone by the name of Euhmeris writes, 'I wouldn't waste my time finding what Britain represents now. I admire what it was!' The outlandish sounding JD Spoonworthy tells us that none of these comments are correct, but he or she fails to add any further ideas to the discussion.

In regards to British tolerance, the American author, Bill Bryson, has suggested that communism would have fared better had it been tested by the British rather than by the Russians. His humorous reasoning for this is based on our national character traits which he states are second nature to the British: a like of going without, a greatness at pulling together in the face of adversity, and we will queue patiently for long periods and are happy to accept rationing. He has also suggested that we are comfortable with faceless bureaucracies and we are tolerant of dictatorships, making reference to Margaret Thatcher's government!

England and Scotland remained as separate countries up

until the 1707 Treaty of Union which created a United Kingdom with a single parliament. The Kingdom of England already included Wales, but in 1801 Ireland merged to form The United Kingdom of Great Britain and Ireland. In 1922, most of Ireland succeeded from the United Kingdom and the state was renamed as the United Kingdom of Great Britain and Northern Ireland. For the purposes of this book, whenever I refer to Britain or Great Britain, I am making reference to the United Kingdom of Great Britain and Northern Ireland.

Scottish and Welsh people are more likely to say that they are from their respective countries than from Great Britain. Years of alleged oppression and aloofness by the English have perhaps left their mark. The Scots held a national referendum on independence in September 2014, which saw the 'yes' campaign defeated with 55.3 per cent of voters voting for 'no independence' and 44.7 per cent voting for it. A passionate Scottish independence quest looks set to remain for many years to come. It has certainly had a boost since Britain declared its intention to exit from the EU in the 2016 Referendum.

With the Scottish Parliament and Welsh Assembly, England is the only part of Great Britain with no devolved assembly or parliament, although there has been a recent push for the creation of an English Assembly. For many years, the English identity lay strangely suppressed. The country's flag was seldom seen, having been allegedly appropriated by the far right. St George's Day was not marked by any celebration of particular significance. Recent years have seen a resurgence in the English identity, and the cross of St George is now seen much more frequently.

One thing that is for certain about the nations that make

up the Union of Great Britain – England, Scotland, Wales and Northern Ireland – is that the English have always had the most dominant role. The English always had the upper hand in the Union, not only because it was they who created it, but because the capital city, London, lies in England. London is not a capital city like so many others around the world in as much as it is just the Government administration centre; London is effectively a city-state. So much business and administration happens there that it effectively dominates and often overshadows almost everywhere else in Great Britain. London was the world's first mega-city, and today over eight and a half million people live in the Greater London area.

The increasing urbanisation of London and other British cities is part of a worldwide trend which saw more people living in the world's cities than rural areas for the first time in the year 2000. Along with New York, London is the world's most important centre of financial services, and it boasts arguably the world's greatest ethnic diversity. In terms of the population of Greater London, its nearest British rivals come nowhere close.

It is important to note that within England itself, all is not harmonious. There is the 'North-South divide' – an invisible line on the map that denotes much cultural difference and economic disparity. This divide is widely agreed to cut across the English Midlands from the northern Welsh border north of Birmingham right across to Hull on the east coast. It also broadly encompasses the difference in voting habits with the South voting largely Conservative, and the North voting predominantly for Labour (although there are notable exceptions – London, for example).

The English North-South divide has increased as

northern industries have died out, whether due to increased competition from abroad or closures that are widely seen as politically motivated such as the closure of many coal pits in the 1980s. On a British level, the North-South divide is also perpetuated by a lack of private investment extending much further out than southern England.

Northern accents from Great Britain have largely been absent from many areas of British media broadcasting such as television and radio. A more recent trend has seen an effort to reverse this with the employment of many more presenters with regional accents. The British Broadcasting Corporation has recently undergone a huge decentralisation from London, taking many jobs up north to a new base of MediaCityUK at Salford, Greater Manchester.

People from Northern England and the rest of Great Britain are regarded by many as being more friendly and community-spirited than the Southerners (in particular the South-Eastern Southerners!), who are often regarded as emotionally cold, aloof, and not particularly friendly. Stereotypes of Northern people often portray a hardier character than their southern counterparts. A friend of mine from 'up North' put this view succinctly to me one time after sharing a few drinks at a bar: 'Northern twats versus Southern poofs!' was his summing up of the situation, and when everyone had had a few too many beers the phrase was repeated out, mantra-like, as if it were some ancient battle cry! One thing for certain though is that whatever side of the North-South divide you are on, there remain key traits shared by all Britons, and one that I think is worthy of celebration is our creativity.

Britain's musical heritage is celebrated around the world. Popular music and British culture have become greatly enmeshed. Britain has borrowed musical styles from America such as the blues, built upon them, and then exported them back to America and the rest of the world. Few bands are held in higher esteem around the world than The Beatles or The Rolling Stones. It is interesting to note that huge American bands such as The Beach Boys and Aerosmith actually modelled themselves on these British acts. The broadcaster and writer Jeremy Paxman has commented that he believes it is the British weather that has forced teenagers to stay indoors in winter instead of going to the beach or skiing, and this has made music an attractive pastime. I think his observation has some merit.

According to the British Council, Great Britain's international organisation for educational opportunities and cultural relations, Great Britain has the largest creative sector in the European Union. In terms of GDP, it is the largest in the world, and according to UNESCO, it is the most successful exporter of cultural goods and services in the world, even beating the United States. One creative area we have always excelled at is the written word. Indeed, Britain arguably has more famous writers than any other country. From Chaucer through to Shakespeare, Austen, Dickens, Peter Ackroyd and JK Rowling, Britain has always been a commander of the written word on the world stage. More books are published per capita in Britain than in any other country around the world.

Britain has more newspapers per head than almost any other nation on earth. *The Sun* and *The Daily Mail* are the biggest circulation newspapers and both are predominantly right-wing. *The Sun* is an easy to digest paper broadly viewed as being more of a working-class newspaper. Its preoccupation with sleazy sex stories sits largely at odds with its allegedly proud upholding of family values. On the other hand, *The Daily Mail* is regarded as a bastion of the middle class, despite the fact that it largely exploits this role and becomes more a terrifier of the middle class. In the views and opinions of this paper, the British middle class appears to be under constant threat whether it be from immigrants, Europhiles, paedophiles and possibly even your next-door neighbour ('but they appeared so normal!').

Whilst a feebly controlled immigration policy has caused much consternation in Britain over recent years, and has certainly set much of the public against immigration, at a time when Europe faces the greatest wave of immigration since the Second World War due to the Syrian civil war, one wonders how much mileage can be gotten from newspapers and the media trawling up the same panicked subject of immigration so regularly. However, if being frightened is what so many of us appear to enjoy then with mammoth sales it doesn't look like *The Daily Mail* is going to stop shocking Britain's middle-class readers anytime soon. The philosopher and *Guardian* writer, Julian Baggini, has come up with a formula he uses to express a link between *The Sun* and *The Daily Mail* newspapers: *The Sun* + money + fear = *The Daily Mail*.

Of all the British newspapers, the most toxic one can no doubt have been *The News Of The World*. The overzealous and downright illegal activities of *The News of the World's* 'investigations' which famously included phone hacking are what led to the closing of the newspaper in July 2011 and the memorable humbling of media mogul Rupert Murdoch. Murdoch's British newspaper operation was centred around sleazy headlines and the manipulation of British politics and police. Having such a powerful figure pretty much determining the outcome of elections produced a parliament of politicians living in fear and a British people feeling somewhat conned out of their own democracy.

Whilst British newspapers have largely seen their circulations dropping as more people go online for their news, television remains popular, and radio is positively thriving. British television is awash with reality shows with one of the main ones being *Big Brother*. The very fact that these shows hire psychologists to interview their own contestants has illustrated that the production companies are well aware of the risks. Other shows like *The Only Way Is Essex* have made millionaires of their stars. These shows tie into our celebrity-obsessed culture and have helped give rise to the relatively recent phenomenon of 'being famous for fame's sake'.

Simon Cowell's popular show *The X Factor* has a cruel obsession with ridiculing people of dubious talent. Whilst many relished in the schadenfreude of laughing at less fortunate people being vilified by Cowell and co, few members of the public questioned the fact that these people had been approved to go through to the next stage by Cowell's selection team, thus setting them up for a humiliating fall. When Andy Warhol said that; 'in the future, everyone will be world-famous for 15 minutes', he fully understood what drives people to seek the limelight. I cannot imagine many people who would enjoy the throwaway culture and overnight success and failure offered by the reality television and the Internet of today more than Warhol.

Out of all media formats, television can be seen as the one having the greatest impact on people. Whilst offering an incredibly powerful communications tool, television has been criticised since the days it first became widespread. Professor George Gerbner, Dean of the Annenberg School of Communications at the University of Pennsylvania, was a pioneer of Cultivation Theory. Cultivation Theorists started to study how watching television may influence viewers' ideas of what the everyday world is like. Whilst much of Cultivation Theory centred around the analysis of the effects of too much violence on television, a contemporary conspiracy theorist might put the idea forth that today's British television with its preponderance of pro-entrepreneurial shows such as *Dragon's Den, The Apprentice, The Secret Millionaire* and *Tycoon* might be orchestrated to change Britain's traditional cynicism of the wealthy and successful and help earn the government more tax revenue!

Since 1967, Gerbner concentrated on analysing the effect of prevailing images on American television with their prevalence in real life. He reported that the TV world was much more violent than the everyday world and demonstrated that about 12 per cent of all males on US television held law enforcement jobs whilst in the real world it was only one per cent. Gerbner demonstrated that such distortions on TV helped increase the amount of crime people perceived to be happening in the real world.

The British have often had a contradictory viewpoint in relation to mainland Europe and the USA. Whilst some Brits talk in a disdainful way of our European counterparts – whether it be jokes about German military conquests, French garlic sellers or hairy continental female armpits, we aspire to the family values and healthy lifestyles of most Europeans. Our roads are crammed full of German, French, Spanish, and Italian cars. Our shopping baskets are full of French cheeses, continental wines, and condiments, and we flock on holiday in droves to the mainland: 17 million of us a year to France and 12 million a year to Spain. Compare this to less than four million visits to the USA. All of this lies in stark contrast to our relationship with the USA. Our 'special relationship' appears to transcend the fact that the British generally regard American gastronomy as a bit of a joke, their cars a gas-guzzling novelty, and many of us Brits do not seem too interested in their attitudes to family and work life either.

The Internet has emerged with such revolutionary gusto that almost overnight all the other media formats suddenly became labelled 'old media' as if a giant stamp had rained down on their appeals, condemning them to a slow death. The reality is that the Internet allows people seemingly limitless information on demand, so it was always going to be the clear winner as a media format. Despite this, one in eight adult Britons has never used the Internet, and it has been estimated that 60 per cent of Britons over the age of 70 have never used the Internet. With banks and post offices closing down, there is a real risk that many people, mostly from the older generations, are going to become excluded from society even further. As it has done to much of the rest of the world, the Internet has changed so much about Britain. I'll be looking at the Internet, some of the influential people behind parts of it and how it has changed modern Britain, later on during my journey.

When it comes to how the British spend their time, the Office for National Statistics has got the answer. Their Adult Engagement in Culture and Sport published the result of a survey of 14000 adults for the year 2009/2010. According to this, 45-50 per cent of Britons visited a museum or gallery in the last 12 months; 75-80 per cent of Britons participated in art or art events; 70 per cent of Britons made a visit to a heritage site in the last 12 months, and 90 per cent of Britons have been involved in a sport or physical activity in the last four weeks.

Britain has a wealth of historical treasures and art from our own lands and others stacked into a whole gamut of museums and collections. The British Museum and Tate Modern each have upwards of five million visitors per year. The National Gallery and the Natural History Museum have annual visitor numbers just below five million each. London is home to the world's largest theatre district. Popular pastimes range from cooking - Britain seems to have become the world's celebrity chef heaven – or hell - to rambling. The Ramblers (formerly the Ramblers Association) has around 123,000 members, and scores of Britons can be seen out walking or hiking throughout the British countryside on the weekends.

In 2011, the number of bike owners reached 13 million, and cycling alone generated three billion pounds towards the economy. A love of British history and heritage can be seen by way of the astronomical rise of the National Trust. Set up in 1895 by three Victorian philanthropists to look after the nation's voluminous collection of stately homes, gardens, parks, ancient monuments and areas of stunning countryside, the National Trust's membership has rocketed from one million in 1981 to a staggering 3.6 million in 2011, making it one of the most popular paid membership organisations in the world. The most visited National Trust place, Wakehurst Place Garden, attracts almost 450,000 people per annum. Not bad considering it is a place that the majority of Britons have probably never heard of!

Britain is a nation of obsessive collectors. We collect

everything from postage stamps, old cigarette cards, vinyl records and toys to militaria and bottle tops. If you can name it, then we collect it! We are also a nation of anoraks! Birdwatching, train, plane, and truck spotting remain popular and are particularly British. Of all the spotting groups in Great Britain, the RSPB is probably the largest. This group, which promotes the spotting of all wildlife, not just birds, has amassed over one million members and can call on an army of over 12,200 volunteers. So bizarre was the idea to the Greek authorities in 2000 that Britons were watching planes and not spying at an airport in Kalamata, that sentences of up to three years imprisonment were handed out by the Greek courts. The plane enthusiast group which comprised twelve Britons and two Dutch were following the movements of NATO warplanes, and it was their scribbling of notes that landed them in trouble. A diplomatic struggle ensued as the two NATO countries of Britain and Holland tried to rescue their nationals from incarceration. Lawyers representing the plane spotters had to explain the hobby to the Greek authorities as plane spotting is not a widely recognised pursuit in their country. After a protracted battle with the Greek authorities, the spying charges were dropped.

Driving through British towns and seeing the huge numbers of fast food chains, burger and kebab shops and fish and chip shops, one cannot fail to realise that another British obsession is food. Many visitors to Britain might actually redefine that: not just food, but sometimes bad food and big portions of it! We British have a slightly strange attitude to food. We are generally more concerned with quantity over quality. Those vinyl letters that spell out 'All you can eat for £4.99' will probably be more appealing to many Britons than the exacting quality of the food on the menu. Just in case you were wondering, during their lifetime, the average Briton munches their way through 10,354 bars of chocolate, four and a half cows, 1,201 chickens and 5,272 apples. To help this all go down, they will guzzle their way through 10,351 pints of beer, 1,694 bottles of wine and 16,000 pints of milk. Still feeling hungry or thirsty?

As a creator of many of the world's sports including football, badminton, cricket, rugby, lawn tennis, snooker, squash, the list goes on ... you'd think the British would have an obsession with attempting to master them. However, this is simply not the case, and our ability to play many sports at an inconsistent level seems to have become a bane of being British. Just why the British have taken a laissez-faire attitude to winning is not well known. Perhaps it has something to do with our legendary support for the underdog.

Along with the mainstream sports played by the British, there are sports so wacky and eccentric that they could only have ever been dreamt up by the British. Take bog snorkelling, cheese chasing, black pudding throwing, The World Coal Carrying Championships, coracle racing, and lawn-mower racing. These don't seem like the type of sports that might get taken up abroad overnight. One suspects that these sports are perhaps invented for one cold and calculating reason only: we are alone in these sports, and we are, therefore, the only ones who can win at them! However, even our most wackiest sports are now attracting an international following!

One of the most popular eccentric British sports is cheese chasing. The tradition of cheese rolling here is at least 200 years old. The most famous event is the Cooper's Hill Cheese-Rolling and Wake held on the Spring Bank Holiday at Cooper's Hill in the Cotswolds near Gloucester. Although the event is traditionally for the people in the nearby village of Brockworth, it attracts spectators and competitors from all around the world. The event is beautifully simple. A seven pound round of Double Gloucester is rolled from the top of the very steep hill. About a second later, the Master of Ceremonies gives the command and the competitors race after the cheese which can reach speeds of over 70 miles an hour. The first person to cross the line at the bottom wins the cheese. In 2009, the event attracted 15,000 spectators, and the ensuing mayhem on local roads and the prospect of damage to field fences led to the event being cancelled in 2010 and 2011. Since then it has carried on in an unofficial form.

Of all sports in Britain, the most popular is undeniably football. Britain's Premier League is the most watched and most lucrative football league in the world. The 2013-14 season alone generated a turnover of over £3 billion. Kicking a ball with the feet has been happening for thousands of years but football, as we know it today, has its roots in Britain. Chaucer referred to football in *The Canterbury Tales*, and the first description of basic rules of the game can be found in Francis Willoughby's *Book of Sports* circa 1660. It can be arguably considered that football is Britain's greatest export. The 'beautiful game' is played all over the world with almost every nation in the world having a national football team. Football is by far the most popular sport throughout much of Europe, Latin America, and Asia. It has become increasingly popular and high profile in North America and Australasia too.

It was the British who introduced football to many parts of the world for the first time. The first recorded game of football outside Europe occurred in Argentina in 1867 and involved English workers in the country. On October 26th, 1863, the Football Association was founded in London. Club football was now established, and it wasn't long before playing against international teams became an attractive idea. The first international match was England vs Scotland in November 1872. The game ended in a disappointing 0-0. In recent years, the sport has been criticised for becoming highly monetised. Despite the fact that football is widely regarded as a working man's game, the cost of following the sport has become prohibitively expensive for many.

British football has a long, ugly and unfortunate association with hooliganism. The violence became more widespread in the 1960s, and so great in England that a term was even invented for it: 'the English disease'. Seeing English football hooligans wreaking havoc in the picturesque centres of many European towns and cities became a common sight throughout much of the 1980s and 1990s. Many of the hooligans had apparently little love for the beautiful game. The association between football and violence in Britain actually goes back a long way. Medieval football had few rules, and games often descended into major disputes and riots. In 1314, the Lord Mayor of London banned the sport declaring 'There is great noise in the city caused by hustling over large footballs in the fields of the public.'

Perhaps it should come as no surprise at all that violence might become associated with various sports. After all, most sports have their origins in the violent but necessary act of hunting. The world-renowned zoologist and people watcher Desmond Morris has commented on how sporting activities are essentially derived from hunting behaviour. He sees the modern footballer as a member of a hunting pack who, if he scores, enjoys the hunter's triumph of killing his prey.

Morris points out that when our ancient ancestors effectively abandoned over a million years' worth of co-operative hunting in favour of farming about ten thousand years ago, the hunting skills and hunting urges remained and demanded new outlets. Blood sports became popular where the chase became exposed as an end in itself. Cockfighting, bear fighting and dog fighting were introduced as gruesome spectator sports, and the Romans brought the hunt to the masses in the city. Thousands could watch close-quarters prey killing in huge arenas. The Spanish invented their own spectacle: the bullfight.

The final transformation came about with the lack of need to eat the prey. Winning took over as a symbolic killing, and the Ancient Greek solution was athletics. Field sports such as track running, jumping, and throwing provided the thrill of the chase, and the winner would be declared as the symbolic killer. Morris points out how the all-important hunter's action of aiming became more dominant in the world of modern sport than anything else. The best examples of this can be seen in the sports of javelin throwing, darts, and archery.

The popularity of sports today can be seen as a direct result of mankind moving far away from his hunting heritage. This is particularly true for adult males, most of whom do not even experience much physical behaviour in the workplace in Britain anymore. Adult males in today's Britain are more likely to be sat at a computer than working in a field or a labour intensive factory. This might go some way to explaining the increased violence and drunkenness all too apparent in British towns and cities. Morris believes that the more successful males in society have less demand for the pseudo-hunt that is the world of sport. He believes this is because the successful male is much closer to the hunting pattern. His work involves the hunt for ideas, the capturing of contracts, and the aims of his organisation.

Before I move on to the next chapter, I thought it best if I leave you with some statistics about the Brits to mull over. A baby is born every 40 seconds in Britain, and someone dies every 60 seconds. The people of Britain are living longer. The number of centenarians in Great Britain has more than quadrupled from 2600 in 1981 to 11600 in 2009. This number is set to reach 80,000 by mid-2033. The average UK house price is £286,000, and the average salary is £26,500. The average British female will be 27 years old when she has her first child, and she will spend an average of eight years of her life shopping. The average British man will be 30 years old when he gets married and 39 if he gets divorced. The average cost of raising a child in Britain from birth until the age of 21 is £230,000, and don't go thinking that you can escape all these burdensome statistics by burying yourself in your work: one in four Britons say that they hate their workmates!

Great Britain has the world's sixth largest economy and a total net worth of £7.6 trillion at the end of 2013. £4.7 trillion of this value is in housing, making it by far Britain's most valuable asset. To put this differently, it has been estimated that Windsor Castle alone is worth one billion pounds. According to this, Britain is worth 7600 Windsor Castles. Well, they say an Englishman's home is his castle! Of the British government's estimated 2015 spending of over £759 billion, £110 billion was on welfare, £138 billion on health, £89 billion on education and £45 billion was spent on defence. Worryingly, £47 billion was spent on debt interest. The 2008 recession hit Britain very hard, and the recovery has been slow and painful. It remains to be seen how Britain's economy will fare in the years after it has left the European Union.

Despite the efforts of recent governments, social inequality has spiralled to levels not seen since the 1930s. Recent years have seen Britain's poorest fall further behind whilst the richest have moved further ahead. According to the Equality Trust, Britain's richest 10 per cent of households hold 45 per cent of all wealth. The poorest 50 per cent, by contrast, own just 8.7 per cent. According to Oxfam, one in five Britons lives below our official poverty line. Inner London has the greatest division of wealth, having the highest proportion of people on a low income and the highest proportion of people on a high income within Britain. Indeed, London epitomises the social polarisation in Britain today.

CHAPTER 2

Standing out from the Crowd

In 2002, the BBC conducted a public poll to discover the 100 greatest Britons. The top ten greats, as revealed by this poll, were: Oliver Cromwell, Horatio Nelson, John Lennon, Queen Elizabeth I, Isaac Newton, William Shakespeare, Charles Darwin, Diana, Princess of Wales, Isambard Kingdom Brunel and, in top position, Winston Churchill. It is perhaps rather unsurprising that Winston Churchill reached the top. It is also great to see an engineer, a scientist, and a biologist in the top ten. If Winston Churchill could be said to have spoken for the nation at one time, it could also be said that it was Isambard Kingdom Brunel who built much of our nation. Both these two people sum up what is truly great about being British. They represent a 'can do' attitude, struggled against adversity, and both were the builders of bridges, albeit in different guises.

It is also interesting to note that there is not one single living person in this list. In fact, the highest ranking living Briton at the time the list was published was Margaret Thatcher in 16th position. Channel 4 ran a tongue-in-cheek response to this poll with their own 100 worst Britons list. Margaret Thatcher landed in the number one spot, thus showing her ability to polarise people. All of the Beatles featured in the top 100 except for poor old Ringo Starr - so carries on the widely held perception of the drummer being at the bottom of the band fame list! I believe that drummers have the real short straw in music; not only do they have the most kit to pack away at the end of the night, but they are also the butt of many jokes. On being asked how many members are in his rock band, my uncle can often be overheard saying 'three musicians and a drummer!'

There are, however, problems with these types of lists. The fact of the matter is, it is mostly only those people who have received a lot publicity in the past that are going to be nominated. There are probably scores of Britons that we would consider for this list because of their good deeds, but they are not widely known. History has not been kind to everyone, and as the old adage goes, 'history is written by the winners' or at least by those with the best PR team. One thing is clear from the list: no one is on there simply because they are a celebrity. It would be a fool who confuses celebrity Britons with the greatest Britons. Unfortunately, media attention and much of the public's obsession with some celebrity airheads has helped close the gap between who is simply famous and who is truly great.

Politicians are always likely to divide people's opinions, so they are unlikely to be contenders for being one of the greatest Britons, although we may look back in hindsight and realise their greatness later on, even if we did not see it at the time. I'll be looking at the business people and eccentrics that shine brightly in Britain later, but first I want to look at the remarkable people who don't shout about it as much as the rest. They are the true unsung heroes of Britain, and no doubt the most important. If you look at the values that many Britons hold highest: honour, sense of duty, courage, and a sense of humour in adversity, then you'll see why this next bunch are truly remarkable.

Launched by *The Daily Mirror* in 1999, *The Pride of Britain Awards* is the most prestigious awards ceremony in Britain that gives recognition to all kinds of remarkable people or to use another phrase 'unsung heroes'. Around eight million viewers tune in to this annual awards show that is screened on ITV and is hosted by Carol Vorderman in London. Around 20,000 nominations for remarkable people from throughout Britain are made. *The Pride of Britain Awards* believe that their show is so popular because it gives lie to the idea that we live in a selfish, cheap, materialistic society where no one cares for their neighbours. There are many categories for entry, including: Outstanding Bravery, Child of Courage, Teenager of Courage, Emergency Services, Teacher of the Year and Special Recognition.

Awards like *The Pride of Britain* are crucial because people from disadvantaged backgrounds and/or with physical disadvantages themselves have a much greater struggle for success or recognition than the more privileged. We've all heard the phrase 'it's not what you know, but who you know'. The fact is that an old Etonian on his downers probably has a readymade network of old chums he can call for advice and maybe for another chance or lucky break. People from impoverished backgrounds have no such network. Hard graft and a strong sense of purpose are always required to a greater degree by those who have few or even no others around them to inspire and help them on their journey, wherever they want to go in life.

Great Britain has proportionally more children living in poverty than most developed nations. According to The Joseph Rowntree Foundation, a body set up to monitor and help fight against child poverty in Britain, child poverty costs the Exchequer £25 billion each year, much from reduced gross domestic product. It seems that there is a real financial as well as an ethical need to ending child poverty. Statistics on children's welfare are shockingly sketchy in a developed nation like Britain.

In 2010, the BBC published the results of a survey of 4029 pupils from ten UK secondary schools. The survey was designed by academics at the University of Nottingham, and the questions asked the children about the types of caring they undertook for unwell family members. Eight per cent of those who responded said that they had carried out 'personal care' for someone in their home either 'a lot of the time' or 'some of the time' over the previous month. 29 per cent of the pupils said that they had carried out 'emotional care' of someone in their home either 'a lot of the time' or 'some of the time' over the preceding month.

The BBC survey suggests that there could be about 700,000 young carers in the UK as a whole. This stands in sharp contrast to the 175,000 young carers identified by the Government's 2001 Census. Campaigners have pointed out that the results of the 2001 Census were based on replies by parents, rather than children, and made no mention of more stigmatised conditions such as poor mental health, substance misuse or HIV/Aids. According to the Disabled Living Foundation, over ten million people in the UK have disabilities, and two million have sight problems. The fact of the matter is that the government missed some of the most crucial factors that lead to children having to provide care.

The charity Alcohol Concern believes there are three million dependent drinkers in the UK and around 1.38 million dependent drug users. According to the NHS, one in four people in the UK will experience a mental health problem at some point in their lives, and 250,000 people are admitted to psychiatric hospitals every year. An estimated 103,700 people were living with HIV in the UK in 2014. Around 400 to 500 people die from HIV in the UK per year, a figure that would be far higher if it had not been for the introduction of combination antiretroviral treatment in the mid-1990s.

With the cost of providing free healthcare on the NHS set to rocket, one can only imagine the importance of this army of silent young carers who are making a sterling job of an often demanding situation. The fact is that this army of young carers, along with the care provided by adults saves the Government billions of pounds in extra care provision. These people often get little help from the Government despite the very challenging tasks many of them face. The dire economic scene since the global recession of 2008 has led to a situation where carers are facing cuts to the funding and service provision they need.

There are many other awards ceremonies in the UK which give rare praise to the most extraordinary people who live amongst us. The WellChild Awards is a high-profile event for courageous children. The Royal Humane Society issues awards to the RNLI, The Royal Life Saving Society and other lifesavers. There are also the The Police Bravery Awards and the Honours and Gallantry Awards for services to the Ministry of Defence. One of the other most prestigious events is the New Year's Honours in which the Queen or another member of the royal family awards knighthoods and other titles to British and some foreign nationals. A list of around 1350 names is published twice a year, and candidates are selected by the Government, private bodies, the general public, and sometimes by the Royal family themselves.

The awards go to a wide variety of people including extraordinary people, business people, and people in the public eye. Many of those who receive knighthoods are often very successful people and already very wealthy. This, combined with the fact that the awards are issued by the British Monarchy, has led to a split in the way the public view the awards. Honour nominations have been the subject of much speculation as to how they are influenced and acquired. An article in *The Sunday Times* in 2006 revealed that every donor who had given a million pounds or more to The Labour Party since 1997 was given a knighthood or a peerage. Many others who had donated smaller sums had received honours. Despite an investigation by the Crown Prosecution Service, no charges were made.

Mick Jagger's knighthood caused disappointment for some Rolling Stones' fans, who thought that accepting the honour contradicted his and his band's anti-establishment stance. Rather amusingly, his rakish sidekick Keith Richards showed irritation at Jagger's knighthood and remarked that he did not want to take the stage with someone wearing a 'coronet and sporting the old ermine. It's not what the Stones is about, is it?' Jagger retorted: 'I think he would probably like to get the same honour himself. It's like being given an ice cream – one gets one, and they all want one.'

In 2011 'Mr Saturday Night' Bruce Forsyth was given a knighthood at the age of 83 after nearly 70 years in the entertainment industry. The knighthood came after many years of people wondering why this man, who is practically a British institution, had not got one. Even an online petition was set up demanding that Bruce receive the honour. Many people had started to believe that people in entertainment were being shunned by the Queen's honours list.

As I have mentioned earlier, Britain has a preponderance of business-focused television programmes, and whilst personal fortune is not the aim of every Briton, it is probably the aim of a lot more than would be prepared to admit it. Like so much else in life, one of the key ingredients to the success of many of Britain's top business people has simply been down to luck. Well-known *Dragon's Den* tycoon, Duncan Bannatyne could not believe how the best pitch for an ice cream van was not sought out by a rival in his hometown of Stockton-on-Tees (Bannatyne made his initial fortune from ice cream vans). The disgraced publicist Max Clifford started work at EMI records at the tender age of 19 and soon after was put in charge of the publicity of 'some average band' called The Beatles. Needless to say, this introduced him to many of the contacts he would need to go it alone in the world of publicity.

The late publishing tycoon and one of Britain's richest men, Felix Dennis, saw a remarkable boost to his early career when, shortly after writing a biography of martial arts film legend Bruce Lee, Lee died sending sales soaring. Perhaps this is one of the most extreme examples of the old dictum 'one man's loss is another man's gain'. Of the incident, Dennis commented, 'It was perched on Bruce Lee's metaphorical shoulders that I first tasted real money and built my first successful business.' The entertainment impresario Simon Cowell was provided with a foot in the door in the music industry by his father who was an executive at EMI Music Publishing and managed to get his ambitious son a job in the coveted mail room.

It no doubt didn't hinder the progress of British music 'super producer' Mark Ronson that his father was a band manager and his mother a socialite butterfly. In fact, Ronson is descended from New York socialite royalty. About a decade ago, *Tatler* magazine suggested that anyone who didn't know the Ronsons should consider leaving Manhattan entirely. Obviously, few of these well-known people would admit that it was anything other than their raw talent and sheer hard work that got them to where they are today – connections or no connections.

Luck doesn't just help tycoons earn money. Lucky Briton Les Carvell earned the honourable title 'Britain's luckiest man' for a short while in the media after he netted thousands of pounds by picking five correct numbers on three separate occasions in the National Lottery. He then won a £1.1 million lottery jackpot and went on to scoop another £74,000 after betting just five pounds after five horses he backed in an accumulator all romped home. Luck indeed!

Whilst luck is one of the most welcome things, it can never be disputed that the quest for fame or fortune, or both, does not require some talent. Sometimes people have talent in bucket-loads, and we may even say of them that they possess 'genius'. However, it would seem that even genius can be quantified. The British-born Canadian non-fiction writer and journalist Malcolm Gladwell argues that genius is the product of a degree of luck combined with 10,000 hours of hard graft. To make his point, he draws upon the success of The Beatles and Mozart as examples of talented people who spent many hours honing their craft. He reasons that The Beatles clocked up their 10,000 hours of playing and songwriting early on in their careers, not least helped by having played up to eight hours every night during their Hamburg years. Similarly, Mozart clocked up his 10,000 hours pretty fast too as a performing boy genius, who was always in demand.

Gladwell asserts that no one is ever born to be the best, and there is no such thing as a born genius. Clearly this leaves quite a big part for luck to play. As I have already asserted, who you know is often more important than what you know. Middle-class and upper-class families have a great tradition of nurturing or even pushing their youngsters who are talented. Not only are the poor less able to fund a child's hobby, but they may also be associated with a somewhat stereotypical mindset of 'that kind of thing isn't for us'. Such a mindset may seem quite ridiculous, but its existence helps explain why football has mainly been labelled as the 'working man's game' and playing the violin after school may be viewed as more of a middle-class pastime. Views are changing because fewer people today regard themselves as coming from a particular class.

The psychologist Rob Yeung PhD has examined the attributes that make up the mind of the extremely successful. With regards to creativity, he notes how psychologists believe that 'the more knowledge, information, and concepts we have in our brains, the more likely we are to be creative.' He says that although we do not know how what we've accumulated *allows* us to generate new ideas, they swirl about inside the mind and generate new ones. Another attribute that Yeung spots in exceptional people is the 'T' shaped mind. This mindset is exhibited by those people who not only have a deep understanding of their own field of expertise but also read information outside of their field. This often leads to a situation where new applications become apparent as people draw ideas and techniques from one field and combine them with another.

One thing that has always been apparent to me is that

exceptional people don't just work hard because they love making lots of money. They do it because they love what they do. Given that we spend so much of our lives at work (the average Briton spends around ten solid years of their lives at work during their lifetime), enjoying your job is a massive bonus. Take pity on those who spend this time in an effective self-enforced prison. Exceptional people are, of course, also very good at what they do, and they are often ardent networkers. They also tend to be very positive people.

No doubt genetics will be a major factor in providing people with the skills required to be exceptional. Psychologists led by Mark Brosnan at the University of Bath discovered that schoolchildren with long ring fingers and shorter index fingers would be more likely to excel in numeracy, and schoolchildren with short ring fingers and long index fingers would be better at literacy. The length of fingers is believed to be controlled by exposure to levels of the hormones oestrogen and testosterone in the womb. It is surprising how little we know about the human brain but, as research into it continues, so our understanding of how it impacts us in our outlook and aspirations may be revealed.

Felix Dennis was once Britain's 151st richest man. He made his estimated £500 million fortune in magazine publishing, and was an advocate of 'making your own luck'. He talked about the importance of making the leap from the financial security of a good job to going it alone rather than the intense regret of looking back on your life, realising that you should have been braver and made different decisions. Cornell University researcher Thomas Gilovich has spent much time studying the psychology of regret. Asking people about the biggest regrets they had in their lives, Gilovich found that 75 per cent of people regret *not doing* something as opposed to only 25 per cent of people who regret *doing* something. Dennis sums up this attitude by proclaiming 'if only' …. are the two saddest words in the English language.'

Felix Dennis told wannabe millionaires to be wary of conventional wisdom, believing that it contains much 'fool's gold' along with the 'nuggets of wisdom'. He once said: 'conventional wisdom daunts initiative and offers far too many convenient reasons for inaction, especially for those with a great deal to lose.' He was not alone with this opinion. The economic whizz John Kenneth Galbraith coined the phrase 'conventional wisdom', and did not consider this term a compliment. He argued that humans associate truth with convenience and find ideas that contribute to self-esteem as more acceptable. He shrewdly noted that 'we adhere, as though to a raft, to those ideas which represent our understanding.'

When asked if they would like to be rich, many people will say 'it's not for me'. I argue that if you are not making yourself rich, then you're probably making somebody else rich. Think for a moment about the young people toiling in MacDonald's fast-food restaurants and similar multi-national chains. They may not crave riches themselves, but they are helping generate them in abundance for senior managers and directors in the company. In our capitalist society, even the 'lowliest members of stock', many of whom are not in the slightest bit interested in any sort of wealth for themselves, are engaged nonetheless, in serious wealth creation. A sobering thought, isn't it? I also answer to those who say they would never like to be rich by commenting that they can always give lots of their money away to charity.

Anyone who has followed the TV show *Dragon's Den* over the years may well remember hearing Duncan

Bannatyne say 'Don't think outside the box, think inside the box!' Serious money is not routinely made by those who come up with new ideas. It is generally made by those who are quick and clever at implementing them. Another key attribute of the exceptional business person is the ability to delegate tasks and incentivise employees. I will leave you with my favourite saying by Dennis: 'The world is full of money. Some of it has my name on it. All I have to do is collect it.' However, he implores you to remember to give all your money away once you're done with it.

Another common trait of many of the super-rich is a lack of any higher education. Richard Branson, Felix Dennis, David Ogilvy, Frederick Henry Royce (of Rolls-Royce fame), Duncan Bannatyne, Philip Green and many others all did not receive any further education. It seems that getting into the 'real world' at an early age did them no harm and in many ways may have helped. Entrepreneurs who took apprenticeships or vocational training instead of the higher education route include mobile phones tycoon John Caudwell, *Dragon's Den* star Deborah Meaden, expletive-strewn chef Gordon Ramsay, diamond dealer Laurence Graff, and JCB founder Sir Anthony Bamford.

Although I believe Felix Dennis had a point when he says that ideas alone are unlikely to lead to riches, there are a few British entrepreneurs who have bucked this trend. Inventor James Dyson developed the bagless vacuum cleaner and now sits on an estimated fortune of £1.45 billion. He was previously known for inventing the Ballbarrow and has more recently put his name to incredibly fast and efficient washing machines, hand dryers and fans. Dyson is probably the nearest link we have to the great British inventors of old such as Isambard Kingdom Brunel.

Trevor Baylis invented the wind-up radio which has been a major benefit, particularly to developing countries. He came up with the idea as a response to the need to communicate information about AIDS in Africa. Clive Sinclair, or simply 'The Brain' to many of his admirers and employees, has developed many forward-looking products including computers and the famous 'flop': the Sinclair C5, a one person electrically assisted pedal tricycle, which was regarded by many as being way too ahead of its time.

As I have shown, Britain is home to a whole host of exceptional people from carers, inventors, designers, scientists, engineers through to business visionaries. I will be in the midst of some of these people during my journey along the Thames. I look forward to telling you the stories of many of them. Perhaps I may bump into one or two.

CHAPTER 3

Into Eccentrica

Celebrity culture has unleashed a whole army of 'wannabees' who crave the limelight. Huge amounts of media coverage are given to celebrity and the pursuit of it. At the extreme end of the 'limelight hugging' spectrum lies a tactic which probably raises eyebrows higher than most others. We've all been there; you sit down to watch that football, tennis, cricket or snooker match and then, all of a sudden, it happens. Even the cameraman can't keep the sensationalism away from us until they come to their senses and realise that what they are seeing is not in the greatest taste, not least to the family audience. The camera quickly pans away. Welcome to the world of the streaker.

The act of streaking is massively effective and relatively simple to carry out. Not only do streakers draw attention to themselves by staging their own surprise invasion, they also amaze us by producing a naked public spectacle which we mostly associate with extreme embarrassment. After all, being seen naked in public is what most of us would probably fear. Streaking is a fascinating phenomenon. The shock is as much to do with being amazed at somebody's lack of societal inhibition as it is with our shock of seeing a complete stranger naked.

Think about it. Just how incredibly devastatingly effective public nudity is. One moment you could be seated at Wimbledon Centre Court, and within 30 seconds you could be naked running across the court in front of hundreds of millions of shocked or amused viewers worldwide. Viewers that *you* just shocked or amused. Then think about all the media footage in print and online about your spectacle. Think about how many millions of pounds advertisers would have to pay to secure that same space. Think about the international tennis stars and all the celebrities and members of the public in the audience who are never going to forget that day. That day *you* went naked. You then get symbolically arrested by a security official or policeman - who secretly might well find it amusing. You then probably get a caution and you go home. I, like many people, have never let the idea of myself streaking get past the uptight, prudish, and wholly clothed gatekeepers of my conscience, but I understand those who choose to do it. I really do.

Mark Roberts is the world's most prolific streaker. What's more, he's British. Roberts, from Liverpool, has performed over 150 streaks at events ranging from football and snooker right through to American Football. Let's just say he is no stranger to Wembley, although to be fair, Wembley has become a little stranger because of him! Roberts, who started streaking in 1993, has even done streaks to raise money for charity. According to him, he was approached by the Guinness Book of World Records, who gave him the label of the world's number one streaker. However, at the last minute, they decided not to publish his entry in their book as they did not want to encourage such vulgar behaviour!

Unsurprisingly enough, it appears that streaking is yet another British invention. On 5th July 1799, a naked man was arrested at Mansion House, London. He explained that he had done it after accepting a wager of ten guineas to run naked from Cornhill to Cheapside. Streaking is now a worldwide phenomenon, and the imagery of the streaker's naked body will continue to be a well-seasoned comedy device even if it were to be eradicated from the sports field.

Perhaps the most famous image ever recorded of a streaker was that of the long-haired and bearded Australian Michael O'Brien. On April 20th 1974, O'Brien ran out naked at Twickenham, interrupting an England vs France Rugby Union match. He was captured by PC Bruce Perry, who quickly came up with the ingenious idea of covering up O'Brien's genitals with a police helmet. The helmet now takes pride of place in the rugby museum at Twickenham.

Many people in Britain stand out because they 'go against the flow' in terms of their lifestyle. It seems that whilst the majority of the inhabitants of these islands and, for that matter, the Western World, have embarked upon some form of wealth accumulation, there is a significant minority for whom it is positively strange and even viewed negatively. The last 30 or so years in Britain have seen the rise of a new group of people who have rejected capitalism or simply rejected consumerism and materialism at the very least. In the late 1990s, one man came to symbolise the resistance against the 'onward advance' of capitalism: Swampy.

After holding out in a series of underground tunnels to prevent the use of machinery above ground, Swampy was apprehended by police as the protest against the construction of a new extension to the A30 road in Fairmile, Devon, was brought to an end. Swampy - real name Daniel Hooper - became a star overnight and came to exemplify a growing breed of people known as the eco-warriors. These people were not prepared to sit back and let what they saw as capitalistic greed and corruption take over Britain and, indeed, the world.

Eco-warriors and eco-campaigners arrived on the back of increasing global awareness of issues such as the greenhouse effect. It is easy to forget in our consumerist age about those who have abandoned the 'standard capitalist way of life'. Not everyone accepts the nine-to-five work ethic and the 2.4 children that often accompany it. Dwindling world resources and increasing populations have forced many in the West to re-evaluate how they view the world. Though the roots of environmentalism as we know it today were established soon after the Industrial Revolution, it wasn't until the 1970s that widespread concern about the environment and the founding of a large-scale environmental movement became well-established in Western nations.

Celebrities, business people, politicians, campaigners, exceptional people, and even streakers are all people who stand out from the crowd in an often spectacular fashion. However, there is one group of people who often like standing alone, not attracting too much attention, but their views and actions often draw attention to themselves anyway. I am talking here of that truly remarkable person and perhaps most quintessentially British of them all: the eccentric. Any investigation into eccentrics would surely start with the question 'exactly what is an eccentric?'

According to the Edinburgh-based psychologist Dr David Weeks, who is renowned as the greatest authority on eccentrics, there are distinctive characteristics that can be used to differentiate between an eccentric and a 'normal person'. These are: a nonconforming attitude; idealistic; intense curiosity, and a happy obsession with a hobby or hobbies. Eccentrics know very early on in their childhood that they are different from others. They are often highly intelligent, opinionated and outspoken, have unusual living or eating habits, are not interested in the opinions or company of others and they have a mischievous sense of humour. Maybe you recognise yourself in many of these characteristics?

The term 'eccentric' is derived from the Greek 'ekkentros' meaning 'out of centre'. Britain is probably more associated with eccentrics than any other nation, and it would seem that many people believe Britain is a nation crammed full of eccentrics. Dr Weeks, however, has come up with what many might find a surprising statistic. He believes that only one in 10,000 Britons is truly eccentric. So even if you answered 'yes' to most of the questions above, Dr Weeks would still probably assign you with that much maligned and troubling condition: normality! I'm hoping that quite a few of you reading this book are true eccentrics, as according to Dr Weeks' figure, it means that I have sold quite a few books! Many celebrities have decided to take on the persona of being eccentric, the pop star Lady Gaga being a good example. However, I believe this has much to do with maintaining an effective sharp public image in a world saturated full of media content.

Eccentricity is often associated with genius, intellectualism, and creativity. Given the huge amount of creativity in the UK, the preponderance of eccentrics comes as no surprise. As the English utilitarian thinker, John Stuart Mill once remarked, 'The amount of eccentricity in a society has generally been proportional to the amount of genius, mental vigour, and moral courage which it contained.' Little research has been done into why the British in particular are so eccentric. Reasons put forward include our class system which has encouraged the upper classes to develop bizarre personal habits that would have to be tolerated by those in the lower classes and the ideas that eccentrics care less than most about what other people think about them and can also laugh at themselves.

Although eccentrics are often loners, they are held in great affection by much of the population. British eccentrics have become part of the fabric of British life, not least because of their acknowledged role in the Industrial Revolution, the British Empire, and British life in general. Much of our greatness is built upon the work of many a 'mad' scientist, inventor, and wandering explorer. The British eccentric has come to personify much of the spirit and character of these islands. The British have always valued individualism highly and have a strong sense of individual liberty. Few people hold higher the banner of the individual mindset than the great British eccentric.

After all this talk of individualism and the loner lifestyle of the fully qualified eccentric, it may come as a surprise that The Eccentric Club (UK) exists. Originally founded in 1781, this London-based club has had many incarnations since including The Illustrious Society of Eccentrics, The Everlasting Society of Eccentrics, The Eccentric Society Club and the Eccentric Club Limited. It strikes me as quite amusing that someone came along and changed the club's name from 'The Everlasting Society of Eccentrics' - surely that's one title that you would want to keep, well, forever! The last incarnation of the club closed in 1984, and it was not until August 2008 that the club was re-launched. The club has HRH Prince Philip, Duke of Edinburgh, as its patron and boasted HRH Prince Charles, Lord Montagu, former London Mayor Boris Johnson, and Elton John amongst many others as people who congratulated the club upon its re-opening.

Whilst many of us may be hard pushed to admit to personally knowing a true eccentric Briton, most people could probably put a name to one or two in the public realm. I would imagine that a few of the following may be high up on many people's lists: The Marquis of Bath (he of the many 'wifelets'); the late astronomer Patrick Moore; general showbiz personality and Oscar Wilde fan, Stephen Fry; the late film director and bon viveur Michael Winner; black dog hounded premier Winston Churchill; rock star Elton John; transvestite and surreal comic Eddie Izzard, transvestite and surreal artist, Grayson Perry; electroconvulsive therapy patient look-alike Ken Dodd; conspiracy theorist and former professional goalkeeper David Icke (he of the shape-shifting lizard theory); eccentrically hirsute horse racing pundit and former tic-tac man, John McCrirrick, and former Who drummer and general 'psychopath' Keith Moon. These are all people who would probably find themselves on a list of those Britons considered to be eccentric.

One of the classic examples of the British eccentric is that of the British inventor. One of these, Derek Imrie (born 1969), invented a special device that could detect other gay men wearing the device. Fitted down the trousers, he believed that the vibrating device could help gay men meet. Although the outlook for the device was promising, work on its development was halted when it was discovered that the device's signal attracted various wild animals, particularly badgers. He was delighted, however, after receiving a large order from Australia. Every year, there is the British Inventions Show held in London which gives exposure to up and coming inventors from both Britain and around the world. There is also the British Inventors Society which was formed in December 2003. Whether or not Derek Imrie is a member of this, I do not know!

The Scottish eccentric James Duff (c1720-88) entered himself into a horse race, unsurprisingly finishing last! Duff then developed a taste for ceremonial dress and melancholic occasions which saw him attend every funeral in Edinburgh for 40 years. Another melancholic was the landed gentleman George Selwyn (1719-91) who was only interested in crime, death, and executions. When his friend Lord Holland lay apparently dying, he said to his servant 'The next time Mr Selwyn calls, show him up; if I am alive I shall be delighted to see him, and if I am dead he'll be glad to see me.'

The poverty-stricken bookseller Soloman Pottesman (1904-78) sold only enough books to stay alive. He disconnected his lavatory cistern in fear that a flood might destroy his book collection. He distracted other bidders at book auctions by talking to them about recent purchases he had made during bids, took up to 15 minutes to write a cheque and was known to go to the cinema seven nights in a row to see the same film. Unsurprisingly, Pottesman attracted the nickname 'potty'.

The adrenaline junkie Ian Ashpole, not content with mundane feats such as tightrope walking, decided to float 11,000 feet above the Cambridgeshire countryside attached to nothing but 600 helium party balloons. The artist Mark McGowan from Peckham pushed a monkey nut for seven miles to Downing Street with his nose. He more recently attempted to cartwheel from Brighton to London to protest about people taking stones from beaches. Another British eccentric is the busker Charlie Cavey who squeezes, with his guitar, into a tiny metal litter bin in Cambridge city centre and proceeds to play his songs. He admits to having to climb out every five or so songs to stretch himself!

Some other Britons who may qualify for being eccentric: Polish-born street cleaner Ziggy Dust demonstrates some funky Michael Jackson-esque dance moves on the streets of Chiswick as he is sweeping the streets much to the amusement of locals. Another street sweeper, Steve Fox, carves out thoughts for the day into giant sand messages with his brush. His antics have brought much adulation from the people of Exmouth, Devon, many of whom flock down to the seafront to read his motivational messages. He even had passers-by cuddling each other after carving one message which read 'hug somebody'. Some eccentrics are to be found amongst Britain's tramps and homeless. 78-year-old Gordon Roberts has been given the name 'super-tramp' by the people of his hometown of Bournemouth due to his ability to tell the exact time at any point in the day without the need to look at a watch. The librarian Thomas Birch (1705-66) would go fishing dressed as a tree insisting that any movement would 'be taken by a fish to be the consequence of a mild breeze.'

Many aristocrats are well known for their eccentric behaviour. Francis Henry Egerton, the 8th Earl of Bridgewater (1756-1829), was a recluse who preferred the company of dogs than humans. He believed them to be better behaved and would eat with them at his dinner table each day. Each of his 12 dogs was given a napkin tied around its neck and servants (one per dog) would circulate with silver dishes. Egerton was obsessed with boots, making sets for his dogs and wearing a new pair himself each day. He would arrange the boots around his bedroom, and as they were worn once only, he could use them as a calendar. Susanna Kennedy, Countess of Eglintoune (1696-1787), was one of the great beauties of the 18th century. She claimed to have only ever received true gratitude from animals, and like the eccentric Earl of Bridgewater, would share meal times only with animals. Only in her case, she preferred the company of rats!

A more recent phenomenon has been the emergence of a whole breed of 'superheroes' who stalk the streets of British towns mostly at night. I would put many, if not most, of these forward for consideration as eccentric. Captain Beany claims that he hails from the planet Beanus, but most people claim that he has the considerably less fantastical origin of South Wales. Captain Beanus, or Barry Kirk as he is also known, spends his time dressed as a baked bean and drives around in his orange painted VW Beetle. Beany claims that he is no longer called Barry Kirk as he changed his name by beanpole. He got the idea for Captain Beany after sitting in a bath of baked beans for charity.

Other eccentric hero characters include Darkslay, a caped crusader who dedicates himself to 'tackling any issues in Greenwich from petty crime to chatting to people about their concerns.' A superhero called Statesman patrols the streets of Birmingham at night. This crusader dresses in a Union Flag T-shirt and a black Zorro-style face mask. By day he works in a bank. Others include a man known as Ciderman and The West Country Hairy Fairy Man (yes, he does have wings, a tutu, and a magic pink wand!) who does good deeds for local people including helping women by carrying their shopping. The Essex town of Colchester can lay claim to perhaps the strangest superhero of them all. The Human Shrub first emerged in mid-2009 doing some guerrilla gardening: the herbaceous hero was making a protest against the local council which was planning to turf over some plant beds in an effort to cut costs.

One can only assume that, even if only one in 10,000 Britons is a true eccentric, there are far more people who express eccentric characteristics. For these people, there are a whole host of eccentric clubs and associations that can be joined in order for eccentric sports and hobbies to be pursued. Amongst Britain's most eccentric clubs there is the British Boomerang Society, The Pylon Appreciation Society, the Handlebar Club and many more. In case you were wondering, the Handlebar Club is dedicated to the handlebar moustache. According to their website, their qualification for membership is 'a hirsute appendage of the upper lip, with graspable extremities.' Beards are strictly forbidden! Many of the clubs are recent creations, further exemplifying the ingenuity of the British when it comes to creating things.

One of the wackiest hobbies to come from these shores is Extreme Ironing, or simply EI. This sport involves people taking an ironing board to a remote and often perilous environment and then ironing an item of clothing. According to the official website, Extreme Ironing is 'the latest danger sport that combines the thrills of an extreme outdoor activity with the satisfaction of a well-pressed shirt.' Purists of the sport agree that it was created in Leicester in 1997 by Phil Shaw in his back garden. The sport has attracted a worldwide following and has inspired the creation of similar themes including Extreme Cello playing and Extreme Lilo, where participants race down rapids on nothing more than inflatable lilos!

The British calendar is peppered with eccentric events. Starting in Spring, one could attend the Pooh Sticks World Championships at Day's Lock, Little Wittenham, near Didcot, Oxfordshire (up to 2000 serious contestants turn up); The Bacup Nutters Dance in Lancashire; the Furry Dance in Cornwall; Worm Charming in Devon and the Potwalloping Festival in Devon (Potwalloping is the painting of pebbles and the returning of them to their sea defence ridge). Moving into Summer, one could attend the Great Knaresborough Bed Race in Yorkshire; the Giant Yorkshire Pudding Race in (you guessed it!) Yorkshire; the Garlic Festival on the Isle of Wight; the Lawnmower Grand Prix in Sussex, and also the Bognor Birdman challenge in Sussex and the World Plank Walking Championships in Kent.

Moving into Autumn, one could attend the World Conker Championships in Northamptonshire; the Gurning Championships in Cumbria; the Cider Barrel Rolling Race in Somerset, and also the Biggest Liar in the World Competition in Cumbria. Moving into Winter, one could attend the Flambeaux Procession in Perthshire; the Annual Bath Race in Dorset; Loonydook in Carmarthenshire, where around 50 brave souls jump into the freezing Firth of Forth on January 3rd; the Annual Clown Service in London; the Up Helly Aa in Shetland, a procession and Viking boat burning, and the Moonraking Festival in Slaithwaite, Yorkshire, where a giant paper moon is unravelled on a canal and then carried around the village in a procession by people dressed as gnomes!

One act that is particularly British is the phenomenon of doing an 'end to ender'. This is the common term for the scores of Britons who, each year, set off from the British mainland's most southern point, Land's End, for the British mainland's most Northern point, John O' Groats. This adventure was popular even way back in the 1800s, and since then literally tens of thousands of people have attempted it. Many of those who attempt this feat do it in the most eccentric fashion, attracting much media attention along the way. A recent end to ender who attracted much publicity was Stephen Gough, the naked rambler who has walked the route twice 2003-2004 and again in 2005-2006. Gough was arrested many times during his walks.

Whilst walking, running, and cycling are the most popular ways of doing an end to ender, attempts have been made in specialised adapted vehicles including a garden shed, a skip, a turbo-charged JCB digger, and a Harrier jump jet. Someone even posted himself by 1st class mail! The record for running is held by Andi Rivett who completed the journey in just nine days and two hours. In 1986 Michael Arets and Mike Day set a record 14 days 12 hours and 41 minutes for travelling 880 miles between the two ends on unicycles. Wayne Booth became the first person to complete the challenge by motorbike without stopping. He completed it in 15 hours on a modified Honda motorbike which had a huge 74 litre petrol tank to avoid the need for refuelling. The challenge has attracted celebrities including cricket legend Ian Botham, *Top Gear's* James May and radio big man, Chris Moyles.

Britons seem to be almost alone in having such a desire to traverse their own lands from one end to the other. Whilst the popularity of the end to ender stems from the elongated shape of the nation, there seems to be no urgency to perform similar feats in other nations with similar 'geographically elongated' conditions. For example, Italy, Norway, Sweden, Chile, and Vietnam do not appear to have an end to ender tradition equivalent. That said, it can no doubt be expected that there have been individuals in these nations who have undertaken end to ender feats.

The only equivalent to the Land's End to John O' Groats journey of any similarity, appears to be the Malin to Mizen in Ireland. This has attracted walkers, runners, cyclists, and even an attempt by four men using longboards, a type of skateboard. East to West Coast traverses are popular in the United States, and various routes, such as the legendary 2448 mile-long Route 66 attract people in their thousands every year, even if the goal isn't quite the end to end equivalent as in Britain. As an end to ender myself, I know what a feat this journey would be to undertake solely under human self-propulsion. Even using the slight advantage of having a car for propulsion, I arrived at John O' Groats in a sorry state, my legs beyond remedy from any more stretches and my hands contorted into a claw-like clamp position from gripping the steering wheel. Maybe one day I'll give it a go using a slightly more eccentric means. Maybe I will bump into some of Britain's great eccentrics on my journey down the River Thames. I hope so.

CHAPTER 4
Broken Britain?

The hulk had decided that this minor goading was destined for punishment. A tingling shiver went down my spine as he lurched forward aggressively shouting at the passer-by whose comments he did not like. The truth is that they were both evidently drunk and the bigger man, at least, was definitely looking for a fight. The passing man mustered up some courage and strode forward to confront the hulk. The hulk kicked the man hard, and punches were thrown. The streets were busy with mostly inebriated youths, mostly from the club the hulk had just left and mostly oblivious to the angry confrontation now at full throttle.

The truth is that my friend Mark and I had specifically come to this street after a work colleague had informed me about the spectacular mini-riots that were occurring at turf - out time around two a.m. on this street in Reading town centre. These 'riots' that had been occurring involved dozens of youths fighting pitched battles with the police. Not long before, there had been a major incident in Henley-on-Thames, not far from here, where dozens of youths had fought a battle with the police in the centre of the otherwise genteel and very affluent quintessentially British town.

Whilst there was no mini-riot in Reading on that night, it was clear that anger and a devil-may-care attitude were prevailing and, to be honest, as the hulk got ever closer to us, we thought our standing and staring behaviour might get us involved. We unimaginatively turned to each other as if we just happened to be in conversation on the pavement and had been doing this all along. It worked, and the hulk continued to beat the man instead of turning on us. My friend is karate trained, but I could sense even he was intimidated by the thought of an alcohol-fuelled onslaught of violence. God knows who else would have joined in. It was a horrible sight. The assaulted man was visibly injured but managed to run away. With his 'summary justice' dispensed, the hulk re-joined his friends triumphantly. It was time for us to leave. We didn't want to outstay the welcome we never had.

This is Reading on a Saturday night, but it could be any town or city in Britain for that matter. The drunkenness, nastiness and pathetic exhibitionism abounded, and I had no doubt the Accident and Emergency department of the local Royal Berkshire Hospital would be full of injured drunk people and full of contempt and drunken abuse for the nurses who were trying to fix these idiots' self-inflicted injuries. The truth is, I was often drunk in my youth, and I could occasionally be verbally abusive, but I never went looking for a fight; I've always had a level of respect for other human beings. Why abuse somebody who would try to help you? What is causing all this? Well, in around 2007, somebody came up with a definitive cause for Britain's seemingly irreversible social malaise. It was called 'Broken Britain'. We now knew what we were dealing with.

'Broken Britain' was a term that first found widespread use in *The Sun* newspaper. It was seized upon by the Conservative Party who used it to describe a perceived widespread state of social decay in Britain. 'Broken Britain' was used to describe many unpleasant facets of modern British life but principally focused upon binge/underage drinking, violent crime, particularly gang, knife, and gun crime, child neglect, the loss of the British identity and teenage pregnancy. The Wikitionary description for 'Broken Britain' is: 'Britain viewed as a crime-ridden state where society and common sense have failed.' The 'Broken Britain' concept filtered into television drama plots and became a running theme on many news programmes. 'Broken Britain' became popular in media terms because, like all scaremongering, it could help the media organisations sell stuff. It benefited the Conservatives because they had an election coming up.

Whilst many symptoms of this so-called 'Broken Britain epidemic' have been put forward, fewer causal reasons have been discussed. Those that have been mooted as potential causes include a generation of spoilt youngsters that has manifested itself in a lack of respect and discipline; a too greater emphasis on human rights which has led to a fear of telling children off; a selfish compensation culture; a too lenient sentencing of criminals, and the impact of the 1960s 'swinging sixties' generation whose frequent different aspirations and rebelliousness towards traditional values has had a direct impact on today's youngsters. Features of modern life such as television and television dependence, video games and the Internet are also regularly blamed.

More recently, 'Broken Britain' has made a return in a slightly different guise. Following the shocking 2011 England riots, the then Prime Minister, David Cameron, referred to Britain's 'Broken Society' in which he deplored 'irresponsibility, selfishness, children without fathers, schools without discipline and rights without responsibilities,' amongst other things. To their credit, the Conservatives have at least shown a willingness to at least address the underlying causes of such issues in Britain, with former party leader Iain Duncan Smith setting up the Centre for Social Justice (CSJ), an independent, not-for-profit think-tank. The CSJ involves people from across the political spectrum including Labour politicians Frank Field and John Reid and the Liberal Democrats' Menzies Campbell. The CSJ conducts social research to provide evidence and solutions that will help to overcome the causes of poverty and to promote social justice.

Trying to repair the damage caused by family breakdown and child abuse may require a longer term strategy. These issues are often tied up with, or compounded by, other issues such as poverty, health problems, and addiction. As for crime, many people have seen this as an area where immediate action can be taken to help prevent it. This action comes in the form of harsher sentencing and tougher policing. Many people believe that if such policy was driven through we would all have a much safer nation. Time and time again, outrage is caused amongst the public when judges hand down sentencing which is seen as too soft. Many judges themselves have expressed outrage at their own sentencing guidelines.

It is easy in today's Britain, with all the unhappiness at the so-called 'soft sentencing' that is thought to be at work, to forget that Britain was once a very harsh place indeed for criminals, and 'criminals' of all ages for that matter. In 1750, Benjamin Beckonfield was hanged at Tyburn for stealing a hat. John Harris, a 15-year-old orphan was hanged at Tyburn on 27th June 1777 for stealing two and a half guineas. In 1782, a 14-year-old girl was hanged for being in the company of gypsies. In 1814, the vagrant John Bibby was hanged for sheep stealing on the Duke of Richmond's estate. As he ran up the ladder to the scaffold, he shouted 'I am the Duke of Wellington!' presumably to try to get the hanging halted.

In 1816, four boys aged between nine and thirteen were hanged in London for begging. It wasn't until The Criminal Law Consolidation Act of 1861 that some common sense was put into practice. Now the number of capital crimes was reduced to four: treason, piracy, mutiny, and murder. In 1908, people under the age of 16 could no longer be executed; in 1931, pregnant women could no longer be hanged, and 1964 saw the last British hangings – those of Peter Anthony Allen and Gwynne Owen Evans for murder in the course of a theft. In December 1969, Parliament abolished capital punishment for murder.

Whilst nobody could seriously condone the death of a child for begging or an adult for stealing a sheep, it is argued that today we have swung too far in the opposite direction. There can be no doubt that harsher sentencing would be a deterrent to many would-be criminals, but even the issues behind locking people up are complex. Many doubt whether prisons are particularly effective forms of punishment for many types of offenders at all. In late 2010, the Ministry of Justice disclosed that 14 prisons in England and Wales had re-conviction rates of over 70 per cent. Statistics such as these do little to reassure anyone that Britain's overcrowded prison population of over 85,000 is going to change significantly anytime soon.

In June 2010 the Minister for Justice, Kenneth Clarke, put an end to many short prison sentences after warning that it was 'virtually impossible' to rehabilitate an inmate in less than 12 months. Whilst being based upon valid evidence,

Clarke's policy caused trouble amongst his colleagues in a party renowned for its tough stance on law and order. Clarke caused further outrage by reversing the Conservative Party election pledge that anyone caught carrying a knife illegally would be sent to prison. Knife crime is often cited by people of many different political persuasions as one of the most worrying and challenging serious problems affecting the streets of Britain today.

Many of the people found within Britain's overcrowded prisons represent the difficulty and entrenchment of social distortion and the effects of family breakdown and poverty. The 2010 survey by the Ministry of Justice included a survey of 1435 prisoners, 68 per cent of these named having a job as the most important factor in preventing them going back to a life of crime after leaving prison, while for 60 per cent it was having somewhere to live. Compounding all these socio-economic problems inside Britain's prisons is the widespread amount of mental health issues. According to the Social Exclusion Unit, more than 70 per cent of the prison population has two or more mental health disorders. Male prisoners are 14 times more likely to have two or more disorders than men in general, and the suicide rate in prisons is almost 15 times higher than in the general population. Clearly, if we are going to tackle Britain's problematic prisons, then we have to tackle the mental health issue too.

Despite the popularity of the 'Broken Britain' concept, there are many critics of the term. In 2010, *The Guardian* ran a series of articles under the title 'Is Britain Broken?' *The Guardian*'s Amelia Gentleman wrote an article in March 2010 that looked at the validity of the term and focused on the East Glasgow housing estate of Easterhouse where Iain Duncan Smith had visited in 2002 and subsequently became a showcase example of 'Broken Britain'. For all the social problems here, it is clear that the key driving element in common with them all is widespread poverty, much of it extreme. Easterhouse residents can expect to die at just 54 years old, a lower life expectancy than in many African nations. Gentleman visited the estate and talked to many residents about their lives and what they thought of the term 'Broken Britain'.

Whilst focusing mainly on the policies of Iain Duncan Smith and the Conservatives, Gentleman acknowledged that Labour had a crucial part to play in the increasing social division within Britain and the failure of their 13 years in office, and their much trumpeted Social Exclusion Unit that opened in 1997 and made areas like Easterhouse a priority. Gentleman notes that the 'Broken Britain' policy was too incendiary for the Conservatives to drop it in the build up to the 2010 General Election, in which the Conservatives won a majority and went on to form a predictably uneasy coalition with the Liberal Democrats. She believes that 'Broken Britain' has been a convenient term which the Conservatives have used to fit different definitions depending on 'what the major worry of the hour is – youth crime, teenage pregnancy or anti-social behaviour.' She points out that there is real hostility to 'being tarred as a broken society,' and quotes one interviewed man who points out: 'To say something is broken implies that it was working in the first place.' There are many residents who tell her that there is no place that they would rather live, and it is low self-esteem and the day-to-day hardships of living in poverty which are to blame. One resident tells of the enormous stress of not being able to allow her children a meal in MacDonald's or to go to the cinema - things that most children take for granted.

Perhaps the most persuasive argument against the concept of 'Broken Britain' is the fact that despite much opinion, particularly that portrayed by much of Britain's press, many aspects of British life are actually improving. After all, the murder rate is much lower than it has been for a decade, gun crime is down, and violent crime and domestic burglaries have dropped since 1995. An article from February 4th, 2010 in the leading editorial section of *The Economist* examines the extent to which Britain really is 'broken'. It states downward crime trends, adding that child homicides have fallen by more than two-thirds since the 1970s. It also states that even the onset of recession did not reverse the downward trend of crime.

It goes on that after many years of increase, there are 'tentative' signs that Britons are drinking less alcohol; in fact, it has been estimated that around one fifth of Britain's young adults do not consume any alcohol at all. Many types of drugs are consumed less - although some, like cocaine, have increased - and rates of smoking are now among the lowest in Europe. Whilst divorce has become much more common, domestic abuse has dropped. *The Economist* argues that one of the main reasons young people are falling behind is because schools are failing to give their pupils the adequate skills they need to enable youngsters to get and hold a job. It reiterates the problems of a prevalence of low self-esteem in youngsters and argues that the 'Broken Britain myth' is 'worse than scaremongering – it glosses over those who need help the most.'

The modern age creates a paradox; whilst technology is constantly being created to enable us to do jobs quicker, it is also opening up more distractions and interruptions.

Consider the mobile phone. Once there was a time when you could only make a phone call from a landline. You could not be in contact when you travelled or in many places that you spent away from home. Then there came the time when a few wealthy people carried huge battery packs around, enabling them to make the odd call, but now, almost everyone from the age of five upwards seems to have a mobile phone, making them, in theory, contactable anytime and all the time. This can cause huge problems.

Even if you are capable of holding out for a meal or meeting with somebody, you still feel the urgency to check your mobile for missed calls and messages. The quicker you respond, the more people generally expect you to respond. In the 'good old days' of the landline, you made an appointment and stuck to it, knowing that making any alterations much nearer the time would be difficult. Today, having a mobile creates a huge distraction and allows people to make last minute alterations. Of course, there are some benefits; mobiles have helped increase the survival rates of many seriously injured people, whether from road accidents or other injuries. Calls can often be made from the scene of the incident, whereas before, people were reliant on finding the nearest telephone or payphone.

Mobile phones are an example of how technology can add to the phenomenon which has become known as 'time poverty'. We often hear that our society and Western ones like it, are 'cash rich, but time poor'. Many of us lead hectic lifestyles, spending much of our time chasing after financial gain, but we have little time left to relax, or spend our money on carefully considered items, for that matter. The American author, journalist and biographer James Gleick has studied the issues of time poverty in detail. He argues that modern society has been driven to a point where 'multitasking' has become very commonplace.

People may choose to watch movies at home rather than the cinema because they can do different things like look at their mobile phones and cook whilst watching the films. I wonder if a similar issue is at work with respect to the alarming decline in the numbers and popularity of British pubs. Whilst the main reason behind their decline is due to the availability of super cheap alcohol in shops and supermarkets, I suspect that drinking at home also allows some people to multitask.

Gleick points out lots of things to emphasise the reality of time poverty: shampoos that offer speeded up hair drying times; super-fast elevators; politicians coached to speak in ten second sound bites, and people who punch 88 on the microwave instead of 90 to save a fraction of the time. Gleick has commented on an underlying reason why people spend so long checking their mobile phones and social networking sites. He has stated, 'You may think you are checking on your portfolio, but deep down you are checking on your existence.' Gleick also talks about boredom. He observes that boredom is a relatively modern phenomenon; the word boredom barely existed even a century ago. He relates boredom to our cultural approach to time - if we are not constantly doing 'something', then we must be bored.

For me, a good example of how many people relieve boredom is using the social networking site, Twitter. A lot of people frequently update mostly mundane stuff about what they are doing and where they are. Their followers then log on to check out what's going on. And so proceeds an endless cycle of a huge amount of not very important information, wasting more of our precious little time. The next logical step from Twitter would surely be a social networking site where webcams are strapped onto celebrities so that the followers can literally follow them around everywhere in real time, making suggestions and remarks as they do. Now there's an idea!

If we are not spending an inordinate amount of time pursuing our career, then we seem to be spending a startling amount of time fascinated by the careers of others. I'm not talking in the main about truly fascinating careers such as those of scientists and researchers working on cutting-edge science; I'm talking about the relatively mundane world of 'celebrities'. In the same way that we often use the term 'youth is wasted on the young', I think we also need to add that 'media time is wasted on the celebrity'. Never has so much air time been given to people with so little to say. In Chapter Two, I looked at how the power of networks enables people to get ahead. Associate Professor Elizabeth Currid-Halkett of the University of Southern California has researched the phenomenon of celebrities, and discovered a network that was much better connected than others.

Most people in the world are six steps away from another person, the mathematically proven 'six degrees of separation'. Currid-Halkett's research showed that top celebrities exhibit just 3.26 degrees of separation. She discovered that not only do celebrities show up in the same key cities - London, Los Angeles, and New York - they also travel off the beaten track to be seen with other A-listers, even if the event they go to has little or no relevance to themselves. By keeping in close-knit circles, the A-listers are able to prevent many others from entering their niche. This is why celebrities who reach the top are often followed round by the media, sometimes long after their star has apparently 'fallen'.

So what impact does this have on our society? Well, it means that celebrities often act in a certain prescribed and structured way. There is no real need to set any particular example as it is not this that keeps you in the spotlight. It is the networking that goes with it that helps fuel the media fishbowl frenzy. Currid-Halkett asserts that it is the public's need to share in intimate moments of celebrities lives, such as a kiss on the beach, that transcends their contributions as professionals. This explains how 'famous for being famous' celebrities like Paris Hilton maintain their celebrity despite an apparent lack of talent.

Having spent time researching celebrities, you would expect Currid-Halkett to be scathing about them, but she is not. Few people would dispute why celebrities exist – the public wants gossip, but she states that celebrity is like glue that enables an increasingly globalised and anonymous society to bond together. She also points out celebrity is a phenomenon that creates a multi-billion pound industry and sustains vast numbers of jobs in the media and the wider reaches of society. It is this interest in celebrities, combined with other features, that led author Ferdinand Mount to believe that modern Britain and the West has become much like ancient Greece and Rome.

On the face of it, it seems like Mount has a point. He states that a resurgent interest in going down the gym, adventurous food, political debate and tolerance to homosexuality are all things that make us like the Ancients. On top of this, he asserts that there is also a resurgence in scientific enquiry and the belief by the likes of Leucippus and Democratus that the world is made up of infinitesimally small particles is the forerunner of modern physics. For me, the most interesting point is that Mount feels that our society has changed enough to make it worth trying to contrast with a different age.

The philosopher Alain de Botton is someone who has spent a lot of time thinking about modern Western life and the ills that accompany it. He offers the issue of status anxiety as being one which causes many problems in Western societies. De Botton raises many issues that are caused by status anxiety, a problem arising from those who fear losing their status in society, or it being transcended by others. He points out the affliction as being a major worry for some. As causes of status anxiety, de Botton points out the anxiety that most of us feel about our position in the world. He highlights problems caused by snobbery, materialism, peer groups, envy, pessimism, meritocracy and dependence upon fickle talent, luck, employment, profitability and the global economy.

Philosophers have long been pointing out the issues causing so much melancholia in a Western society that surely should be spending most of its time celebrating the advantages and freedom it has when compared to the majority of the rest of the world. Bertrand Russell believed that joy was to be gained from people doing things for themselves; he said, 'It is far better to do something badly yourself than to watch someone else doing it well.' Jean-Paul Sartre believed that humans could never be free from desire, but instead they could embrace it without acting upon it.

The breakdown of family life is often cited as a key component in the cause of many of the societal problems facing Britain. According to some statistics, Britain has the world's fourth-highest divorce rate. Behavioural problems are higher amongst those children from 'broken families', and the issue of 'broken' families is frequently run alongside 'Broken Britain'. Marriage has become a political hot potato. All political parties tend to be wary of how they approach the issue of marriage. Whilst they note the benefits of the important bond between people that marriage certainly is, they are careful not to alienate the many people who will leave marriage until much later on in life or never marry at all.

Many people have cited an exodus of people leaving Britain as hard evidence to substantiate their claim that 'Broken Britain' is a place that many seek to escape. A recent study by the Institute for Public Policy Research has suggested that one in twelve British nationals may now be living abroad. More British people live abroad, proportionally, than any other nationality. There are 41 countries with more than 10,000 British living there. Levels of emigration are now back to those of the late 1950s and early 1960s when the 'Ten Pound Poms' left in their droves for Australia, enticed by economic incentives. However, whilst we hear about the numbers that are flocking abroad, we hear less about the amount that decide to return. Known as 'boomerang Brits', many people discover that their life in Australia was simply a case of 'the grass is greener'.

Those trying to escape worries and problems back home in 'Blighty' often discover that problems often follow you around, however much you try to escape them. Others find that life in the southern hemisphere is too lacklustre and miss the hustle and bustle that signifies the northern hemisphere of the world, where 90 per cent of the world's population live. Britain is an expensive place to live; our roads are very busy, and whilst not suffering from the world's most extreme weather, what we experience is wildly unpredictable. These three factors are as likely contributors as any others in why some people seem so desperate to escape Britain.

The notion of 'Broken Britain' is not just a handy political tool. Newspapers and other news media cling to the concept because it helps their products to sell. Many people remember that 'it was never like this is in my day', but they forget to remember that neither was the media. People like Rupert Murdoch changed the face of the media in Britain and focused more on sensationalism and scandal. Spin doctors were employed by politicians to direct inflammatory stories to discredit other political parties and their policies. This focus on scandal and sensationalism has informed an audience to become less shocked by outrage, and so it is that we have reality TV shows and documentaries whose main objective has become to shock the audience rather than inform it.

British society has become more wealth-orientated with shows such as *The Apprentice*, *Dragon's Den* and others which effectively and quite rightly shout out 'anyone can do it'. Indeed anyone can do it, but often at tremendous self-sacrifice and in tandem with some well-timed luck. Wealth creation has become a means to an end for many and has given rise to a new snob-elitism based simply on what you own. There is change in the air, though, and Western governments are beginning to focus more on what makes their people happy as well as what can make them wealthy.

On July 19, 2011, the United Nations General Assembly passed a resolution about world happiness. Former Prime Minister David Cameron's Government expressed an interest in looking at how happiness affects people in Britain and the current Prime Minister, Theresa May, is sure to continue this interest. Currently, the Office for National Statistics is drawing up plans of how to conduct widespread surveys of happiness and what to do with the results. A trial survey of over 4000 people was carried out by the ONS between April and August 2011. The results revealed that three-quarters of Britons place themselves at seven out of ten or higher on a scale of well-being.

The World Happiness Report is a measure of happiness published by the United Nations Sustainable Development Solutions Network. In 2013 it identified Switzerland as being home to the world's happiest people. This was followed by Iceland and Denmark. Outside of Europe, Brazil was the highest scorer, coming in at fifth position. Important contributory factors to happiness include a healthy work-life balance and low unemployment. Britain came in at a poor twenty-first position. The most fundamental criticism of happiness economics lies with its dependence on cardinal utility – the concept that personal preferences are measurable and comparable in an objective nature by an outside observer. However, I'm sure that there is some merit to what the World Happiness Report is trying to achieve. For too long, many people have associated increased happiness solely with increased wealth. Surely it is time to banish the 'Broken-Britain' concept and get Britain in to the top ten of this report.

CHAPTER 5

The Source (The Journey Begins)

Once a major Roman settlement along with St Albans and Colchester, Cirencester retains its importance in today's world by virtue of its significant road networks to Gloucester, Cheltenham, Bristol, Bath, Oxford, Swindon, Stroud, and Wantage. In fact, this explains why this small town of around 19,000 people is encased by a ring road which unexpectedly greets the road visitor. Being located just a few miles from the source of the River Thames, it made sense to pop into this charming and important town to collect provisions for the journey.

Known as the 'capital of the Cotswolds', Cirencester attracts many visitors who have come to visit the Cotswolds, a region appealing enough to be called 'home' by many a social butterfly. The list includes Prince Charles whose country home is at nearby Highgrove, Jilly Cooper, Damien Hirst, Kate Winslet, Liz Hurley, and Kate Moss. Just in case you were thinking that a social gathering of this schmoozing bunch might get a bit out of hand, do not fear, for this area was also once home to Air Chief Marshal Sir Arthur 'Bomber' Harris. If carpet bombing these socialites might seem a little harsh, you could instead opt for wishing upon them the calamitous pranks of another Cotswolds resident: comedian Dom Joly.

I have learned from previous experience that I normally

The Source (The Journey Begins)

buy things that turn out to be wholly inappropriate for long journeys. I forced myself to employ some common sense in buying provisions for my trip: bottled water, sandwiches, crisps, pork pies and, in an effort to entertain some form of vitamins, apples. Leaving the shop, I now have a bigger worry on my mind. I have an accomplice you see. Not the most normal of people! Toby is an old friend, a friend I 'won' in a silly game I used to play with my old school mates: 'now who can befriend the weirdest person possible' game.

Toby didn't go to a state school like me; he went to a rather prestigious public school where he didn't shine academically, but he had a talent for the arts. Still, his oddness brought him to the attention of my school friends who seemed to revel in the particular character that they perceived to exist in Britain's public schools.

I was walking towards Toby sat in his car. He is very much still here, and his neurosis was strictly next-level. The truth is that despite his highly unusual demeanour and unbelievably overblown repeat questioning 'is this the right road? Is this the right road, Thomas?' Toby is a harmless chap. I've got to quite like him over the years and would never dream of telling him that he was the 'winning card' in part of a silly competition between old friends many years ago. In fact, when he's not in full neurotic meltdown, I prefer him to most of my other friends. The other advantage Toby has is that his aunt lives around these parts, and he's got a car that can buzz me around to visit various places that are a little bit off the beaten Thames track. And so we drove out of Cirencester past all the wonderful yellow Cotswold stone shops and houses.

Anyone who has visited the source of the River Thames will probably tell you the same thing: it is, in fact, actually quite hard to find. It was only after obtaining some detailed directions from the landlady at the Thames Head Inn that we knew where to look. The drizzle had begun to change into more of a downpour. I stopped under some trees to allow Toby to catch up. An InterCity train thundered past us along the rail line that runs parallel to the footpath. Just as I had thought, Toby decided to stop at the rail crossing. I tried to encourage him to visit the source with me, only because I thought it would be good for him to see it after coming all this way but, after a few moments hesitation, he decided to stay put.

The rain was probably putting him off as much as the walking, or maybe his neurosis was focusing on a possible near death rail line crossing blunder! I told him I'd call him at his aunt's later on and headed across the double rail lines. There's always a slightly unnerving feeling to crossing a high-speed rail line, despite the fact I could see a good few hundred metres in either direction. I hurried through a field with quite a steep incline, and I could start to make out a copse from the bottom which certainly seemed like one I had seen from images of the source of the Thames.

The second field had a pleasant hummocky feel to it. The cows seemed disinterested in me, which was all just fine as far as I was concerned. The grass was peppered with cow pats, and the field was lined with a world-weary dry stone wall. I guessed this was the fabled Trewsbury Mead that gives life to England's most important river. The rain was coming down harder, but I could feel the excitement as I closed in on the copse. I could then make out the stone monument beneath an ash tree. Finally, I reached its shaded sanctuary. No one else was there. Upon the stone was carved the words 'The conservators of the River Thames 1857-

The Source (The Journey Begins)

1974. This stone was placed here to mark the source of the River Thames.'

Next to the monument lies a wooden signpost that proclaims 'Thames path public footpath'. Beneath this, another wooden arrow indicates 'Thames barrier 184 miles 294 km'. The Thames Barrier at Charlton, East London, marks the end of the Thames Path. Despite all these proclamations, it is actually disputed whether Thames Head is really the true source of the River Thames. Many people believe that the River Churn is actually the true source of the Thames. Thames Head is, however, the 'official' source of the Thames, and so it is that this place is the main destination for many an intrepid Thames traveller like myself.

The River Thames is actually 215 miles in total length (as opposed to the shorter Thames Footpath) measured from Thames Head. Thames Head is located around three miles south-west of Cirencester and around ten miles north-west of Swindon. A small cluster of stones, positioned only a few metres from the monument at Thames Head, marks one of four springs which give life to the Thames. The Thames springs up from groundwater in its initial stages, so the visible 'wet source' of the Thames is constantly in a changing place. In fact, it emerges anywhere along a 20-mile route from Thames Head depending upon weather and water table conditions. Thames Head has no visible water for most of the year, although it can turn into a lake after particularly heavy rain.

It was mid-summer, and this rainy weather is just about as likely as any sunshine on this excitingly unpredictable island. As the comedian, Billy Connolly likes to say, 'There is no such thing as bad weather, just the wrong clothes!' The rain had subsided, and I decided to step out from beneath the shaded bough. It is a strange feeling thinking that all this ends in a huge river that scythes London into two. A river that has witnessed so many of the historical events that have shaped England, Great Britain and indeed the world. It reflects our own history just as it reflected the seething flames of the Great Fire of London.

This mighty river also embodies the joviality of the British from Jerome K Jerome's *Three Men in a Boat* through to the world-famous regattas. A whole new pastime was built around such rivers giving rise to that most coveted of British pastimes, 'messing about on the river'. There may have been more water sloshing about in bottled form in my heavy backpack than I could see there, or even far into the distance, but I found myself humming 'Waterloo Sunset' by the Kinks, nonetheless.

This first stretch of the Thames would be an easy walk as I was meeting up with Toby again in just a couple of hours in the village of Kemble. Ahead, I could clearly see the spire of Kemble church. This spire dates back to 1450, and the rest of the church was built several hundred years earlier. It never ceases to amaze me, the sheer volume of historic stuff we have crammed onto our islands. In this small stretch of the Thames Path, I had also crossed the ancient Fosse Way, a Roman road that leads from Cirencester towards Devon. I had barely started on an 184-mile journey and already I was overwhelmed by history! The Thames Path is the longest river walk in Europe, and I was thankful for being able to undertake a journey that would keep me by the banks of this great river for almost all its entire length.

I reached the north side of Kemble and made my way into town. I met Toby at The Tavern Inn opposite the railway station. He was parked up and waiting for me. We drove the short distance to take a look at nearby Kemble airfield. Formerly RAF Kemble, all military flying ceased in March 1993. In March 2001, the airfield was purchased from the MOD by local businessman Ronan Harvey. Commercial aviation continues at the airport, and in September 2009, Kemble airfield was renamed as Cotswold Airport.

Over the years, RAF Kemble has been used as an important aircraft maintenance base for both British and American air forces. For 16 years, it was home to the Red Arrows, and huge crowds would form to watch their daily aerobatics training. What has attracted me to Kemble airfield, however, is not so much to do with the goings on of aircraft during their working lives, but what happens to them at the end of their working lives.

We parked up outside two huge hangars, and I got out to take a look. With no evident sign of a site office, I walked up to peer into the vast cavernous space inside one of the hangars. Huge crates containing all sorts of commercial aircraft parts were stacked up. I could make out a large jet engine cowling. There was an airliner, possibly a Boeing 737, parked up outside.

These hangars are owned by a company called Aircraft Salvage International (ASI). They are key players in an aviation salvage industry worth an estimated £80 million in Britain alone. Whilst the scrap aluminium from a Boeing 747 may be worth around £30,000, each salvaged engine can be worth upwards of a million pounds. Scrapping large commercial aircraft is quite a complex and dangerous task, and ASI is one of only a handful of British-based companies capable of doing it. Kemble is reputedly the busiest aircraft scrapyard in the world. As I walked out of the hangar and back to Toby's car, I reflected on the important work being carried out by companies like ASI. I considered how they are playing their part in Britain's multi-billion pound recycling industry.

Every year, British households produce over 30 million tonnes of waste. Britain is one of the poorest performing recyclers in Europe. According to DEFRA, we recycle only 17 per cent of waste, compared to some of our neighbouring European countries which recycle over 50 per cent. Up to 60 per cent of the rubbish that we put in our dustbins can be recycled. According to DEFRA, nine out of ten people would recycle more if it were made easier.

Each year, Britons throw away £36 million pounds worth of aluminium; each family uses an average of 500 glass bottles and jars and gets through 38 kilograms of newspapers. Recycling isn't just about the re-using of materials; it also vastly reduces the demand on energy which is used in the manufacture of virgin products. Recycling aluminium uses only five per cent of the energy required by virgin production and recycled paper produces 73 per cent less air pollution than if it was made from raw materials. It is time for us all to fully embrace the three 'R's' of sustainable living: reduce, reuse, recycle.

The recycling industry in Britain has an annual turnover of approximately £17 billion and directly and indirectly supports around 100,000 jobs. Whilst recycling may appear to be a modern phenomenon, it has, in fact, been going on since pre-industrial times. The term 'dustmen' is derived from the people who collected dust and ash from coal fires to be used in brick making. It wasn't until the 19th century that recycling really took off when railroads purchased and sold scrap metal.

The Source (The Journey Begins)

The automobile industry purchased scrap metal in the early 20th century, and a whole industry grew as scrap metal peddlers and 'rag and bone' men became commonplace in industrial societies. The 1970s saw the next big investment in recycling as legislation was brought in. Household waste recycling is required by law across the UK, although recycling rules differ between different councils. The internet has revolutionised the idea of 'free-cycling' whereby items such as household furniture can be collected and found a new home for free.

The recycling industry does have its critics, however. Many argue that the energy and chemicals required to recycle products mean that the environmental benefit can often be negligible. In Britain, we are constantly being exhorted to recycle but little emphasis seems to be given to cutting down in the first place. Food has become a throwaway commodity, and it has been estimated that around 20 per cent of the food we buy ends up being discarded. The only real attempt to cut down on the amount of packaging used tends to focus on shopping bags themselves. I think it is time to review the huge amounts of packaging used on products but maybe we are simply too stuck in our ways. Progress was made on the 5th October 2015, when the British government brought in the compulsory five pence bag charge.

Toby picked me up from the village of Kemble, and we headed off to Swindon. After a brief but entertaining drive through the pleasantly undulating North Wiltshire countryside, we entered the outskirts of the town. Despite being a much-maligned place, in particular by former Monty Python member Terry Jones who gave Swindon a poor review in his book *Evil Machines,* Swindon is a key economic component of that very British version of 'the Silicon

Valley'; the M4 corridor. Once a thriving centre of industry and employment, Swindon has been deeply affected by the recession, and in early 2009 its unemployment rate overtook the national average for the first time in 30 years.

One of the best known things about Swindon is that this is where one-time pop star and Dr Who's sidekick, Billie Piper comes from. Included in this list of famous people associated with Swindon can be added: Irish born, Swindon raised singer/songwriter Gilbert O' Sullivan; television presenter Mark Lamarr; actress and sex goddess Diana Dors; actor and comedian Julian Clary; television presenter and former glamour model, Melinda Messenger; PR guru and businessman Nick Hewer of TV's *The Apprentice* fame, and the writer Ralph Bates, to name a few.

Arguably Swindon's most important resident was David Murray John, the town's clerk from 1938 until 1974 and a driving force behind Swindon's development. His memory lives on in an imposing wide-bodied 83-metre tall building in the centre of town. The David Murray John building can be seen for miles around, and its looming presence came into view as Toby and I approached ever closer.

Before long, we had stumbled upon something which I was hoping we might luckily avoid – Swindon's infamous Magic Roundabout. Constructed in 1972, this innovative 'super roundabout' consists of five mini-roundabouts arranged in a circle. Surprisingly, this is not the only magic roundabout in Britain - others can be found in High Wycombe, Colchester and Hemel Hempstead - but it is Swindon's which has become the most notorious. Our apprehension was, however, somewhat dispelled as we managed to glide over the confusing carbuncle with relative ease. Toby said it was down to his driving finesse; I told him that I put it down to sheer luck!

The Swindon urban area has a population of over 185,000 people and around 300,000 people are said to live within just 20 minutes driving distance from the centre of town. Not long ago, Swindon could boast full employment and it was a boomtown, certainly one of Britain's most successful towns. Major employers in the town include Honda and BMW who both have a manufacturing plants. Motorola, WH Smith, Nationwide, Zurich Financial Services and energy company RWE also have significant presences in the town. Swindon is also home to the registered head office of the National Trust.

Swindon is referred to in the *Domesday Book* as 'Suindune', most probably originating from the Anglo-Saxon words 'swine' and 'dun', literally meaning 'pig hill'. Swindon Old Town sits atop a hill in the centre of the existing town. The Industrial Revolution led to a rapid expansion of the town outside of these limits. The creation of two canals led to an increased population and, in 1840, Isambard Kingdom Brunel chose Swindon as the base for his railworks in the construction of the Great Western Railway (GWR). The GWR would eventually lead to the employment of more than 14,500 people making it one of Britain's biggest employers. In 1871, the GWR management set up a healthcare service for its personnel using a small amount of pay deducted from each worker's weekly pay. This innovative service would go on to provide a blueprint for the NHS.

I took a look at the covered market out on the fringes of the shopping area. I have always found that covered markets promote the spirit of the independent shopping experience more than any other. Fantastic smells of fresh produce mingle with the hustle and bustle of the market atmosphere. Swindon market is housed in a striking white yurt-like construction making it look like something more from Mongolia than from Northern Wiltshire. However, inside it felt like the place was in terminal decline. Many of the stores looked shut or empty, and the footfall was dire. It's a real shame for the independent businesses here, but it comes as no surprise to me.

I think the big conglomerates of the town centre are making too good a job of vacuuming up any available cash for people to be able to make it out to the independents. Surely there must be a Swindonian out there who can make a success of their local market? Maybe a big marketing scheme in the town centre to get people out to visit it; nothing grand, just some people with flyers and vision. A vision for what independent markets can and should be; I simply don't believe the general public don't care enough about this town.

I traipsed back to the car with my shopping. I'd bought some unusual condiments from a fantastic Thai shop in the market to make my culinary experience down the Thames that bit more exciting. I met Toby back at the car park, and we started on our return journey to the river. Our second encounter with the Magic Roundabout did not go quite as well as the first. I have only ever been in one major car crash before, and that was with my good friend Toby behind the wheel! Both cars involved were written off, and everybody escaped with just some cuts, bruises, and a few tears for some passengers. As we got near to the roundabout I noticed that there didn't seem to be any road directions in sight. We must have missed them earlier on somehow. We nervously edged towards and then darted across the intimidating mini roundabouts one by one and emerged mentally scarred the other side. It was more by luck than design that we found ourselves on the correct road out of town.

Something that people may find almost as bizarre as the maddening Magic Roundabout is the fact that Swindon has no university. In fact, Swindon is the UK's largest centre of population without its own university. Proposals were put forward in 2008 by former Swindon MP, Anne Snelgrove, to establish a university-level institution in the town. Likely names for the university are the obvious 'University of Swindon' and 'The Murray John University'. All plans for a Swindon university are currently shelved. No doubt the issue will persist for years to come and, from my point of view, it is only a matter of time before it happens, if not only due to the demands of an expanding population. One thing that would no doubt be championed by a new university would be IT as Swindon is home to many hi-tech companies. The Museum of Computing in Swindon was the first computer museum in the UK.

Swindon gained notoriety in 2010 when it was revealed that the town had won a competition to twin it with Walt Disney World in Florida. The popular BBC television quiz show *Have I Got News For You* played upon the incongruity of a town such as Swindon being twinned with the likes of Walt Disney World. The fact is that any British town of similar size would have likely raised eyebrows by such a comparison. Swindon also played its part in giving one of Britain's most well-known bands their name. Britpop legends Oasis took their name after singer Liam Gallagher saw Swindon's music and leisure centre 'The Oasis Centre' on a poster. Oasis themselves never performed there but, in 2011, 20 years after naming his band after the centre, Liam

Gallagher's band Beady Eye gigged there. He certainly did have a beady eye grabbing the band's name from that poster!

As anyone who has ever been in a band will testify, getting the band name right is crucially important, and after much deliberation, a name is often found from the most abstract source. Brave is the band who, without looking, open a dictionary and point to any old word for a name. If that were the case, then the band that I would now be in would be called; 'Prepossess', thanks to *The University English Dictionary,* date unknown, as the front cover and some of the front pages of my copy are missing! Personally, I was never taken by the great Britpop battle between Blur and Oasis; I was too interested in the likes of Suede and Shed 7. Those guys never waged any war between them that I was aware of. Swindon's most famous home-grown band is XTC, and the town also gave us Rick Davis, founder and member of the band Supertramp and Justin Hayward, lead guitarist, vocalist, and composer for The Moody Blues.

After a busy day, I was looking forward to being able to stop over the night at Toby's aunt's house just outside Cirencester. Once inside, Toby excitedly showed me round the oak-panelled rooms, rushing around like an excited child. I marvelled at what looked like Afghan rugs hung from the walls. 'Oh, they collect those,' he boomed across. He lanced towards me with his upper body and demonically whispered, 'They're worth thousands each!' An air of awkwardness hung thick in the kitchen. Toby's aunt asked me only a few questions, making the silences unbearably awkward. Toby was normally a motormouth, but even he seemed lost for words. 'You were meant to be here four hours ago for lunch, Toby,' his aunt announced. Another awkward silence followed.

The Source (The Journey Begins)

The following morning, Toby dropped me back to the Thames Path. I was on my own today and had a fair few miles to walk and a few villages to pass through before reaching Cricklade. I set off from the point near Kemble I had left yesterday and continued my journey down the path. I walked past tranquil scenes of cows chewing the cud at Ewen and past the first weir on the river. I stopped to marvel at the first water in the Thames. After this point, patches of water appeared more and more frequently.

I savoured the scene of a single log bridge placed over the infant Thames stream as I knew that very soon they would mostly be made of brick or stone. I could see the village of Somerford Keynes across a meadow, and it wasn't long before I was walking between the large lakes that make up the Cotswolds Water Park, the largest man-made inland water feature in Europe. These popular lakes are used for all forms of recreational water sports and were created from abandoned gravel pits.

Ashton Keynes is the first village that actually sits on the River Thames. This place is simply fascinating. The river flows in a channel between some beautiful old houses and then down the high road where it is constantly bridged to allow access to the properties. There are around 20 bridges here, and they all add to the picturesque scene. This is the first place that I stumbled across some fellow Thames travellers. They too were quite taken aback by the beauty of the place. This village, along with Poole Keynes and Somerford Keynes, gets its name from the Keynes family who established 12th century Ashton Keynes Castle in the northern part of this settlement. Unfortunately, all that is left of the castle today is a few mounds and ditches that mark the spot where it once stood.

After Ashton Keynes, the Thames is joined by Swill Brook which adds a welcome increase to the infant Thames' volume. The path widens out, and it is now in fact following the old Midland and South Western Junction Railway line between Cheltenham and Andover. The tracks are no longer here, but I could almost hear the sound of hissing steam pass through the trees. Soon I would be in Cricklade, the first town on the River Thames.

CHAPTER 6

Minted

Cricklade is a 9th century Saxon town. It was home to the Saxon Royal Mint from 979 until 1100. I jumped up onto the bridge at the north end of the town and trekked the short distance down to the High Street. After buying some provisions, I went to the Red Lion pub for a well-earned beer. This pub is on the site where the Cricklade Mint once stood and, as I supped my pint, I started thinking about how Cricklade has been keeping up with the world, and in particular, the world of money.

If Cricklade had been important as the one-time home of the Royal Mint, it would later crop up again with a significant money-creating proposition, but this time in the Internet Age. The Million Dollar Homepage was a website conceived in 2005 by Cricklade resident Alex Tew who was looking to raise money for his university fees for his business degree at Nottingham University. Not only would it generate over a million dollars for Tew in an incredibly brief amount of time, but it would garner praise from the likes of *The Wall Street Journal* and the international tech community. Tew would be interviewed by everyone from Richard and Judy through to the USA's Fox News Channel about his remarkable but shockingly simple website idea.

Launched on 26th August 2005, The Million Dollar Homepage had an incredibly simple strategy. The homepage had a million pixel window that was up for sale. Ten by ten blocks of pixels could be purchased for a dollar. Each advertiser would use an image-based link so that once clicked on, the link would take you through to the advertiser's website. After initially selling a small amount of pixel blocks to friends and family, the website began to receive attention from much farther afield. Tew had sent out a press release that was picked up by the BBC. Influential online tech sites also began to feature articles on the website, and it wasn't long before huge amounts of advertising space was being sold.

At its peak, The Million Dollar Homepage was receiving up to 25,000 visitors every hour and had become the world's 127th most popular website. The website made a gross total of USD $1,037,100 in just five months. After costs, taxes, and donations to charity, Tew was reported to have earned at least half a million dollars for his efforts. Ironically, Tew decided to quit his business degree that the site was set up to fund. Naturally, he has decided to carry on building innovative websites.

So what was the key to Tew's success with The Million Dollar Homepage? Well, the answer, as with many things, lies predominantly with the idea. Great web ideas stand out from the crowd, and the nature of web-based ideas means that they can spread with eye-watering rapidity. By focussing purely on advertising, Tew has no 'physical' products that he needs to ship anywhere. He invented a clever web idea that the media would love. With only one page, the minimalism of the website demonstrated how incredibly easy it could be to have success online provided that you have the right idea.

One of the people who witnessed Tew's meteoric success with his website is the former *Guardian* New Media columnist Paul Carr. Carr has explained how Tew gambled that the idea would be quirky enough to get huge media attention. He has recounted how Tew told him that there is no secret to having good ideas. According to Carr, Tew grabs a notepad and writes down a list of every idea that he thinks might make a lot of money. Once he has whittled the list down to the serious contenders, he then gets to the hardest part: choosing which idea to follow.

Alex Tew's website demonstrates how quickly success can be found on the Internet and how quickly ideas are talked about and spread. Few people would disagree that the Internet has revolutionised so many aspects of our lives. Perhaps the greatest implication has been with the accessibility of knowledge. The academic no longer needs access to a big library to find documents. The consumer no longer needs to listen to a salesperson talking about the functions of various products – they can find all the information they need online. News spreads incredibly fast and can be disseminated in many different formats, so much so that governments find it very difficult to keep track of.

The Internet, and in particular, social networking sites such as Facebook, have played a significant role in the downfall of dictators such as Colonel Gaddafi of Libya and the uprising of many people against other regimes such as in the Arab Spring of 2011. Even terrorist organisations such as the FARC guerrillas in Colombia have come up against mass opposition organised through Facebook. The Internet revolution has meant that the cost of communication between people has been dramatically reduced and open sourced networks allow many people to collaborate on projects from almost anywhere around the globe.

With the Internet playing such a massive role in most of

our lives in the West, it is easy to forget the humble origins and fascinating journey that the Internet has taken up to this point. In 1968, an essay was published by J.C.R. Licklider and Robert W.Taylor titled *'The Computer as a Communication Device'*. In it, the authors suggested that online communities would be 'not of common location, but of common interest.' They also pointed out that 'You will not send a letter or a telegram; you will simply identify the people whose files should be linked to yours.' Taylor was an employee of the Advanced Research Projects Agency of the Department of Defense, USA, and he helped set up ARPAnet, which would lead to the establishment of the Internet.

The first mention of the word 'Internet' appeared in 1974 as an abbreviation of the term 'internetworking'. It wasn't until around a decade later that pioneers started to experiment with the idea of online communities. In 1979, two American students set up Usenet which allowed people to post messages to groups dedicated to specific topics. NASA developed a sophisticated network that could connect space scientists to data and information stored anywhere in the world. From 1984 onwards, the European Organization for Nuclear Research or CERN, as it is more commonly known, began installing a system that would interconnect its major internal computing systems. It was while at CERN in 1989 that Briton Tim Berners-Lee invented a network that he released for the public to use. It would go on to form the World Wide Web. For his work in developing the World Wide Web, Berners-Lee received the Millennium Technology Prize in 2004.

A major alteration occurred in 1992 when US Congress passed the Scientific and Advanced Technology Act which allowed some existing computer networks to interconnect with commercial networks. Up until this point, the Internet had been mainly focussed on academic and educational roles. In April 1995, the final restrictions on carrying commercial traffic ended. Commercial enterprises clamoured to make a presence on 'the net'. Venture capitalists and entrepreneurs raced to get a foothold on the back of this new technology. In March 2000, the dot.com bubble burst. Many companies were hugely overvalued, and the inexperience of many entrepreneurs showed in this marketplace. Large numbers of online businesses were stamped out as strong existing brands developed their own internet presence and took customers away.

One of the features of today's Internet that will come as little surprise to anyone is the huge dominance of Google. In 2015, Google had 66 per cent of the global search engine market share. Usage in Britain has been estimated to be near 90 per cent. In the late 1990s, search engines such as Netscape Navigator, Lycos, Yahoo, and Altavista dominated the field. Founded in 1998, Google was late to the competition, but its new approaches to relevancy ranking helped to quickly secure its industry dominance. Relevancy ranking had been an issue for search engines since the mid-90s, as it had become impractical to view full lists of results in the old directory based systems. Google founders Larry Page and Sergey Brin came up with an algorithm for relevancy ranking that would put some listings of results above others.

The Google founders realised that relevancy was the key – you had to give internet users the best possible results for what they were looking for. By remaining innovative, Google look set to be around for a long time. Predicting internet trends and staying ahead of the game will remain crucial for this company who are the front runners in an industry that sees both growth and destruction develop at astonishing speed.

Naturally, a game-changer as significant as the Internet has caused distress to many traditional business models. Many people get their news online now instead of buying newspapers. Everything from books to brochures are now generally available in digital format, and we are no doubt going to see a significant drop in the volume of printed paper products used by each individual throughout the world over the coming years. Music and video are available online, cutting out the once vast profits created back in the era when most music and video was transported by physical products such as the Compact Disc or the DVD.

The ease of storing and disseminating digital files online has vastly increased the amount of copyright infringement issues. Whilst 'piracy' was always a problem, the Internet has given rise to an age where the vast majority of music and film downloads are illegal. In 2009, a report by the International Federation of the Phonographic Industry calculated that 95 per cent of all internet music downloads online were illegal. The Internet has had a particularly profound effect on the music industry in which the outcome situation could be described as being like a double-edged sword. Not only is most music downloaded illegally for free, but many individual tracks are now purchased instead of entire albums.

I remember a time when many people bought an album by a band they liked just to get hold of a couple of songs! That was back in the day when the music companies were raking the profits in. On the upside, bands have an easy platform on the Internet to promote themselves in a way that was near impossible just over a decade ago. Impressive profiles can be built on Myspace or Facebook for free; tracks can be loaded up for sale on online music selling sites such as iTunes, and videos can be put up onto video sharing websites such as YouTube for free. In short, a band can establish a presence online, promote, publish, and build up a business much in the same way as a music company does. A quirky music video can attract a huge audience.

In 2006, the relatively unknown US band OK GO uploaded a video for their latest song 'Here It Goes Again' featuring an elaborately choreographed dance on fitness treadmills. The video has clocked up over 52 million views on YouTube alone and brought the band success. The OK GO story demonstrates that if you have a good idea and just a small amount of marketing knowledge, then the sky can really be the limit. YouTube has been an internet success story, establishing itself as the most dominant player in the video viewing arena in much the same way as Google (YouTube's owner) has established itself as the most dominant player in the search engine field. YouTube is, in fact, the world's second largest search engine after Google.

The Internet has revolutionised retailing, and the amount of people in Britain purchasing goods online is rising by the year. According to the online retail industry association IMRG, £133 billion was spent online with UK retailers, and online sales are predicted to overtake high street sales in just five years time. Without the need for costly shops filled with display products and staff, it has become much cheaper to open an online retail business. No longer bound by the challenges of having to travel distances to view and collect products from shops, the Internet has allowed the consumer to view the same products by many different retailers. This has given rise to great competitiveness between high street retailers and 'e-tailers' or 'clicks versus bricks'. Price comparison sites put the consumer onto the lowest price that a product can be found at. The net result is that profit margins for branded products across the retail sector have been squeezed, and this has led to many high street traders and independent shops being forced to close.

Recent years have seen a resurgence of interest in regenerating the high street. In May 2011, the retail guru Mary Portas was appointed by Prime Minister David Cameron and Deputy Prime Minister Nick Clegg to lead an independent review into the future of the British high street. Portas has stated that she aims to 'put the heart back into our high streets, re-imagined as destinations for socialising, culture, health, well-being, creativity and learning.' I say good luck to her – with a few changes, I believe that the British high street can make a return to being an important social hub, though with the increasing dominance of the Internet, I think the glory days of the great British high street are probably over.

Many people see the Internet in a negative light, and there is no doubt that 'the net' has made it easier for many subversive activities to be carried out. With well in excess of a trillion individual web pages, the Internet has become very difficult to police. Paedophiles can distribute and access vast quantities of vile images and videos of children being abused. They can cleverly hide their files behind security devices such as encryption and mask them beneath websites that seem outwardly innocent. They can chat and network with other paedophiles in secure chat rooms and can 'groom' potential victims using false identities, so that the child may think that they are innocently chatting to another child.

Internet pornography is easy to access, and many sites are free to use. There is concern about the ease with which children can access pornography. Parents have to use increasingly sophisticated safety filters on computers to stop children from being able to access porn online. The fact that many of them can view pornography on their friends' mobile phones or their home computers means that stopping youngsters from viewing such material will always be an uphill task.

Another unwelcome internet phenomenon is known as trolling. People can leave unwholesome and unnecessary comments about people or services on online blogs, or even people's websites. Because there is no need to leave any real identification or details about who you are, trolls are very hard to trace. Trolls leave unsavoury and most often unnecessary comments about everyone from supposed friends, work colleagues, actors and actresses, and perhaps most controversially, they have been known to make comments on tribute pages to people who have died in tragic circumstances.

In 2011, the troll Sean Duffy wrote vile comments and even mocking cartoons of a 15-year-old girl who had committed suicide. He left the comments on a condolence page set up by the girl's family. Reading magistrates heard how the alcoholic, who suffers from Asperger's Syndrome - a form of autism in which sufferers have difficulties with communication and social interaction - trawled the Internet looking for tribute sites. The magistrates sentenced Duffy to 18 weeks in prison and banned him from using social networking sites for five years. Historically, internet businesses have been slow to crack down on trolls and subversive behaviour in general.

Cyber crime has been identified by many governments including Britain's as presenting an extreme threat in the future. With so much covert and confidential information online, the stakes are high. A successful cyber attack could knock out everything from nuclear power stations through to transport networks and military communications. With the invention of cyber warfare, the wars of the future could take on a very different nature to those of today. Most Britons will be familiar with computer crime taking the form of spam emails. I am sure most of us have had emails from long lost relatives begging for help, or people telling us they can send money to us if we give them our bank details! Email actually predates the Internet and was a crucial tool in creating it. It dates back to 1965 as a means of communication for multiple users of the same mainframe system. In 1971, Ray Tomlinson created what was to become the standard email address format using the '@' sign to separate the username from the host name.

As technology develops, we will see ever more remarkable innovations use the Internet as their platform. As the Internet becomes increasingly saturated with similar websites, businesses will continue to use ever more advanced technology to stay ahead of the game. The stiff competition will continue to drive brilliant new ideas for how websites can work, attract people to them, and keep their new audience engaged. We are already seeing more relevant news, even bespoke news tailored to the individual. Already newsfeeds on social networks such as Facebook give people news from the sites and individuals relevant to them.

Voice recognition technology has advanced significantly over recent years, and we can expect more and more websites on the Internet to use spoken command recognition. We can simply tell some search engines what we are looking for and give simple voice commands such as 'banking' or 'billing' to log straight onto our private information. Blogs and even websites themselves could be written solely using voice commands. Science fiction films and comics often feature people speaking into their watches or rings, but in the coming years, this might be something that we will no doubt witness for real. As technology is delivered in ever increasingly smaller packages, it is only logical that it may soon find itself packaged in a small device on our hands. The ultimate must-have desirable for the rich and famous might one day be a jewel-encrusted wedding ring that is crammed full with the latest internet capable software.

Augmented Reality or AR has also been an exciting area of development in recent years. AR is a live, direct or indirect, view of a physical, real-world environment whose elements are augmented by computer-generated sensory input such as sound, video, graphics or GPS data. In 2016, the free-to-play GPS-based augmented reality game Pokémon took the world by storm, with the game being downloaded more than five hundred million times worldwide.

As the Internet and related technologies become increasingly integrated into our lives, it is not unreasonable to see internet-linked technology finding its way into more and more products. This is known as the 'Internet of Things'. Our fridges might contain gadgetry that helps select and order new foodstuffs, helps plan a healthy lifestyle and even issues a stern warning from a digital personal trainer when someone visits the fridge a little too often!

Digital display screens will find their way into ever more

locations. Chopping boards might have an integrated screen to help with recipes and menus. Ovens might be linked to databases to fine tune cooking as if it were carried out by a Michelin-starred chef. The trend for ever more immediate information might carry on to surprising new levels.

Some commentators have wondered whether the Internet will have any long-term psychological effects. The technology writer Nicholas G. Carr has been highly critical of the Internet's effects on cognition. He believes that the Internet might diminish the capacity for concentration and contemplation. What we do know is that with the Internet still in relative infancy, there has been little time for any psychological effects to show up. Little research has been conducted into this area, but it would be fair to suggest that heavy long-term internet usage might alter our psychological state.

With so many links and distractions on almost every website, our attention is constantly being courted. With increasing communication possibilities and reduced costs, we are evermore distracted by phone calls and emails. Already there is speculation that internet usage is leading to an increased lack of sleep whereby it serves as yet another distraction in an already cluttered world. Whether you see the Internet as a source of good or evil, one thing is for sure, it will continue to develop at rapid speed, and the whole world will become ever smaller, intrigued or shocked as a result of its continual development.

* * * * *

After all these thoughts about technology and our inevitably mind-boggling technological future, I welcomed the extreme tranquility of the scene before me. Cricklade Town Bridge is the limit of navigational rights on the River Thames. At some point soon, I guessed, I might chance upon the first river craft plying its way down the river, although the Thames still seems too shallow for anything much larger than a canoe. Shortly after re-joining the Thames at Cricklade, I could see the confluence of the River Churn with the Thames. Many people see the River Churn as the true source of the River Thames. Whilst I am aware that there is a very noble logic behind this, I feel a sense of pride in my journey so far, and I cannot help feeling that that old stone monument at Thames Head is in the right place. I guess it's all about what you are familiar with. I'm sure that had I grew up along the banks of the Churn, I might see things differently!

Not far outside of Cricklade, I passed under the busy A419 which roared overhead and gave me a preview of the increasing industrialisation I would start to encounter on my journey in the not too distant future. Away from the road, I was back in the beautiful Cotswold countryside. With nothing but the occasional wooden bridge to cross and bobbing dog walker, my journey was serene and pleasant.

I occasionally stopped to drink up the sights, smells, and sounds. I have long been entranced by water – I think it is something deep inside. I guess it is probably a good thing that humans might be hardwired to appreciate water; after all, we all know we can't survive for long without it. Shimmering reeds and weeds beneath the water appeared like translucent strands of emerald. The gravelly river bed showed off its glossy surface from beneath its glass-like case. It's the simplest things like this that can make you feel so alive.

After an hour and a half or so of meandering and

passing a lone canoeist, the first river craft I had stumbled across, I entered the village of Castle Eaton. Many of the buildings in this remote village date from about 1650, and part of the village has been made a Conservation Area to protect its historical and architectural importance. The bridge at Castle Eaton has been described as one of the ugliest on the River Thames. However, I quite like this grizzly iron girder construction. There is something a bit 'Mississippi Delta' about it.

Reasoning that I may very well need a drink, I headed across to the Red Lion pub just a stone's throw away. This is a truly great place, and I loved its gently sloping gardens which tail off into the emerald Thames. I 'accidentally' stopped here for a couple of pints. I felt it would be totally out of order not to have stopped here as this is the first public house actually situated on the banks of the River Thames!

Shortly after leaving Castle Eaton, I was reminded by the growl of jet engines that I was not far from the mighty airbase of RAF Fairford. I have visited the Fairford Airshow before. The Airshow here is the largest of its kind in the world. RAF Fairford was built in 1944 as a base for the British and American air forces involved in the Normandy landings, and it had a pivotal role in the Cold War when B-47 bombers were stationed here. Today it remains a key base for the US Air Force and has been home to all sorts of impressive aircraft from B-52 and B-2 Stealth bombers through to huge transport and tanker aircraft. RAF Fairford is a leading NATO airbase and the diminutive Thames round these parts feels a little overwhelmed by it all.

A short distance from Castle Eaton lies the village of Kempsford. The huge monolithic square tapering tower of its wonderful church loomed ahead for much of my journey here. This village is steeped in history. It once formed the boundary between the Saxon kingdoms of Mercia (north bank) and Wessex (south bank). An important castle once stood here, and the impressive village church was built by John of Gaunt, the son of Edward III, as a memorial to his wife.

Pushing onwards towards Lechlade, I left the towering Kempsford church behind. I had a fair walk ahead before getting to my destination. I stopped to admire the characterful Hannington Bridge with its three beautiful stone arches. Shortly afterwards, I passed another river craft – this time a small dinghy piloted by two young lovebirds. I nodded knowingly as we looked slightly awkward to have chanced upon each other.

Across the other side of the river, I looked into the tiny village of Inglesham. A beautiful house sits within its comfortable surroundings. There is a swimming pool and what I eventually deduced to be the property's own island in the middle of the river connected to the lawn by a footbridge. Now that's what I call a property portfolio! Some people would be more than happy with just a bigger house, but a massive pile on the river with a swimming pool and its own island? Now we're talking! I imagined some Richard Branson-type could well be living here. Maybe they were in their house right at that moment pondering whether it might be better to go for a swim in their pool or just best to pop outside in the sun on their own mini Necker Island in the middle of the Thames!

I have always loved the way that small coves form along the stretches of some rivers. The banks occasionally give way to a small area of silt and shingle that looks like a mini-beach. You often see cows accessing the river at these points. The river meanders tightly, and the Inglesham Roundhouse came into view. The Roundhouse is where the lock-keeper for the first lock on the Thames and Severn canal used to live. Today this canal lies abandoned, though recent enthusiasm for Britain's canal network has raised the prospect that it might one day be restored. Inglesham Roundhouse marks the head of navigation for the river. Although boats are allowed to travel further than this point, anything much larger than a canoe or dinghy would soon encounter some problems.

A row of narrowboats and small pleasure cruisers lined up on the bank, and I could see the outskirts of Lechlade. I passed a small marina, and was soon presented with the wonderful humpback of Halfpenny Bridge. I crossed this bridge, stopping on top to drink up the scenes. It was early evening, and the sunset was phenomenal; I must have spent a good ten minutes admiring it. I felt pleased with myself for yomping my way there, and I was looking forward to exploring this intriguing place the next day. I got down from the bridge and strolled into The Riverside pub. I ordered the first of quite a few drinks and booked a room.

CHAPTER 7

Tales from the Riverbank

I woke up early and tucked into a stunning full English breakfast. A refreshing cuppa helped welcome me into the land of the living. After breakfast, I set out, eager to take a look at this most charming of towns: Lechlade. Outside The Riverside pub, I stopped to take another look at the quaint bow-shaped Halfpenny Bridge. This bridge was built in 1792 and took its name from the halfpenny toll levied to cross it. The roof of the bridge was built high to allow the vastly increased traffic that passed through Lechlade to or from the now defunct Thames and Severn canal. Lechlade prospered with the river trade and the wharves built on the river. The stone used in the construction of the roof of St Paul's Cathedral in London was loaded at Lechlade.

Today, this town prospers from tourists who have come to explore the river or the local Cotswold area. Halfpenny Bridge is also important because it is very close to the Head of Navigation. Many walkers and boats begin their journey down the Thames from here, and it was at Halfpenny Bridge in September 2011 that the comedian David Walliams started his epic eight-day swim down the river to Westminster Bridge in London. Thousands of people came down to the banks of the River Thames to cheer Walliams along, and his remarkable feat raised over one million pounds for the charity Sport Relief.

Lechlade town centre is a short walk from the bridge, and it oozes character. It wasn't long until I was lost in my own world exploring a couple of antique shops and a bookshop. Behind the marketplace lies the majestic church of St Lawrence. It was here in this churchyard that the poet Percy Bysshe Shelley was inspired to compose 'A Summer Evening Churchyard, Lechlade'. The path he walked along is named Shelley's Walk, and there is a commemorative plaque on the wall marking the occasion. Shelley spent a couple of nights in the town, and his visit adds to Lechlade's charm and mystique. I stopped along the path and imagined Shelley walking along here, his mind putting the sights, smells, and emotions into words. What a delightful little corner of Britain it is here.

I wanted to get some good walking down the Thames Path achieved that day. There were no more towns on the river until I reached Oxford, and I was sure to be greeted with more of the pastoral sublimity that I had experienced on my journey so far. I followed the meandering Thames through a lush green meadow. The occasional pillboxes were scattered along the banks of the river. These concrete monoliths were constructed in 1940 to reinforce the river as a line of defence against a German invasion after the fall of France. The idea was to protect London by using natural barriers where possible. Ditches were also dug as an extra defence against German tanks. The River Thames provided an awesome natural barrier against an invading force, and a good portion of the twelve hundred plus pillboxes that remain today can be found scattered along the banks of the Thames.

Along the bank of the river, I chanced upon an elderly fellow dragging a small net amongst the reeds. It seemed a strange way to fish – surely he was looking for something particular. 'Caught anything?' I asked, realising I must be using an age-old classic line to get into conversation with a fisherman. It turned out that he was looking for tiddlers for his garden pond. As we talked, a large kite flew low over the far side of the riverbank. I turned my gaze back to the distant spire in Lechlade with the meadows in front and drank up the quite ravishing view. The fisherman paused and looked too. 'That's one of the finest views in the whole of England,' he enthused. I could only agree.

A brightly painted narrowboat coughed and spluttered past as I neared the busy St John's Lock, the first and highest lock on the River Thames. At the heart of this lock lies a reclining elderly bearded man carved from stone. Resting upon his plinth, and with a shovel loosely hanging over his shoulder, this is Old Father Thames. The statue was carved by Italian sculptor Rafaelle Monti for the Great Exhibition of 1851. Following the fire at Crystal Palace in 1936, Old Father Thames was moved to the source of the River Thames. The sculpture was moved to St John's Lock from Thames Head in 1974.

Old Father Thames was sadly being vandalised in the secluded location of Thames Head but now, right in front of the lock and the lock-keeper's cottage, hopefully this old man can finally get the peace and respect that he deserves. I took a couple of photographs of this evocative stone carving and respectfully carried on my way. I passed under the brick-built arch of St John's bridge built in 1886 and back out into the meadows.

It was not long before I caught fleeting glimpses of the village of Buscot, which is now largely owned by the National Trust. The Old Parsonage here was built in 1703, and it was later sold to the American author Peter Stuckley who lived here with his partner Mr Mussett. Upon his death, Stuckley gave the house to the National Trust on the condition that future tenants must have American literary connections. It appears that the current tenant remains a closely-guarded secret.

Not far from the tiny Buscot Lock is the majestic Buscot Park. This pile was built in 1779 for Edward Loveden Townsend. It was owned by a gold mining magnate and then passed onto the successful financier Alexander Henderson who was given the title Baron Faringdon in 1916. Although the house is today in the hands of the National Trust, it is leased to the Faringdon family who continue to live there. Buscot Park is famous for its stunning water gardens laid out by Harold Peto.

After a short amble through the countryside, another huge country pile came into view. Kelmscott Manor was once the home of William Morris, the great artist, designer, writer, and social reformer of the Victorian era. Born in 1834, Morris founded a design firm with the artist Edward Burne-Jones and the poet and artist Dante Gabriel Rosetti. This business would go on to profoundly influence home interiors for years to come. Even today, William Morris is a name frequently bandied about by devotees the nation over. Britain is still in love with William Morris, but his ambitions went far further than wanting to design wallpapers and fabrics.

As an author, Morris would help to establish the modern fantasy genre, and he was a major influence on the writer J.R.R.Tolkein as well as James Joyce. Morris was the first author whose works were set in an entirely invented fantasy world. He was approached with an offer of Poet

Laureateship after the death of Tennyson in 1982 but declined. Morris was also an important figure in the emergence of socialism in Britain, founding the Socialist League in 1884. Kelmscott Manor would become famous itself as a result of the Kelmscott Press. Morris rejected much that was on offer from industrial processes and became a proponent of handcraftsmanship. He believed that the craftsman was of equal importance to the artist. Morris would go on to form Morris & Co, a brand which survives to this day under licence to Sanderson and Sons and Liberty of London. Morris also founded the Society for the Protection of Ancient Buildings in 1877 along with Philip Webb and J.J. Stevenson.

In the 1870s, Morris began to become interested in politics. Some historians have indicated that Morris was an important early proponent of modern environmentalism. He sought to protect planet Earth from the ravages of pollution and increasing industrialism. Morris spent the last years of his life engrossed in the Kelmscott Press. The 1891 Kelmscott edition of the Works of Geoffrey Chaucer is considered a masterpiece of book design. Morris died at Kelmscott House, Hammersmith in 1896. He is buried in Kelmscott village churchyard.

Today, William Morris' legacy continues through the William Morris Society. He has fans not only in the field of interior design but also of his literary works, which have found a resurgence since the great fantasy revival of the 1960s. There is a public museum in Walthamstow dedicated to Morris' life, and his fondness for true artisanship and worldly compassion are as relevant today as ever.

For me, Morris represents a truly inspirational figure. Much of his life was spent appraising values of the past, such as craftsmanship, but his embracing of environmental sentiment was looking to the future, past industrialism. It is a sign of his eclectic genius that almost everything that Morris concerned himself with is of great concern today. We live in a world that craves authenticity amongst industrial ubiquity, and a world which is finally coming to terms with the environmental consequences of its past and present industrial indulgences.

William Morris was one of an increasing amount of people who were growing concerned with the Industrial Revolution, and its effect on communities. He believed in leading a simple life based upon community, authenticity, and an element of romanticism. He championed the cottage industry, and its simple, carefully crafted wares. The cottage industry was based on handmade products, whereas industrial mass-production issued bland products mainly made by machine. It is interesting to note that there are few references to ugly landscapes in British literature before around 1800. The Industrial Revolution changed many towns and cities in Britain into smog-filled grim places. The mass production of goods was facilitated by a whole army of people who simply became machine operators repeating the same processes day in, day out.

Along with the architect Charles Voysey, William Morris led the Arts and Crafts Movement. This international design movement would flourish for a 50-year period from 1860 onwards. Inspired by the writings of John Ruskin and Augustus Pugin, the movement stood for traditional craftsmanship and the usage of medieval, folk, and romantic styles of decoration. Although it developed first in Britain, the movement soon spread to include Europe and North America. The movement was a revolt against the onward advancement of machine production and the ever-increasing ugliness associated with the Industrial Revolution.

William Morris championed the establishment of ideal communities which based life around co-operation. In many ways, his principles are still relevant today. Many people continue to feel alienated by an increasingly corporate Britain in which nearly every town high street looks the same. Gone are many of the friendly local stores and the happy market traders. Their replacements are the machine-like supermarket behemoths. A certain vibrancy has gone and compounded by the ever-ubiquitous Internet; the British high street fades ever closer to insignificance. Sure, we hear about social revolutions such as social networking and how they are changing our world, but they are no substitute for the real world, and they are the marketeers greatest friend.

'Dear Neighbour', the letter begins, 'As a future neighbour, I am pleased to let you know that we propose to open a Tesco Express convenience store ....'. This is the much-feared letter that many people in Britain seem to hope never to receive. I got hold of a copy of this letter from a neighbour when the inevitable ambition of Tesco reached my neck of the woods. I'm not sure if Tesco like their letters being mooted about, but I'm sure they must be pretty used to it by now. Well over one hundred people protested against the store, but it opened anyway.

The truth of the matter is that, little over a year after opening, the store appears to be thriving, and it hasn't yet shut down all the local shops. Tesco point out the benefits of having a local cheap convenience store. They highlight the benefits of people not having to drive long distances to go food shopping; the fact that they will be creating approximately 20 new full and part-time jobs for local people, and that the presence of their store will act as a deterrent to anti-social behaviour.

As far as I am concerned, the opportunity for independent convenience stores to compete with the likes of Tesco vanished many years ago. First, there were the out-of-town shopping centres which pulled in their customers from both the inside and outside of British towns and cities. Then the big supermarkets decided to muscle into Britain's smaller towns and villages, competing and replacing the independent shops with smaller metro-style stores.

The sheer economies of scale and buying power of these supermarket giants have squeezed the profit margins of many independent convenience stores too far. Owning an independent convenience store involves working incredibly long hours from opening at dawn to sell newspapers right through to putting up with intimidating yobbos late in the evening. Hardworking and determined Asian families have long been adept at running these enterprises, and their dedication is admirable, particularly in their brave defences of their stores against armed robbers and other undesirables, footage of which regularly graces our television screens in both the national and regional news across Britain. Admittedly the 'big boys' like Tesco should not be made to shoulder all the blame for the demise of Britain's independent shops, after all, we can all choose where we shop.

Recent years have seen a resurgence of interest in independent shops and interesting schemes have been dreamt up to rejuvenate Britain's towns and villages. One example of these schemes is 'Pub is the Hub'. This scheme helps rural communities by placing community information and even small convenience stores within pubs. This 'not for profit' scheme, which was initially inspired by the Prince of Wales, has been running since 2001 and has worked with over 500 pubs. The scheme has also given many British pubs a lifeline by helping them achieve alternative revenue streams such as from the sale of provisions.

Freedom from having to earn the large amounts of money required to live in advanced capitalist countries such as Britain is an increasingly common aspiration. As I have pointed out earlier, wealth rarely leads to greatly increased happiness. Most people are fully aware of this even if popular culture rarely reflects this reality. Maybe it does not have to cost that much to live here in Britain. For example, do we need such a big house or such a large enslaving mortgage? Could we save more money and rely less on the tempting loans and credit offered by those oh-so-friendly banks?

We can always grow our own vegetables, barter with our neighbours and waste less. No longer do all our energies have to be bound up in slaving away just to fulfil the same lifestyle as our peers. Growing your own vegetables is incredible fun, and bartering for goods and services with your neighbours eliminates the money that is always expended on capitalism's ubiquitous middlemen.

Getting to know your neighbours is just part of a growing trend of reconnecting with the local rather than the global. For many decades, the Western world seemed obsessed with the idea of globalisation, and that is how we have ended up with our land of 'identikit' towns or 'clone' towns. There is increasing demand for the independent trader in the local community. Throughout Britain, local community groups have been set up, and many towns have embarked on remodelling or gentrifying their centres in an effort to entice people back.

Interestingly, there has been a more recent online trend for regional social networking groups, where people can communicate with people within their own communities as opposed to with anyone from around the world. There appears to be a sea change and, whilst globalisation will carry on for obvious reasons, the local community will become increasingly important and relevant.

Capitalist commerce increasingly flatters the masses with compliments about anyone and everyone. It shouts out 'Because you're worth it' and it tells us when to slow down, when to relax, and how to do it, what we should be doing, and why we should be doing it. It has assumed emperor-like power, and it knows that we can be cajoled into doing things if we know that's what our peers are doing. This is the very antithesis of living for the moment. I have always respected and even been slightly jealous of my friends and colleagues who exhibit an almost canine-like love for doing things on the spur of the moment. Planning is often necessary, but it increases burden and anxiety on people. Anxiety is a too common curse of Western life. I am not rejecting Western consumer culture entirely, just highlighting its limitations in what it can offer humans in terms of emotional reward.

The pursuit of personal perfection seems to have gained almost as much attention in the West as the pursuit of money. Fuelled by an obsession with celebrities and celebrity lifestyles, many young girls want to attain a dangerously low weight. Whilst keeping fit is a good idea, many people insist upon aggressive gym regimes. Youngsters can feel excluded if they do not have the latest computer games or designer sportswear. To cut it short, consumerism in Britain and much of the rest of the world has won. It has taken advantage of insecurities about the way we look and stolen a lead on us. We are even sometimes told by means of slick marketing that junk food can be good for us!

Time and again, we hear that the excuse for some act of mindless vandalism by some feral youths is boredom. The word boredom would appear to be a relatively modern invention; in fact, it wasn't until 1760 that the word was first used in English. The reality is that there are plenty of things that can alleviate boredom. Learning to play an instrument, a sport, or how to make things are all worthy pastimes. Shopping has become the national pastime and, as a result, a mountain of debt has been allowed to pile up. Needless to say, alongside this mountain of debt is a mountain of unwanted or little-used goods. The whole scene is really quite tragic.

We spend huge amounts of money on vastly overpriced goods, only to end up not really wanting many of them. Contrast this, I ask, with the world's estimated two billion people living below the poverty line. Not only do these people not have regular access to basic things such as clean drinking water, they would benefit so much more if we could give them the monetary equivalent of our huge wastage here in the West. Charity has been shown to make the benefactor feel good about themselves, often more so than spending the equivalent money on themselves. This Christmas, I ask you: why not consider helping a child or a family in a poor nation as a present for someone, rather than spend it on some gift of questionable worthiness that will probably end up unused and unloved?

The paradox of modern life is that no matter how much wealth can be obtained, many people keep on pushing themselves to obtain more. By living beyond their means, rather than enjoying the freedoms often associated with wealth, people often get caught up in a self-imposed cycle of never having enough money to finance their lifestyle. By rejecting that bigger house and bigger mortgage, those latest must-have accessories and the expectations of celebrity culture and peer pressure, we can all benefit from less stress and time poverty. Growing your own vegetables in your garden or allotment; being creative; introducing the kids to the wonders and wilds of your local woods; visiting Britain's heritage; going to museums, galleries and exciting parts of the country are all things that have a calming effect on the mind.

Yes, shopping is fun, but we do not have to own everything that we discover. Giving to charity, being polite, and showing respect and manners to other human beings can be a rewarding experience. Think about the tiny things we take for granted ourselves and how they can bring huge rewards and enjoyments to those less fortunate than us. The millionaires should relish giving away their wealth to help others. The average man or woman on Britain's streets should think about how massively fortunate they have been to have been born into one of the wealthiest nations on earth.

So what about those who have escaped from 'conventional society' altogether? It is difficult to put a figure on the amount of people that live in communes and alternative communities in Britain. It has been estimated there are around 150 alternative communities in Britain. Many of these are based around religious principles; for others, the main focus is based around sustainable living and sharing. The vast majority of alternative lifestyles in Britain are conducted in the shadow of 'conventional society'. For example; the nudist is bound by majority moral values and sometimes even law, so they are only likely to be found in their 'natural element', tucked out of the sight of mainstream society with their fellow nudists.

* * * * *

Today, Kelmscott Manor is owned by the Society of Antiquaries of London. As I walked past, I imagined Morris at his printing press or his loom thinking about how the world around him was changing. We think that we live in a fast-changing world today, but the fact of the matter is that the world was rapidly changing well over a hundred years ago. Whilst its appeal to the masses worldwide continues to wane (despite socialism being given a major boost in Britain by the election of Jeremy Corbyn to Leader of the Labour Party on 12th September 2015), it is easy to forget that in Morris' day, the realities of life were much harsher.

The gap between the rich and the poor in Britain remains too large, but in the early Victorian era it was common for children to be forced into labour such as down hazardous coal mines, for people to go starving for days, and for basic human rights to be widely ignored. The socialists wanted to address the needs of the poor and disadvantaged, and they helped counterbalance against the emergence of the new super-wealthy industrial elite.

With Kelmscott Manor fading into the distance, I continued through wonderfully peaceful meadows and only passed the occasional rivercraft and fellow walkers. To my south, I caught glimpses of the church at Eaton Hastings. Its population of 80 or so residents is considerably less than the number of people who once lived here. This rare example of de-population can be attributed to the Bubonic Plague or

Black Death as it was charmingly known. This 14th-century nightmare plague killed an estimated 25 million people in Europe, and is believed to have accounted for the termination of somewhere between 30 to 60 per cent of Europe's total population.

I will resolve never to complain again about having a cold, despite being male! Some have speculated whether the Black Death was, in fact, an Ebola-like virus. The Ebola virus devastated a large area of West Africa from late 2013 until 2016, killing over 11,000 people before a large-scale international relief effort helped contain the virus.

Soon the distinctive Gothic arches of Radcot Bridge, the oldest bridge on the River Thames, came into view. The Battle of Radcot Bridge was fought on 19th December 1387 between troops loyal to Richard II and an army captained by Henry Bolingbroke, Earl of Derby. The triumphant Bolingbroke went on to become Henry IV. I decided that a battle-worn bridge that was built over 800 years ago was as good a place as any to have an excuse for a break. There are two bridges at this point in the river as it splits, forming an island in the middle. Feeling inquisitive, I went for a stroll along the island and caught some equally inquisitive glances back from the garden of The Swan pub across the river.

Just north of here lies the village of Clanfield, a village of around 850 residents. Anyone thinking of moving to this charming village should be warned that the Thames often moves into the village too in the form of flooding as it did in July 2007. A little further down the winding river, past the quaint Rushey Lock with its amusing topiary frog in the lock keeper's garden, is the elegantly pleasing arch of Tadpole Bridge. A short distance to the north of here lies the village of Bampton. A village of around 2,500 people, Bampton was an important settlement in Saxon and Medieval times. It will be familiar to many people as a substitute for North Yorkshire in ITV's hit 2011-2012 period drama series *Downtown Abbey*.

Bampton has an eclectic mix of people, who clearly keep themselves busy and presumably rather amused. After all, they boast having a tradition of Morris dancing that is believed to go back as far as 600 years. They play the traditional throwing game Aunt Sally. They dress up in nightgowns and push each other in trolleys, visiting each pub in the village, and making sure they down a beer at each stop. To cap all these crazy antics off, they have a Pumpkin Club dedicated to the growing and presenting of the largest pumpkins possible (what else would a pumpkin club have to do?). Monies raised from this event are distributed to local old-age pensioners. Quite clearly, just thinking about the village Bampton is enough to make you raise a glass in a toast to humanity!

Moving along the wildly meandering Thames, I passed under some sinister overhead power cables. I never like passing under these things. My map informed me that a short distance to my south lies the huge pile of Buckland House. This Palladian masterpiece was built by John Wood, the Younger, for Sir Robert Throckton in 1757, a 'nice little abode' which has recently undergone a restoration project involving up to 70 craftsmen. The restoration was carried out by its current owner Patrick, or Paddy McNally.

McNally, a former love of the Duchess of York, started life as the Grand Prix reporter for *Autosport* magazine, but he soon made the financially sound decision to move to the commercial side of motorsport. He became a driver manager and then moved on to become a sponsorship consultant with Marlboro. This brought him into close contact with the tycoon and former Formula One boss Bernie Ecclestone. McNally developed a system that gave advertisers the maximum TV exposure and took over the sales of most of F1's trackside advertising. McNally's Allsport Management company is based in Switzerland.

With the sun low in the sky, my thoughts began to focus on the fact that it was around there that I was going to need to pitch down for the night. I could have planned this one a bit better, I thought. I returned to a thought I'd had earlier on in the day, but not considered seriously until now – should I spend the night in an old type 22 pillbox?

Now I think it's time that I should level with you; I have spent some pretty uncomfortable nights sleeping in some unusual places out in the wilds before. For instance I've slept under an upturned fibreglass dinghy boat in someone's back garden - it was after a party, so it was totally excusable! I also once spent an alcohol-sodden night asleep under a sun lounger on a beach on the Costa Del Sol which was quite a surprise for the German sunbather on top and everyone else on the beach as I emerged at 10 a.m. the following morning! Then I've spent spent many an uncomfortable night sleeping in my car. A night spent parked up on a verge on the side of a lane in misty Exmoor was spooky, but a night spent parked up in the howling wind next to the lighthouse at Lizard Point in Cornwall was even spookier. Despite all of these night-time escapades, I have never had to face anything quite as strange as the prospect of spending a night in a Second World War type 22 pillbox!

I traipsed over to the concrete batholith pillbox and decided the only reason I wouldn't do it was if the place smelled of urine. It didn't, so I took off my rucksack, laid out my sleeping bag as best I could and rested up my aching feet, just hoping I didn't bump into any rats. I then jumped up and cracked open a bottle of red wine outside to assuage my trepidation and leant up against the outside of my new home, savouring the last vestiges of sun. When it was near dark, I crawled inside in my well-oiled state and enjoyed the thought of being quite possibly the only person in Britain to be spending the night in a small concrete pillbox (surely there couldn't be anyone else holed up in one of these derelict limpets on that night?). I shut my eyes and embarked upon a quite uncomfortable night's sleep.

My back was a bit sore, but I did get some sleep. Whether that would have been the case had I not drunk the bottle of wine, I am not sure! Ahead of me lay the tiny hamlet of Shifford with its picture-postcard church. It was in a meadow here in AD 890 that King Alfred presided over the first recorded English Parliament. A little further along I got a good view of Harrowdown Hill. There is nothing particularly notable about these small woods atop a shallow hill other than the fact that it was here in 2003 that the weapons expert Dr David Kelly was found dead after apparently committing suicide.

Kelly had disputed what was known as the '45-minute claim' that Saddam Hussain of Iraq was capable of firing battlefield biological and chemical weapons within 45 minutes of an order to use them. Kelly came under intense pressure from the Blair government after it was alleged that he was the source of a news leak about the dubious nature of the claim, which was a pivotal feature in the invasion of Iraq and toppling of Saddam from power in 2003.

Despite a re-opened investigation which has confirmed that the verdict of suicide was indeed correct, many people still believe that Dr Kelly was murdered. The main reasons behind this assertion lie in the fact that very little blood was found at the scene from the slitting of his left wrist and that the amount of Co-proxamol painkillers taken was regarded as insufficient to kill someone. Additionally, no fingerprints were found on the knife that he had used to slit his wrist.

The British epidemiologist Dr Rouse wrote in the *British Medical Journal* that the act of committing suicide by severing wrist arteries was an extremely rare occurrence in a 59-year-old man with no previous psychiatric history. He pointed out that nobody else had died from the exact same causes during the year of Dr Kelly's death. David Kelly is buried in the churchyard of St Mary's in Longworth, which is only a short distance from his former home in Southmoor. The controversy surrounding the decision to invade Iraq by the Bush and Blair governments and the circumstances of Kelly's death are likely to prevail for many more years to come. The Chilcot Inquiry's report into the Iraq War, published on 6th July 2016, was broadly critical of the actions of the British Government and military in making the case for war. It also was critical of the tactics and planning for the aftermath of the Iraq War.

A short distance to the south-east of Longworth lies the exotic sounding village of Kingston Bagpuize. This village of around 2000 inhabitants derives its name from its original name of 'Kingston' plus the surname of Ralph de Bachepuz, a nobleman from Bacquepuis in Normandy who helped William of Normandy in the Norman conquest of England in 1066. Kingston Bagpuize House was built around 1720. I wonder if it was Kingston Bagpuize that was the inspiration for the 1974 old saggy cloth cat children's TV character Bagpuss? Further research shows that I am not alone in thinking this and a conversation with some fellow Thames ramblers reveals that Kingston Bagpuize is often referred to as Bagpuss by the locals! The possible connection between Bagpuss and Bagpuize remains a mystery, but personally I cannot stop thinking of Bagpuss when I think of Kingston Bagpuize!

Kingston Bagpuize caught the world's attention after the release of the romantic comedy film, *Tortoise in Love*, which features a stately home gardener who is helped by the village after he falls in love with a Polish au pair, but is very shy in pursuing her. Guy Browning, the film's locally-based director, presented his idea to produce a film at a village meeting in 2009. The village embraced his idea with aplomb, and many of the locals are featured in the casting. Around 800 village residents invested between £10 and £1000 each towards a total budget of £250,000. The film received its world premiere at Leicester Square.

A short walk brought me to Newbridge, the second oldest bridge across the Thames. This elegant bridge was built in 1250 by monks. There are pubs either side of the river here, but it was too early in the day to be thinking about things like that! An unpleasant sight which greeted me shortly after was the presence of another type 22 pillbox. My back shivered at the thought of another night in one of those. At Babcock Hythe, the north bank of the river is flanked by a seemingly endless caravan park. Shortly after, I was greeted on the right by the built-up banks of the Farmoor reservoir. Built in two stages, the Farmoor reservoir was completed in 1976. It holds around 14 billion litres of water and supplies Swindon as well as many other locations. This reservoir is supplied by the River Thames.

After walking through Pinkhill Lock, I looked to try and

catch glimpses of the village of Farmoor which, according to my map was little more than a quarter mile from the Thames path. After a mile or so of the glistening river, I reached the attractive Swinford Bridge with its wonderful balustrading. Swinford is one of only three functioning toll bridges on the River Thames. The other two can be found at Whitchurch and Dartford. Swinford Bridge was built by the Earl of Abingdon in 1767, and its toll revenues are not subjected to any tax. The bridge was sold at auction in 2009 for just over one million pounds, and it creates a tax-free income of around £100,000 annually. The road over the Thames here takes traffic between Oxford and the village of Eynsham.

Eynsham is one of the oldest villages in Britain. Evidence has been found here of sixth and seventh-century Saxon buildings. A Benedictine abbey was founded here in 1005, and by 1302 Eynsham had a wharf on what became known as Wharf Stream, a tributary of the Thames. Eynsham has suffered a number of fires in its history. One in 1629 destroyed 21 houses and another in 1681 destroyed 20 houses. The two main products of the village today are the strange bedfellows of gravel and superconducting magnets, produced by Siemens Magnet Technology Ltd.

About five miles to the west of Eynsham lies the town of Witney. It is perhaps famous for two things: its woollen blankets made since the Middle Ages and former Prime Minister David Cameron's one time constituency seat. Witney is situated on the River Windrush and suffered its worst flooding for 50 years in 2007. Further flooding here in 2008 contributed to the death of a 17-year-old boy who drowned in a culvert.

Swinford Bridge and Eynsham Lock were now far away in the distance behind me. A particularly pleasant stretch of the river wends its way past the enticing Wytham Great Wood. Wytham Woods are a Site of Special Scientific Interest and owned by The University of Oxford who use them for research in zoology and climate change. The woods are noted for their significant population of badgers, and they frequently featured in the 'Inspector Morse' detective novels by Colin Dexter.

I rambled up through another lock and passed under the busy A34 road bridge. I knew that I was only a short distance from the city centre, and from Oxford's famous 'dreaming spires'. The last stretch of my journey took me across Port Meadow. The spires of Oxford could clearly be seen behind the trees. It was in this tranquil meadow that Charles I's army set up camp during the English Civil War. Few could imagine a welcome to a major city better than the misty calm of Port Meadow.

CHAPTER 8
Dreaming Spires

The cheap B&B wasn't up to much, and the well-worn electric shower was up to even less. The rest was welcomed, however, and almost anything beats a concrete pillbox for a bed! Oxford could well and truly be summed up by the word 'cosmopolitan'. All around me purposeful looking people buzzed past on bicycles and tourists swarmed in droves. The Japanese tourists had their cameras out at the ready, and I suspected that by the end of the day there wouldn't be a square centimetre of the town centre that hadn't been studied by their camera lenses! I wondered how many of their photographs I would end up in; an unsuspecting pedestrian providing part of the background scenery in somebody's holiday snaps.

In Oxford, quiet medieval backstreets open onto bustling streets and brash commercialism sits side-by-side with fine old buildings. Oxford's world famous university seems to surround the town centre. Nearly all routes from Cornmarket Street, the pedestrianised retail centre of Oxford, appear to end up at the gate of some illustrious university building. A pasty from the Hot Pasty Company is about all that I fancied buying on that day from down Cornmarket. Turning the corner into Broad Street, I was at the threshold of a different Oxford. Ahead, I was confronted by rows of parked bicycles, acres of honey stone buildings and walls, and a short parade of quaint shops.

I like this part of Oxford. I like it a lot. The only thing which slightly detracts from the pleasantness of this place is the fact that it was here, where Broad Street is now located, that the Oxford Martyrs were burnt at the stake for their 'heretic' religious beliefs and teachings. The Martyrs were the Anglican bishops Hugh Latimer, Nicholas Ridley, and Thomas Cranmer. Latimer and Ridley were despatched in 1555, and Cranmer was executed the following year. We should all be thankful that Britain, and most of the rest of the world, for that matter, is a far more tolerant place today.

Sometimes when walking down the small historic alleys, it is easy to forget that you are in a city of around 165,000 people. Oxford, or Oxenaforda as it was known, originates from the Saxon times and literally means 'Ford of the Oxen'. The town's diverse economy boasts motor manufacturing, publishing, education, science, and information technology. Many of these industries benefit from the University of Oxford's output of intellectually-gifted people. The precise foundation date of the University of Oxford is not known, but there is evidence that it stretches as far back as 1096. It is the world's second oldest surviving university, following the University of Bologna. Disputes between the students and Oxford townsfolk in 1209 led to academics fleeing Oxford and founding what became the University of Cambridge.

The battle between 'town and gown' was reinvigorated during the English Civil War when the University supported the Royalist cause whilst the town favoured the Parliamentarian cause. It wasn't until the 19th century that women's colleges were established, and these only came into being after substantial activism from the Association for Promoting the Higher Education of Women. Today, from these commendable efforts to establish equal rights, Oxford remains only slightly male dominated with around 52 per cent of students male and the remaining 48 per cent female.

Famous Oxford University 'Oxonians' seem to spring up everywhere. They account for 26 British Prime Ministers, including the current one, Theresa May; over 30 international leaders; 49 Nobel Prize Winners, at least 12 saints and 120 Olympic medal winners. At least 117 Oxonians were elected to Parliament in the 2010 British General Election, and more than 140 sit in the House of Lords. The prevalence of Oxford graduates in some areas of British life has become a little too much for some; in 2012, the soon- to-be-departing director-general of the BBC, Mark Thompson, commented that he was 'disturbed' by the high number of BBC employees who had attended Oxbridge colleges.

My excitement built as I approached the splendid grandeur of Sir Christopher Wren's Sheldonian Theatre. Built from 1664 to 1668, the Sheldonian is used for lectures, music concerts, and university ceremonies. Just past the Sheldonian, I traversed the front of the impressive Bodleian Library with its four massive pillars, where a few tourists were sat on the steps enjoying their lunch. The Bodleian is one of the oldest libraries in Europe and second only in size to the British Library. It is affectionately referred to by many students simply as 'the Bod'. I sped up as I turned the corner past the library as I neared the building that I most want to see: The Radcliffe Camera.

For me, this is the most impressive building in the whole of Oxford. It may not be the largest and by no means the grandest, but there is something about this cylindrical building built in a Palladian style that moves me. The Camera or the 'Rad Cam' as it is often referred to was built in 1737-1749 to house the Radcliffe Science Library. Many found humorous the fact that John Radcliffe, a man who scorned book-learning, bequeathed such a substantial sum of money for the founding of a library. This unusual beginning only adds to the building's allure. The Rad Cam is set in the centre of a quadrangle and surrounded by gated lawns. Quite a sight.

My grumbling stomach started to tell me that getting some lunch wouldn't be a bad idea. Just to my left after passing beneath the suspended walkway known as the Bridge of Sighs, although Hertford Bridge actually resembles Venice's Rialto Bridge, not the Bridge of Sighs, there is a narrow walkway called St Helens Passage. This unassuming narrow conduit conceals from view one of Oxford's oldest and finest pubs: the Turf Tavern. Walking into this pub and its surrounding beer gardens and terraces is like stumbling upon a hidden treasure trove.

A 'hidden gem' would be a suitable description for this pub, and no doubt a description that has been applied to it hundreds of times before. It is an intriguing enough place to engage the hidden explorer in almost anybody; I found myself eagerly exploring this ramshackle old place as soon as I arrived. The low-beamed ceiling in the bar dates from the 17th century, although the foundations of this pub can be traced back to the 13th century.

Pint of Oxfordshire ale in hand, I stepped outside to investigate further. The rear garden is enclosed on two sides by a remaining section of the old Oxford City wall. Due to the illegal activities of its former patrons, the Turf Tavern was situated just outside the city wall to escape the jurisdiction of the local colleges. These fantastically crumbly old walls only add to the security and intimacy of the garden.

Taking my seat at a table in the third and final garden area of the pub, my mind turned to my journey. I had walked over 60 miles and hadn't bargained for my feet blistering along the towpath. I put this down to the extra weight caused by my backpack. It wasn't long before an exceptional plate of battered cod, chips, peas, and a good dollop of tartare sauce was placed in front of me on the slatted wood table. I devoured the food with satisfied zeal. On the table behind me an excitable group of 20- and 30-something foreigners - I guessed Spaniards - gossiped and giggled away.

The Turf Tavern is probably well known to one alleged reformed 'smoker', former US President Bill Clinton. For, if local legend is to be believed, it was here that the Oxford student infamously 'did not inhale' from a spliff. Another world leader who definitely made his mark in the Turf was former Australian Prime Minister Bob Hawke, who set a Guinness World Record for consuming a yard glass of ale in just 11 seconds. Downing a yard of ale wasn't on the agenda for me that lunchtime, nor were any spliffs for that matter. As I walked back up the skinny St Helens Passage, I glanced behind me to take one last look at the Turf before melting back into the streets of Oxford.

After a very pleasant stroll down New College Lane, yet another of Oxford's fine quiet city-centre backstreets, I emerged onto the High Street, a wide, gently curving road of yet more grand buildings and a mixture of expensive looking cafes, art galleries, restaurants, and even a shop devoted to old maps. I had to take a look inside the map shop to satisfy the intrigue of my inner geographer. It's quite clear that Oxford's High Street caters for a more discerning clientele than nearby Cornmarket Street with its well-known branded outlets, or 'clone shops' as many disaffected Britons would probably call them.

A short walk along the High Street brought me to another of Oxford's gems: Oxford Market. This place is a feast for the eyes. I love seeing and smelling fresh meat and fish. You are reminded in an instant that these things come from real living beings, a sense that is far removed from the pre-packaged lumps of plasticised meat found in many of the big supermarkets. My best find was a great little delicatessen. 'Sod it, I'm going to eat like a king on this trip!', my mind brooded. I left the deli with my backpack laden with goodies such as olives, salamis, and luscious smelling bread.

My feet groaned under the extra weight, but my stomach danced for joy at the thought of gorging rich food in the non-too-distant future. It was a real shame that the market was quiet and the clone shops of Cornmarket were busy but, as I have said before, I believe a revolution is coming to Britain: a revolution that will generate a desire for more locally sourced produce. A revolution of interest in the locality. A revolution of the real over the hyped.

Up past the busy intersection of Cornmarket Street and the High Street and the enticing allure of the St Aldates Tavern, I was soon passing the Museum of Modern Art or, to give it its hip acronym, MOMA Oxford. Many people have 'issues' with modern art and, when they are referring to modern art, they are often pointing towards conceptual art. This is art in which the idea or concept presented by the artist is considered more important than the finished product. People can understand the skill and effort made by a fine painter, but they may struggle with accepting the offerings of many conceptual artists.

For me, the difference between fine art and modern art

is not such a quantum leap. In essence, both use ideas as inspiration for their creations, and both usually strive to invoke some kind of feeling within their viewers. However, I strongly suspect that one of the main issues at stake here is the amount of time that has been invested in producing each piece. Whilst even the smallest fine art painting often takes many hours, the conceptual artist can take just seconds to create a piece. Because of this notion, much conceptual art has been branded as 'con-art'.

I feel that the issue isn't about how long a piece of art has taken to create; it just simply boils down to whether you view it as good art or bad art. It is, to be fair, always art, given that we are talking about something of an entirely subjective appreciation. In the same way as a talented fine art painter has to be very methodical and disciplined to make a stunning piece, so the conceptual artist must dream up brilliant ideas for new art that invigorates the viewer and conveys its meaning powerfully. Whilst fine art usually takes a lot of time to physically create, I would point to the fact that great conceptual art may take a lot of time to percolate and develop in an individual's mind before it is ready to be realised. I think that truly great conceptual art is a rare creation, and most conceptual art I have ever seen simply doesn't cut it.

For the last 15 years or so, Britain has seemingly been subjected to a frenzy of conceptual art. Whether you liked it or not, 'Britart' had arrived. In 1988, 16 Goldsmiths students took part in a cheap alternative exhibition called 'Freeze'. The main organiser was Damien Hirst. Whilst Freeze generated little interest itself, it set a precedent for a couple more 'warehouse' exhibitions, and it was these that began the meteoric rise of an influential group of British artists that would become known as the Young British Artists. The artists asked for sponsorship money of a relatively modest £1000 from art world figures including Charles Saatchi.

In what has been described as a 'self-fulfilling prophecy', it wasn't long before Saatchi and other collectors began buying up a lot of the Young British Artists' product. It would seem that the Goldsmiths' graduates' self-promotion had paid off. Indeed, it was producing a good handful of future multi-millionaires including Damien Hirst who would find himself as the world's richest living artist just 20 years later. Hirst's personal fortune today has been estimated at over £200 million.

Damien Hirst's most iconic piece is 'The Physical Impossibility of Death in the Mind of Someone Living' or the 'shark in the tank' as it came to be widely known. This piece became the iconic work of British art in the 1990s and a symbol of Britart worldwide. Using the well-tested means of 'shock art' alongside wild living and having plenty of attitude, the Young British Artists attracted the media and eventual notoriety.

The much lambasted annual Turner Prize propelled the controversial stars of the Young British Artists even further; indeed by the late 1990s and early 2000s you would be hard pressed to avoid the effects of the YBAs. Turner Prize-winning Tracy Emin took public ridicule further with her piece 'My Bed' which consisted of her bed surrounded by condoms, soiled knickers, and other detritus. Many of the public whooped with joy when they heard the news that two Chinese performance artists, Yuan Cai and Jian Xi, had jumped up and down on her bed in an apparent show of disrespect of her work.

Shock art can be an easy ticket for people to get noticed,

and I have always been astounded at the interest people have shown in Hirst's shark, an exhibit that might just as well be home at the Museum of Natural History where, should it be situated here, no doubt few people would ever think of it as an artwork. I just wonder whether many of the people who go to see Hirst's shark and other dissected animals are really more captivated by the fascination of seeing giant carved up beasts than something that they believe is a truly great piece of artistic expression. Artists like Hirst are clever, and his short introspective media sound-bite interviews are designed to keep us fascinated with a man who I think still cannot believe his own luck.

* * * * *

As I paced on from MOMA Oxford (which was closed at the time of my visit), I pondered what the future holds for the next generation of British artists. The YBAs have held court now for too long and need to give way to future talent. Art has played a very important part in recent British culture, and with an estimated 30,000 plus artists based in the East End of London alone, there should be some great talent in both the fine and conceptual fields yet to emerge.

Picking up my pace, I rushed past the nondescript shopping mecca of the Westgate Centre. Here I was, lost in the freedom of the City of Oxford and traipsing my way to the Ashmolean Museum. This was the world's first university museum and, after an extensive and costly renovation, it re-opened in 2009 to wide acclaim. Certainly, it does not fail to impress. Having studied the numerous carvings of people mounted on beautiful swirling marble columns, I was soon beavering my way room to room, studying various antiquities. There are abundant rooms dedicated to ancient

Egyptian, Nubian, Chinese and Indian artefacts, and all sorts of items from all across the globe. I was captivated by the gold mask of Agamemnon, something I've got a picture of on the front of one of my Penguin Classics books.

It's quite amazing to be confronted by these things up close. I was also captivated by various hoards of Roman and Saxon items on show that had been discovered locally to Oxford, many along the banks of the Thames. Apart from a few shoals of schoolchildren enthusiastically taking in their surroundings, I was pretty much left alone to mill about uninterrupted. This place is vast, and you would need to spend a good day here to take it all in properly. My fleeting visit of just a couple of hours left me feeling overwhelmed. I walked out onto the streets of Oxford knowing that I would be coming back to the Ashmolean again.

And so it was with the shops closing all around me and determined commuters dashing around like demented bats to get home for their tea, I forged ahead to my next destination: Oxford Castle. The giant cone-shaped Motte or mound of this castle soon came into view. Built in 1071, on the western edges of Saxon Oxford, Oxford Castle comprises part of an impressive original stone tower sat atop its mound. Thinking about the sort of views I might be afforded by this sizeable man-made hill, I followed a large group of French teenagers through an open gate and up some steps cut into the rugged hillock.

The lack of any authority figures about, coupled with the feeling that maybe we shouldn't have been there, added to the excitement of this excursion. The views over the rooftops and spires of much of Oxford and parts of the Thames Valley were magnificent, and I remained atop to look out over the city for a good while after the teenagers had left. It is near impossible to look out across Oxford without invoking the classic line from Matthew Arnold's poem Thyrsis, 'That sweet city with her dreaming spires.' Although the poem was written overlooking the city from Boars Hill, I couldn't help imagining that the view I was getting right then was equally as captivating. This was a perfect time to visit. The sun was low in the sky, and a light breeze was picking up as dusk approached.

From up there I could ascertain orientation from my map. To my north lies Summertown, where Oxford's most expensive houses are located and where over half the local population has a degree. Further out to the north lies the large village of Kidlington. With over 17,000 people and over 50 shops, Kidlington is one of the largest villages in Europe. However, in classic British style, its residents have ardently resisted proposals to become a town, despite the fact that it clearly qualifies for town status against any criteria. Oxford Airport, which was somewhat bizarrely renamed London Oxford Airport, is also in Kidlington. It has a famous pilot training scheme which has trained thousands of pilots for many different airlines in over 40 countries. For me, it is the presence of the UK headquarters of the chocolatier, Guylian, in the village, which adds the most appeal. If you have never eaten Guylian's shell-shaped chocolates, I urge you to go out and buy a box now!

In a truly bizarre series of events, hundreds of excited Chinese tourists started visiting and photographing two streets in a housing estate in Kidlington in mid-2016. Nobody knows why because no one known to be famous lives on either of the streets. Some of the reasons people have put forward are that the tourists are confusing some of the houses in Benmead Road for ones filmed in a Harry

Potter film, or that they want to visit a typical English village before going on to the nearby Bicester Village outlet shopping centre. Maybe it will always remain a mystery.

To my east lay the much larger suburb of Headington, famous for its rooftop shark sticking out of a residential terrace house. This was installed in 1986, presumably shortly before Damien Hirst had dreamed up any shark related works – could he have been inspired by this Oxford shark art installation? Just to the south of Headington lies the large suburb of Cowley, famous for its ethnic diversity and being the manufacturing home of that most quintessentially British car: the Mini. To my south lay the villages of South Hinksey, New Hinksey, and Kennington, the home of the 'dreaming spires' poet Matthew Arnold. To my east lies the Saxon settlement of Botley which is now effectively a suburb of Oxford.

Climbing down from Oxford Castle's mount, I glanced at my watch a couple of times, surprised to see that I had spent a good half hour up there. I was meeting an old friend of mine and, characteristically, I was running late. Jericho is just a short walk of 20 minutes or so from the castle. A historic suburb of Oxford, this area likely got its pleasant name from the fact that it was once a remote place located outside the city walls. That night I was meeting up with my old pal Mark. He lives locally and can put me up for the night. Mark waved me over to the bar. This is the Jericho Tavern, a tidy bar and music venue with a legendary status to many. It was at the Jericho Tavern that Radiohead played their first ever gig in 1986 under the name 'On a Friday', and it was also here that Supergrass secured a record deal after playing a gig in 1994.

After a couple of jars in the Jericho Tavern we decided

to explore this fascinating little Oxford enclave. We visited a few bars before ending up in the Bookbinders Arms. We half-staggered down the road seeking out more fun. Out of the corner of my eye, I suddenly saw what appeared to be a couple of cardboard boxes moving towards me. Fortunately, Mark had made a move towards the moving boxes first. Closer inspection revealed that this was, in fact, a homeless man who had ingeniously enshrouded himself with a cardboard suit.

We chatted with him for a bit to make sure he was OK and gave him some money to buy some food. We tucked into a delicious kebab from a van parked by the roadside and got a taxi to Mark's house in Abingdon. The next morning, I bid farewell to Mark and found a local shop to buy a can of cola to assuage a slight hangover. These fizzy pop companies may be a load of hot-air marketing, but I really haven't found anything better than that strange, gassy, oily-looking stuff to replenish the soul after a heavy night.

Oxford is full of so many fascinating stories that it is difficult to know where to draw the line. One of the things that intrigues me is that it was home to the dreams and vision of yet another remarkable person called William Morris, Viscount Nuffield, the founder of Morris Motors Ltd. When it comes to motor car manufacturing in Oxford, his is the name to mention. William Morris was born in 1877 and was raised in a modest terraced house in Cowley, near to the location of the current Mini plant. In 1893, he started up a bicycle repair business in the shed at the bottom of his father's garden. In 1912 he designed his first car: the Morris Oxford. Other cars followed including the Morris Minor in 1928 and the Mini in 1959. By 1937, Morris Motors Ltd had become the largest motor car manufacturer in Europe.

Both William Morris, the artist, and William Morris, Viscount Nuffield, were concerned about the welfare and rights of their fellow man, with Viscount Nuffield giving away a large part of his fortune to found Nuffield College at Oxford University, and giving £10 million to found the Nuffield Foundation in 1943 to advance education and social welfare. He made various other donations. In fact, William Morris, Viscount Nuffield, donated the equivalent of £11 billion in today's money. He is recognised by the *'Guinness Book of Records'* as being 'Britain's greatest benefactor'.

Despite becoming one of the world's richest men and the greatest industrialist of his age, Morris was a man of modest means. He is regarded with great esteem by the people of Oxford today. Upon his death in August 1963, he gifted his house, Nuffield Place, to Nuffield College and, in the Spring of 2012, the house was donated to the National Trust, ensuring that the legacy of this great British innovator will be preserved.

* * * * *

It was late morning now, and I had rejoined the towpath back in Oxford. Once I had passed a good distance from the roaring ring road I decided to have a sit down. I tucked into some of my nice grub from Oxford's covered market and had a rest. I hadn't eaten anything since the previous night's kebab, but I resist the use of the word famished as I, like most people in the West, have never been truly facing starvation.

One of the world's most renowned famine relief charities must surely be Oxfam, which was founded in Oxford in 1942 as the Oxford Committee for Famine Relief. In all of their actions, the ultimate goal is to enable people to exercise their rights and manage their own lives. Oxfam works directly with communities and seeks to influence the powerful to ensure that people can improve their lives and have a say in the decisions that affect them. A truly noble cause and one that Oxonians can certainly be proud of.

One of the things that you cannot fail to notice as a feature of the Oxfordshire landscape, particularly around the Thames, is the amount of overhead power pylons there are. Whilst the proposals for more wind turbines in Britain have encouraged much-heated debate about their aesthetic impact on the landscape, we seem to easily forget how nearly all of us have come to accept the presence of over 88,000 overhead power pylons that stride across Britain. Most of these steel lattice pylons stand at 165 foot high and weigh in at around 30 tonnes. In addition, their presence in populated areas has led to a great deal of suspicion over potential serious damage to people's health that may arise from long-term exposure to their magnetic fields.

To be fair, I think most people would agree that the steel lattice power pylons that we are used to seeing marching across Britain make less of a visual impact than the attention grabbing thick–columned wind turbines that we are supposed to be getting used to as they are erected up and down the nation. In addition, wind turbines can often produce a lot of noise as well as being quite hazardous to bird species. It has been estimated that more than 200 miles of new overhead transmission lines will need to be built in the next ten years across Britain in order to connect new nuclear power stations, as well as onshore and offshore wind farms, to the National Grid.

With more power stations planned for Britain, coupled with many smaller sustainable power schemes and a rising population, we will need more power pylons. In May 2010, a pylon design competition was launched by the Department of Energy and Climate Change to find a new design to replace the existing one which has remained unchanged since the 1920s. The winning design was the T-Pylon submitted by the Danish firm Bystrup. The National Grid will be working with Bystrup to further develop the design, which is much shorter than the existing pylons. Alternative designs were chosen for areas where the Bystrup design is not suitable.

In accordance with the British national character's eccentric obsession with clubs and societies, it is heart-warming to know that a society called the Pylon Appreciation Society exists in Britain. No doubt members of the club will be eagerly anticipating the first sighting of the new breed of power Pylons.

A short walk along the towpath brought me to Sandford-on-Thames, a place that got a mention in the *Domesday book* in 1086 and where Roman pottery was discovered. I stopped at the lovely riverside pub, The King's Arms, for another cola. Rather depressingly, Sandford has a long association with drowning. In his book, *Three Men in a Boat*, Jerome K Jerome describes the village of Sandford as 'a very good place to drown yourself in.' The river claimed the lives of three Christ Church students in 1921. One of those killed was Michael Llewelyn Davis, the adopted son of J.M.Barrie, who was the inspiration for Peter Pan. Other students of Christ Church College died at Sandford in separate incidents prior to 1921.

Sandford was also the setting of an innovation that maybe should not be boasted too much about. In 1826, cottages were built that had flat roofs made of tarred paper, a first in Britain. So maybe we can all blame the people of

Sandford for the invention of flat roofs! Sandford's claim to fame other than drownings and roofs that leak is that it was the home of Charlie Walters, former Tottenham Hotspur player and winner's medal holder in the 1921 FA Cup Final.

Continuing downstream, I passed the boathouses of the prestigious Radley College, former educator of one of my comedy heroes, Peter Cook. On the opposite bank, Nuneham House came into view. Built in 1756 for the Earl of Harcourt, the house is now owned by Oxford University and leased to the Brahma Kumaris World Spiritual University. It wasn't long before Abingdon entered my sight. It took frustratingly long to get there, but I was comforted by a Waitrose supermarket upon arrival. Any visitor to the centre of Abingdon cannot fail to be impressed by its Baroque County Hall, which now houses a museum. It has been described as the finest town hall in Britain and was once the county hall of Berkshire back when Abingdon was the county town of Berkshire (It ceded the title to Reading in 1867).

The county boundaries changed in 1974, and Abingdon switched from being in Berkshire to being in Oxfordshire. County Hall sits atop arched pillars giving a handy sheltered area for municipal functions such as the town's market. Abingdon was an important agricultural centre and increased in importance with the arrival of a canal and then the railway. The railway closed to passengers in 1963 and closed completely in 1984, leaving Abingdon as the largest town in Southern England with no rail service. More recently, however, greater importance has been secured as local councillors got approval on 23rd February 2012 to rename the town 'Abingdon-on-Thames'. Abingdon town centre is refreshingly bereft of many of the big chain shops that dominate other towns. However, with new development earmarked, this could soon change.

Abingdon was well known for being the home of MG cars. Well over a million cars were made at the MG plant in Abingdon before British Leyland closed it down in 1980. The town was also the home to Morland Brewery before it was relocated to Bury St Edmunds in 1999. Morland's most famous ale, Old Speckled Hen, was named after an early MG car. I remember drinking a pint or two of Old Speckled Hen back in the day. Like so many other British towns that have had their manufacturing base extracted, Abingdon has come to rely heavily on the service industry.

Major employers in Abingdon today include the headquarters of anti-virus company Sophos and the British headquarters of premium German home appliance company Miele. Abingdon is situated close to many scientific employers such as the United Kingdom Atomic Energy Authority at Culham and the Science and Technology Facilities Council's Rutherford Appleton Laboratory. Rock music fans would be interested by the fact that Radiohead formed whilst studying at the private Abingdon School.

In a sign of our times, Abingdon is having its fair share of disruption caused by the Islamic State terror organisation. In mid-2016, an Abingdon-based recruitment firm called Isis had to change its name to Shine Appointments after clients were too scared to search for it online. Also in Abingdon, Kim Wallis, sewing enthusiast, has been stopped from enjoying her hobby as PayPal has blacklisted her address in Isis Close. The River Thames is called the Isis on the section that runs through Oxford.

On a more jovial note, it would appear that Abingdon was recently home to the UK's worst robber. In August

2012, dim-witted robber James Allan, 28, was sentenced to three years in jail at Oxford Crown Court for raiding a newsagents in Abingdon, the same newsagents he had robbed just days before. After waving a toy gun about and grabbing £134 from the shopkeeper, Allan proceeded to remove his mask in full view of the security cameras before trying to escape by pushing the door instead of pulling it. He tried in vain to kick out the glass, an attempt which sent him sprawling into a drinks display before working out how to operate the door. Three years' jail for just £134; in the case of this chap, it seems crime really doesn't pay!

I re-joined the Thames path and looked forward to a decent summer's day. After a short while, I was walking past the village of Culham. It was at Culham in May 2016 that 16-year-old Ellis Downes drowned whilst swimming in the River Thames. Another drowning added to the grim roll call of this notorious stretch of the river.

I had a brief search through the undergrowth in a couple of copses for a command bunker that a half-cut Oxonian from the pub last night had told me existed there. He seemed to me to be one of those knowledgeable local people; one of those people that really *knows* their local area. Despite my efforts, I couldn't find the bunker. I guessed this would have probably been a good thing had I been an invading German soldier back in the 1940s. I conceded defeat and returned to the path.

CHAPTER 9
Thames Valley Capital

The sun was out as I traipsed along the pathway. Across the fields, over the other side of the river, I saw the huge cooling towers and chimney of Didcot Power Station, and it wasn't long before I came across what I could only presume to be a water intake for the power plant. Apparently, Didcot Power Station can be seen from a distance of up to 30 miles away. Didcot is a fossil fuel burner, obtaining its energy from coal, oil, and natural gas. Despite much opposition to the building of a power plant in this idyllic Thames-side countryside, it was the provision of hundreds of jobs that swung the vote in favour of constructing the plant which began in 1964. The plant was reputedly capable of producing enough electricity to power well over one million homes.

However, Didcot's prominence as a power station was somewhat curtailed on Sunday 27th July 2014 when three of its six iconic cooling towers were demolished at 5.01 a.m. Despite discouragement from RWE Npower, thousands of people turned out locally to watch the demolition from various vantage points, with the Wittenham Clumps proving to be one of the most popular. Many locals were actually sad to see half of Didcot's power station demolished; Kelly Green, who grew up in Didcot, had an image of the power station's towers tattooed on the shin of her leg ahead of the demolition.

The closure of many fossil fuel burning power stations is part of the British Government's attempts to source 15 per cent of its energy for heat, transport, and power from renewable resources by 2020 under the EU Renewable Energy Directive. The UK is a long way off this target, with only seven per cent of energy being supplied by renewables in 2014. However, since Britain's declaration of withdrawal from the EU, it remains to be seen what targets for renewables the Government will now set.

The use of many renewables, for example, wind turbines and solar power, has been very controversial because of the vastly greater area of land required to produce them, and for the sometimes dubious environmental credentials on which they are based. The UK's largest power station, Drax in Yorkshire, has been converted to burn biomass instead of coal, but there are many claims that burning biomass could be worse for the climate than coal!

Didcot Power Station has received considerable media attention in recent years. On 2nd November 2006, 30 Greenpeace activists invaded the plant, some of them chaining themselves to equipment and others scaling the 200ft chimney where they painted the words 'BLAIR'S LEGACY' on the sides. Greenpeace invaded the plant for a second time in 2009, scaling the chimney once again, claiming that Didcot is the second most polluting power station in the country after Drax.

Greenpeace was founded in the early 1970s in Vancouver, British Columbia, and now has offices in over 40 countries. Due to its belief in direct actions, Greenpeace has been described as the most visible environmental organisation in the world. Their actions at Didcot could most certainly be called 'highly visible', and the plant invasion got them national media coverage.

In October 2014, some of the cooling towers at Didcot B caught fire, with two of the towers being completely destroyed in a massive blaze. On 23rd February 2016, a large section of the old boiler house at Didcot A collapsed whilst it was being prepared for demolition. Four people were killed. The remaining section of the boiler house was demolished on 17th July 2016 in a controlled explosion.

Sat beside the power plant lies the town of Didcot itself. Didcot dates back to the Iron Age and sits upon an area of marshland. It was an important town for military logistics during the First World War, though its huge ordnance stockpiles have long been replaced by the power station and a business park. Didcot is well known as a railway town. At Didcot Railway Centre, the Great Western Society has recreated a section of Isambard Kingdom Brunel's broad gauge railway as well as other paraphernalia from the 'grand age' of steam. Like Abingdon, Wallingford, and Wantage, Didcot was a Berkshire town until the county border changes in 1974 transferred it to Oxfordshire.

Didcot is the principal town of South Oxfordshire and it has been earmarked for thousands of new homes. The town was the birthplace of William Bradbery, the first person to cultivate watercress commercially. East Hagbourne sits just outside the southern perimeter of Didcot. This village has been described as the prettiest in Oxfordshire. 6,000 Parliamentarian horsemen were billeted in East Hagbourne during the English Civil War.

To the south, the pleasant village of Sutton Courtenay can be seen over on the opposite river bank. Written records of Sutton Courtenay's history can be found from 688, and the village appeared in the *Domesday Book* of 1086. Once home to the large construction firm Amey Plc, the main employers today are the local scientific establishments and Didcot Power Station. All Saint's Churchyard is the final resting place of Herbert Henry Asquith, the last Liberal Prime Minister; David Astor, of the Astor family dynasty, and the author George Orwell who is buried here under his real name Eric Arthur Blair.

George Orwell is considered perhaps the 20th century's best chronicler of English culture. Regarded as one of Britain's most important writers, his works have offered an incisive look at authoritarian rule and totalitarian regimes. He is best known for his dystopian novel *Nineteen Eighty-Four* and his allegorical novella *Animal Farm* which is understood to be based on the totalitarian regime of the Soviet Union. Both these books have sold more copies than any other two books by any other 20th century author. His work continues to hold great relevance today and words such as 'Orwellian', 'thought crime' and 'thought police' have entered the vernacular. It is also possible that Orwell was the first to use the term 'cold war' which appeared in one of his essays in 1945. He spent his childhood years next to the Thames.

Orwell was raised in Shiplake, a few miles downriver from here, and he attended school in Henley-on-Thames. The term 'Orwellian' seems to crop up when totalitarian governments are discussed and, in Britain, the term is often applied when the British Government announces plans to 'snoop' on the lives of the British people. When she first met him, Orwell's childhood friend, Jacintha Buddicom, recalled Orwell standing on his head in a field at the bottom of her garden. When she asked him why he was doing this, he replied, 'You are noticed more if you stand on your head than if you are the right way up.' Orwell's succinct take on the world and its societies would later ensure he got noticed by a worldwide audience.

The area to which the term 'Orwellian' has been probably applied most, however, is to closed-circuit television. There are reportedly more cameras per person in Britain than in any other country in the world. The estimated number of CCTV cameras operating in Britain by both the authorities and private concerns has been put at somewhere around four million. According to a report by the Cheshire Constabulary, the average person in its jurisdiction is seen by 70 CCTV cameras on a typical day. Figures such as these are difficult to work out for the whole of Britain as the amount of CCTV used in different regions of the country varies greatly. It would be expected that an urban dweller would be caught on CCTV a lot more than someone who lives in a rural area. If the use of CCTV cameras appears sinister to many, then it is worth mentioning that the origins of CCTV are quite sinister too. The first CCTV recording system was installed by Siemens AG in Germany for the observation of V2 rocket launches.

One thing that you cannot fail to notice along this stretch of the Thames, and for that matter anywhere in and around the Chiltern Hills, is the presence of red kites. These majestic creatures make fabulous viewing as they circle around overhead. Their wings ever striving to catch thermal uplifts to keep them airborne; in fact, they hardly ever seem to be using their wings. These birds of prey were reintroduced back to England and Scotland in 1989 by the Nature Conservancy Council. Kite chicks were brought in from Spain, and the breeding programme has been so successful that many people are referring to these majestic birds as pests and a nuisance.

From an initial import of 90 birds, there are now believed to be somewhere between 400-500 breeding pairs. The birds seem to be becoming ever braver; fashion model Kate Hillman from Maidenhead was given the shock of her life recently when one of the giant birds swooped down and tried to pick up her 'handbag dog'. I must confess to a dislike of those 'po-faced' handbag dogs that peer out on the world from their leathery cradles of perfection. Their snobbish gaze is only ever occasionally outclassed by their highly strung carriers, often to be seen tottering around in a blaze of self-glory. On this occasion, I am sorry to say, Kate, that I am with the bird on this one. The best thing for those handbag emperors, as far as I'm concerned, is to become bird feed!

Although the giant towers of Didcot Power Station dominate much of these parts, there are still other sights vying for attention. The distinctive tower of Appleford's Peter and Paul Church is one of them. The name of this church reminds me of that famous saying 'robbing Peter to pay Paul'. The origin of this is likely to have arisen from a period when monies for Saint Peter's Cathedral in Westminster were diverted to pay for repairs to Saint Paul's Cathedral in London. Although the nave of Appleford Church dates from the 12th century, the spire was added in 1885. Two of the church bells here date from the 14th century. Back at the Ashmolean Museum in Oxford, I saw the impressive Appleford Hoard, a collection of 4th-century Roman pewterware that was discovered here in 1968.

Appleford is the final resting place of John Faulkner, the world's oldest jockey who rode in his last race when he was 74 years old. He was an Appleford resident all his life (he died in 1933 aged 104) and outside of being a champion jockey found time to father 32 children! I think the words 'a life lived to the full' might well be applicable to this extraordinary man.

Soon I was passing under the Great Western Railway extension line from Didcot to Oxford. A short walk further brought me close to the village of Long Wittenham. The path follows the Clifton Cut, another piece of engineering designed to make the river more navigable. The village is supposedly named after a Saxon chieftain by the name of Witta. Bronze Age pottery was found here in the 1960s, and the village is recorded in the *Domesday book*. A bit further up, and I was presented with what I think is one of the most charming bridges on the whole river. The red brick Tudor arches of Clifton Hampden Bridge were built by Sir George Gilbert Scott who is believed to have sketched out the bridge's design on his shirt cuff at dinner!

Clifton Hampden was praised as 'a wonderfully pretty village' by Jerome K Jerome, and a short walk into the village revealed some of the most wonderful dainty thatched cottages I have ever seen. This place is magical. Before the bridge was built here, there was a ferry service dating from the 14th century. The village hall, built in 1896, used to play host to the band called 'On A Friday' who, as we know, would go on to seek worldwide fame as Radiohead.

I have to say that the stretch of river the other side of Clifton Hampden is one of the most beautiful. The river sweeps round in a giant arc. The flat floodplain fields afford fantastic views. In the distance, the giant Wittenham Clumps loomed large, and I could not wait to scale these two huge smooth and symmetrical hills. Glimpses of the hamlet of Burcot could be caught on the opposite bank of the river. Burcot was once home to the Poet Laureate John Masefield until his death in 1967. I would imagine that this place is home to quite a few well-heeled individuals today, judging by the hamlet's idyllic positioning and ample gardens.

Just behind Burcot lies the village of Berinsfield. Berinsfield village was built by Bullingdon Rural District Council in 1957, and at the time it became the first English village to be built on virgin land for over two hundred years. Up ahead lay the tower of Dorchester Abbey, an impressive sight as it came into view.

Dorchester, or Dorchester-on-Thames, as it is officially known, was the first city of the ancient kingdom of Wessex. With a population of just 992 according to the 2001 Census, Dorchester's historical significance as a regional powerhouse dwarfs its modern day size. This area has been inhabited since at least the Neolithic times. The site was selected due to its significant natural defences as it is bound on three sides by the river. It was here in 634 that Bishop Birinus was sent by Pope Honorius to convert the Saxons of the Thames Valley to Christianity. This event played a key role in the conversion of England to a Christian country.

Dorchester Abbey acts as the village's Church of England church as well as a tourist attraction housing a museum. Dorchester is well worth a visit, and a drink in one of its old coaching inns or a perusal around one of its antique shops is well advised. Jerome K Jerome wrote of Dorchester being 'a delightfully peaceful old place, nestling in stillness and silence and drowsiness.'

A short distance from the outskirts of Dorchester lies Day's Lock. This lock is the main gauging station for measuring the flow of water in the Thames and is also the home of the annual World Pooh Sticks Championships which attracts thousands of visitors and competitors every spring. Many of the competing teams fly in from all over the world.

Right on top of me was the looming presence of the Wittenham Clumps or Sinodun Hills to give them their official name. Strictly speaking, the name Wittenham Clumps refers to the wooded summits on these hills. The ancient beech trees that make up these small woodland 'caps' were planted in the 1740s. I decided it would be impossible to walk right around these fascinating intrusions without scaling them. The intrigue was simply too much. The Wittenham Clumps are not particularly high, but it is the presence of the two alluring almost perfectly round copses that crown these hills that makes them incredibly enchanting.

Surrounded by the relatively flat land of the Thames flood plain, the Wittenham Clumps are actually two isolated fragments of the Chiltern Hills. Round Hill is the highest, and it is this one that I 'conquered' first. There are great views to be had from the top. I reckoned you can see a good 30 or so miles from up there, and I stood in stone silence as I surveyed the panorama. Below me, Day's Lock looked like a toy, its miniature detail emphasising the sheer minuteness of almost everything all around.

A short hop brought me to Castle Hill, so called because the rather impressive earthworks here were built as part of the defences of an Iron Age hill fort 2 to 3,000 years ago. A quick circumnavigation of the crowning copse on this clump took me past the Poem Tree. Crumbling letters carved into the bark of this fallen dead beech tree are all that now remains of the creative works of Joseph Tubb of nearby Warborough Green. Tubb carved his 20-line poem in the 1840s. A nearby plaque preserves the words for all to see. Although it died in the 1990s, the tree, believed to be around

300 years old, had remained in an upright position until it collapsed in 2012.

Shillingford was as good a place as any to take a break for lunch. It is perched upon a bend in the river, and the commanding position of the Shillingford Bridge Hotel higher up on the other bank lends this spot a slightly alpine feel. I sat on the grass next to the fine balustraded bridge and hoped to catch a glimpse of a good ole' British eccentric. The hamlet of Shillingford can boast a very definitive role in the construction of the great British eccentric persona. Few people could be cited as being a more stellar example of the great British eccentric than the singer, actor, and all round eclectic that was Vivian Stanshall.

Stanshall was born in Shillingford in 1943. He actually hated being called an eccentric because, according to him, it suggested that he was putting on an act. Perhaps most famous as the leading member of the Bonzo Dog Doo-Dah Band, Stanshall was a good friend of Keith 'the loon' Moon, legendary madcap drummer of The Who. Stanshall was the narrator on Mike Oldfield's Tubular Bells and created a surreal exploration of the British upper classes in Sir Henry at Rawlinson End. This eccentric character is etched into my brain as the madcap host of a surreal dinner party in the 1990s television adverts by Ruddles Real Ale, in which the guests of the dinner party used oars to row themselves and their table out of a banqueting hall as Sir Henry exclaimed 'Real Ale' in time with the music.

Vivian recounted his days at Shillingford as being the happiest time of his life. He was also brought up in Walthamstow. It was at the Central School of Art in London that Stanshall formed the Bonzo Dog Doo-Dah Band. The band went on to gig heavily and had a surprise top ten hit with 'I'm the Urban Spaceman'. The band split up six years later, and Stanshall's life had become dogged by alcoholism and panic attacks. He suffered from depression, the black dog that all too often torments the creative mind. He retained his sharp wit and sense of humour and went on many an anarchic wind-up spree with his close friend Keith Moon.

Along with many different pranks, including driving around in a hearse and issuing commands from a hidden loudspeaker, one of the pair's most legendary wind-ups was one they used to play on an unsuspecting tailor's shop. Stanshall would be admiring a pair of trousers when Moon would enter the shop posing as another customer and admire the same pair of trousers. A fight over them would pursue in which the trousers would be ripped in two so that they ended up with one leg each. At that moment, just when the shop owner was in complete dismay, a one-legged actor who had been hired by Moon and Stanshall entered the shop and on seeing the trousers, would proclaim, 'Ah, Just what I was looking for!'

Stanshall was found dead on the 6th March 1995 after a fire caused by faulty wiring at his Muswell Hill flat. He was a true 'one-off' character and a creative humorist that Shillingford should be extremely proud of.

* * * * *

A short distance behind Shillingford stands the village of Warborough. With its half-timbered and thatched houses, Warborough was the home of the Malster Joseph Tubb, the chap who carved the Poem Tree at the Wittenham Clumps.

Up past a boating club and out onto the main road, I was fast approaching the village of Benson. The first thing that most people note about Benson is its airfield, RAF Benson. Home to the headquarters of the RAF's photographic reconnaissance mission in the Second World War, Benson is now home to the RAF's support helicopters. The clock at St Helen's Church in Benson has two 11's as the 9 was accidentally painted on upside down. This led the Nazi traitor Lord Haw Haw to announce a Luftwaffe air raid on 'an airfield near the village whose clock has two elevens.' Benson was bombed shortly afterwards. Due to significant aircraft noise from the nearby base, property values in Benson are significantly lower than in surrounding villages. This could surely be counterbalanced by the fact that the *Domesday Book* noted Benson as being a royal centre of great importance.

Benson has two meteorological relevancies of note. Firstly, it is the final resting place of meteorologist William Henry Dines (1855-1927) who carried out all sorts of experiments with kites and balloons to become the first person to understand the nature of air pockets and their effect upon the flight of aeroplanes (please remember him the next time you get that searing fear from the sudden dropping and diving due to severe turbulence in an aircraft). The second relevancy is probably a mere coincidence: Benson is a well-known frost pocket and often records the lowest night-time temperatures in the whole of the UK.

Back on the river, the distinctive skeletal, though pleasant, spire of St Peter's Church at Wallingford was well within sight. Wallingford Bridge is yet another fine balustraded Thames bridge. I trampled across it with my rucksack across my arched back. The Boathouse pub was a welcome sight and felt even more welcome as I sat in its beautiful garden in silence. I was meeting Toby there for a couple of drinks, nothing too heavy, I promise. 'Christ, this beer is going down well', I sighed. I knew we were in for a good night. I also knew that we had to be. We were camping out under the stars, and, although still novel to Toby, I was getting a bit tired with the old 'camping plus free backache malarkey.' 'Drink up, let's move on...' I said.

Wallingford was once the capital town of Saxon Berkshire. A castle was built here by Robert D'Oyly in 1069 on the orders of William the Conqueror. In 1154, Henry II granted Wallingford a Royal Charter, making it only the second town in England to receive one. The town was the last Royalist stronghold to surrender to Oliver Cromwell during the English Civil War. Unfortunately, the capitulation of the town's Royalist forces, after a siege lasting 16 weeks, also meant the demise of Wallingford Castle, whose stone was used in the construction of various buildings around the town.

Wallingford has a fine marketplace which has seen a market held every Friday right from the time of Henry II's Royal Charter. At the end of the marketplace sits a characterful 17th-century arcaded town hall. The town has been associated with notable people including mystery writer Agatha Christie; Marmite-like comedy writer and presenter Charlie Brooker; world renowned professor of English Law Sir William Blackstone; poets Kevin Bailey and Thomas Tusser; sculptor John Buckley, and plenty of people of historical note who have been given the title 'of Wallingford'. These are the chronicler, John of Wallingford; the mathematician and clockmaker, Richard of Wallingford; an organiser in the Peasant's Revolt, Richard of Wallingford, and the builder of St Albans Cathedral, William of Wallingford.

It would be worth pointing out, seeing as we visited a good few of the town's pubs, that Wallingford was once famous for its beer, with two breweries and 17 maltings once based in the town. The brewing link ended in 2001 with the closing of Paul's Malt. So here's a glass to Wallingford town, yet another fine Thames-side market town of significant historical importance. We walked across the marketplace to the town hall and then stopped for a final beverage at a fine pub called The Ship. I remember this place from the last time I was in Wallingford, during the BunkFest, a raucous music festival that occurs every year in the town which is thoroughly recommendable.

We crossed over the long bridge and made our way into a field. After checking every which way, we laid out the tarpaulin, donned our trusty sleeping bags and bedded down for the night. I kept wondering to myself about what animals could be in this field that we hadn't spotted. And I thought even worse 'what if the farmer is about in his tractor in the morning and decides to flatten what appears to be a sheet of tarpaulin snared on his barbed wire?' Fortunately, the night's sleep didn't turn out to be too uncomfortable.

We got the tarpaulin bagged up and jumped up over the gate by 8 a.m. Toby was joining me for the next stretch of river travel. The plan was to take a hike out to see Jerome K Jerome's grave at Ewelme before getting back to the Thames Path. At around two miles away, Ewelme was a bit of a diversion, but I had been assured that it was a trip well worth taking.

The first part of our journey took us through the village of Crowmarsh Gifford. This is just over the bridge from Wallingford, and I have no doubt it is probably mistaken for being part of Wallingford. We walked past a cul-de-sac of modern houses called Jethro Tull Gardens, and this served as a visible reminder that it was here in 1701 that the agriculturist Jethro Tull invented his revolutionary seed drill using pieces of an old pipe organ that had been dismantled. This contraption, the first of its kind to have been documented, allowed fields to be sown much more quickly and cheaply than before.

Jethro Tull probably had little idea of the complete implications his revolutionary invention would have on the world as it helped spur along the Agricultural Revolution, which in turn influenced the Industrial Revolution and the eventual dominance of the Western nations. From his father's farm in little old Crowmarsh Gifford, Jethro Tull helped change the world!

In 1944, a Royal Canadian Air Force Halifax bomber with a full bomb load caught fire over Wallingford. Whilst most of the crew managed to bail out, Flying Officer Wilding and Sergeant Andrew gave their lives to steer the plane away from the town and crash into the fields of Crowmarsh Gifford. They are commemorated by an obelisk in Wallingford.

After figuring out a way to get across the roundabout on the busy A4074, we wound our way through pleasant country lanes which took us down to the stunning village of Ewelme. On first sighting, I knew that this had been well worth the extra effort. Set in a fold in the Chiltern Hills, Ewelme is the epitome of a rural idyll. Upon entering the village, it feels like you are embarking on a lost world. The church is easy to find in a location climbing up one of the hillsides. After some hunting around the yard, we finally found the humble gravestone on which were inscribed the words 'In Loving Remembrance Of Jerome Klapka Jerome.

Died June 14th 1927 Aged 68 Years And Of His Beloved Wife Ettie Died October 29th 1938 Aged 78 Years.'

We paused in silence looking at his grave. In the distance were the muffled chinks and scratches of an elderly couple tending to a loved one's grave. From the edge of the graveyard, I took in the stunning setting that is the resting place of this comedy genius. I wondered how many of the people resting in this graveyard had lived lives that had turned out dramatically different from the lives they had planned, or at least thought that they might live. I wondered how many of us alive today would lead lives that might stray a long way from the life we had planned, or thought we might live. Jerome K Jerome had set out to write a Thames guide for tourists but ended up writing a comedy masterpiece. Strange the paths our lives have, and the dramatic outcomes they can lead to.

We got back to Wallingford Bridge shortly after noon. Had we had more time, I would have liked to have walked a little further out in the other direction. Just a mile or so out behind Wallingford lies the village of Brightwell-cum-Sotwell. There were originally two villages here until they were joined as the name suggests. Settlers were encouraged by the good soil and probably also by the close proximity to the Wittenham Clumps. There is little doubt that the road here was the main one between Dorchester and Silchester, making it a popular settlement during Roman times. Historical records show that in 1507 a clerk was murdered in St Agatha's Church. In 1666, there was a church collection for victims of the Great Fire of London and, in 1781, King George III rode through the village after returning from a stag hunt.

A short stretch of towpath lead us up to Mongewell

Park. This was once home to the American millionaire Henry Gould, an atheist who had the pathway to the local church sunk into the ground so that he did not have to watch the villagers walking to church. Mongewell was taken over by RAF Bomber Command during the Second World War. From 1948 until 1997, Mongewell was home to Carmel College, the only Jewish boarding school in Europe. Former pupils of Carmel include the retail billionaire Sir Philip Green and Oscar-nominated director of The Killing Fields, Roland Joffe.

Philip Green is well known for being one of Britain's richest men, with a £3.5 billion fortune and for having a brash and aggressive personal style. What is less well known is that the then multi-millionaire Green was not interested in helping when he was approached by a group of former Carmel pupils in 1997 who were trying to raise money to save the College.

What makes Philip Green quite remarkable is the speed with which he accumulated his wealth. In his early 30s, he was a mere rag-trade hopeful with a string of failures to his name. By the age of 40, he had made a few million. However, by the age of 50, he was a billionaire. He had made the fastest billion in British corporate history. In 2005, he paid himself a whopping salary of £1.2 billion.

Green is famous for his corporate tax avoidance. His wealth is held in his wife Tina's name and she is a resident of Monaco. This has cost the British tax authorities many hundreds of millions of pounds in lost revenues. Although Green's tax arrangements are not technically illegal, it was a surprising move when the then recently elected Prime Minister David Cameron appointed Green to carry out a review of government spending and procurement in 2010.

As the recession grated on, Green and his retail empire became the target of the activist group UK Uncut, which protested against his tax avoidance by performing demonstrations outside his shops.

Like many other high street retailers, Green's company has come under attack from anti-sweatshop groups who have criticised his use of poor working conditions and low pay in Britain and overseas. On 15th June 2016, Philip Green was questioned about the BHS pension deficit and the sale of the department store chain to Retail Acquisitions Limited, shortly before it was closed down. It led to Green being labelled as the 'unacceptable face of capitalism' and calls for his knighthood to be removed. Green is a colourful and controversial figure who, for many, epitomises greed and status. I will soon be in London, where greed and status abound!

* * * * *

Up past a couple more pill boxes, none of them appealing enough to tempt me to revisit for a night's sleep, we trundled under the magnificent Moulsford Railway Bridge built by Isambard Kingdom Brunel in 1839 and past the village of North Stoke, glimpses of which can be caught from between the trees. It is the former home of the actor Michael Caine and the final resting place of the singer Dame Clara Butt. North Stoke was given a touch of rock and roll by Deep Purple vocalist Ian Gillan who built a guitar-shaped swimming pool in the grounds of his house which is now The Springs Hotel.

Shortly afterwards, we passed Moulsford, which translates quite simply as 'mules ford'. There is a fine Elizabethan Manor here which was once home to Kevin

Maxwell, son of the old swindler Robert Maxwell. The Beetle and Wedge, an expensive looking restaurant, sits by the side of the river. H. G. Wells stayed here whilst writing 'The History of Mr Polly' and the place was visited by the 'Three Men in a Boat' on their journey along the river. George Bernard Shaw was also a regular visitor back in the day. Moulsford is also home to its eponymous public school.

A little further up and the scenery starts to become quite majestic. Perched up in the Chilterns not far from here lies the village of Woodcote. It holds an annual steam rally and real ale festival - now that sounds like the recipe for a possible disaster! We were entering the Goring Gap where the Berkshire Downs meet the Chiltern Hills. The valley sides are getting steeper here. We passed the Leatherne Bottel, a restaurant I have heard rumoured to be owned by Reading-based businessman and business-collector Sir John Madejski (more about him later). At Cleeve Lock, I took particular interest in the island by its side as it is owned by Pete Townshend of The Who. However, not a single windmilling arm was in sight on that today.

Goring High Street is positively welcoming. We traipsed into the village shop to buy provisions and became quite a long-term patron of a wooden bench, a good place to see village life float past. The relaxed scene does well to hide the village's handful of noisy past and present inhabitants which includes the aforementioned Pete Townshend, George Michael (who tragically passed away on Christmas Day, 2016), and Sir Arthur 'Bomber' Harris, who lived in the village from his retirement up until his death in 1963.

We made our way up over Goring and Streatley Bridge built in 1923. We were on hallowed ground, as this bridge takes both the Ridgeway and the Icknield Way across the river. Before there was a bridge here there was a ferry, but in 1674 the ferry got drawn into the weir and 60 lives were lost. In June 2008, tragedy returned to the river here again as a ten-month-old girl fell into the river at Goring and died shortly after being rescued.

Goring is the location of a proposed exciting new hydroelectricity scheme which will generate enough power for 300 homes. The project will involve the installation of three 3.5 metre diameter Archimedes screws into the weir, that will turn under the force of the water and drive electricity generators. It is designed to have a 50-100 year operational life and will provide a long-term revenue stream to be diverted back into the community. The project will cost in excess of one million pounds and was given the go-ahead in early 2016.

Goring Hydro is an example of a push towards renewable energy that has started to transform Britain and her landscape from the mid-1990s. Once confined to areas such as the Scottish and Welsh Highlands, hydroelectric power has been introduced on a much smaller scale to many of Britain's rivers. A lot of these schemes have been set up in former mills to produce small amounts of power, though Goring Hydro is an example of larger scale production that can be achieved. Certainly, walking down the Thames, you get a real sense of the untapped potential from all the noisy weirs.

Far more conspicuous than hydropower schemes has been the introduction of large-scale wind farms in the UK: in March 2012, the amount of electricity being generated by wind power in Britain was 6,580 megawatts. This figure is expected to rise to 28,000 megawatts of production by 2020. Wind power now produces more electricity than hydropower in the UK. Opponents of wind power have expressed their dissatisfaction with huge stretches of British countryside being 'planted' with these less-than-unassuming turbines. Opponents have also pointed out that these turbines can often be noisy and a danger to wildlife.

Whilst it has to be said that many opponents of wind power would surely agree that the visual impact of a wind farm may not be any greater than the traditional towering fossil fuel or nuclear power stations that they are replacing, it does seem to me that we are having to surrender so much of our countryside to the wind turbine. Perhaps we can combine the seemingly unstoppable march of the wind turbines with other large-scale renewable energy resources.

The villages of Goring and Streatley were home to a spectacular street party for Queen Elizabeth II's Diamond Jubilee in June 2012. Made up from 465 trestle tables and 3,700 seats, the party measured about a kilometre in length, making it one of Britain's longest street parties. By spanning the two high streets in different counties and the river bridge, it certainly made for one of the more unusual Diamond Jubilee celebrations.

The Morrell brewing family originally owned much of Streatley and used to live in Streatley House. Spice girl Geri Halliwell lives here. Streatley High Street is certainly steep and, suckers for additional punishment, we had decided to carry on straight up through the village and see the views afforded by the daunting Streatley Hill. This hill appears as an almost vertical wall as you crane your head up to view it whilst slogging up through Streatley; however, the views are simply magnificent. From the top, we stood masterfully surveying the Goring Gap, where a large selection of the Thames Valley is laid out in the steepness below. Houses bravely creep up the slope to the side.

After our strenuous gander up Streatley Hill, we headed into The Bull, Streatley's only pub, for some refreshment. 'Did you know that Jerome K Jerome and his mates also visited this place?' I exclaimed excitedly to Toby upon entering the rickety-roofed hostelry. 'There is a monk and a nun buried in the garden here after being executed for 'misconduct' in 1440', I confirmed. Toby turned to give me a look that said 'I've had enough of your excitable facts.' He was probably tired, and I was too. I was going to tell him that Danny La Rue once owned the Swan Hotel in Streatley and that an IRA bomb had exploded in a postman's bag on a bicycle in the village in 1979, but I thought it best to keep these little nuggets of history to myself for a while.

It was early evening by now, and the beers had gone down well. A little way outside Goring, we decided to camp out for the night. I had cunningly convinced Toby to camp out with me for another night, and he had drunk just about enough to agree to it. We found a little spot in some woods just tucked around the corner from a moored-up narrowboat. Having tied the guy ropes to some trees, the tarpaulins were roughly in place. I trekked the short distance through the undergrowth to catch a final glimpse of the river in the darkening blue sky. 'Good night' I announced to the wilderness, but Toby did not reply. He was fast asleep, but not before I had convinced him to accompany me on the next leg of my journey down the towpath.

A quick scan of the map revealed that we were only a few twists and turns of the river away from Reading. We passed a few more fine mansions including The Grotto, created for Viscount Fane, Gatehampton Manor and the massive Basildon Park, built in the Palladian style for Sir

Francis Sykes and now owned by the National Trust. Basildon Park may be of interest to many office-bound people as being the inspiration for that famous luxury brand of writing paper, Basildon Bond. We also passed Lower Basildon, the birthplace and final resting place of the agricultural innovator Jethro Tull.

Close to here are also the gravestones of Harold and Ernest Deverell, two young boys who drowned whilst swimming in the Thames - there seems to be an awful lot of drownings on this stretch of the river since Oxford. The path climbs steeply through the Hartslock woods. In fact, it climbs so steeply that steps have been cut into it. The harder work was easily compensated by the magnificent views of the river and of the surrounding area which were by then quite a long way below.

Up ahead on either sides of the river are the villages of Pangbourne and Whitchurch. We took a walk into Pangbourne across the toll bridge, one of few fee paying ones left on The Thames. The Swan is a lovely old pub established around the time of the English Civil War. It was at The Swan that the 'Three Men in a Boat' decided to abandon their homeward trip back from Oxford to Kingston.

Famous Pangbourne residents have included *The Wind in The Willows* author Kenneth Grahame, the book written when he lived further downstream at Cookham; Led Zeppelin guitarist Jimmy Page, and engineer Sir Benjamin Baker, who lived just outside the village. Amongst other things, Baker built the Forth Railway Bridge, the Aswan Dam in Egypt and the Central Line on London's Underground. He also designed the cylindrical vessel used to transport Cleopatra's Needle from Egypt to the Thames

Embankment. I will be passing Cleopatra's Needle later in this book. The writer Lytton Strachey also spent a period living in the village.

My exploratory instinct told me that we weren't witnessing the true opulence of Pangbourne to its fullest, so I left Toby in the busy village centre, and I wandered up the hill to satisfy my curiosity. Half an hour later, I met Toby breathlessly exclaiming 'yep – there sure is some wealth for certain up in those Pangbourne outer reaches.' Some of it was getting positively Beverley Hills! Sitting just to the South-West of the village is Pangbourne Naval College. The college gets its name from its founder Thomas Devitt, who established it in 1917 as The Nautical College, Pangbourne. The Falkland Islands Memorial Chapel was opened here in March 2000 by The Queen. The shape of the chapel resembles a ship.

Just outside of Pangbourne, the path leads onto a serene grass meadow that seemingly has a magnetic attraction for canoeists. For all we could tell, we might as well have been yomping across the tamed wilderness of Patagonia rather than the meadows of Southern England, for the fields around here are home to more than 800 alpacas! Having passed the fine country pile of Hardwick House, we were now closing in on an even more superb mansion, Mapledurham House. Built in 1588, the year of the Spanish Armada, the house pays a deliberate honour to Elizabeth I, by being built in the shape of an 'E'. The home is still in the hands of the original tenants, the Blounts.

At the water's edge lies Mapledurham Mill. This ramshackle yet alluring building had centre stage in the 1976 film *The Eagle Has Landed* which also featured one-time North Stoke resident Michael Caine. The Mill also appeared on the cover of Ozzy Osbourne's 1970 *Black Sabbath* album; I would imagine all the local bats have been keeping a beady eye out for trouble ever since!

Not long after Mapledurham Mill come the suburban streets of Purley, and soon we were walking into town along Reading's famous Oxford Road or 'Okky Road' as it is affectionately known amongst many of the locals. It was along this road in Reading that a herd of elephants broke free and escaped from a carriage of Wombwells Travelling Fair in 1851. According to George Sanger's book, *Seventy Years A Showman* (1927), a fight broke out between Wombwells and Hitchens travelling fairs as both convoys were engaged in a race to be the first to get to the 1851 fair, held in Henley-on-Thames. Sanger recounts that the fight was between the rival showmen that included the Living Skeleton and Fatman. If the thought of these two characters locked in a tussle isn't enough to raise a chuckle, then just imagine the spectacle as a herd of elephants stampeded along the busy street as well! The elephants were eventually rounded up and then taken on to Henley-on-Thames.

And so a Paean of praise to good old Reading town. A Victorian town. At last, we're here amongst the streets of West Reading, and I was excited about meeting an old friend of mine, Jason Hendrix. With fresh beers in hand from the 'Okky Road', we make our way up the hill towards Jason's flat. I'm already feeling kinda free, and Toby's and my own legs could sense a good rest. When you knock on their front doors, most people answer it shortly afterwards, but Jason Hendrix is one of those people who always emerges from their upstairs window first as if to howl at some kids in some street scene from back in the 1940s. Jason bounded down the stairs and greeted us at the door. 'Come on up; I'll put the kettle on.'

The first sip I take I think about the author and itinerant drunk, Charles Bukowski. One of his sayings is amongst my favourites: 'The problem with the world is that the intelligent people are full of doubts, while the stupid ones are full of confidence.' How very true, I feel. Just look at Donald Trump's campaign to be elected US President. Full of sexism, bile, and arrogance, it was a shock to probably most people around the world when he won in the November 2016 United States Presidential Election.

When you feel freedom, your mind is totally in the zone, if you get what I mean. If you don't get what I mean, then let me explain: most of us lead a nine-to-five existence, or at least some kind of imposed routine; a system maybe. Some of us break that mould and do it our own way. Then there is Jason. Jason Hendrix. This guy is a Reading town legend and dances to his own tune. A well-known character on these streets, Jason has been playing in bands in the area for the past 20 years. His latest incarnation is the Jason Hendrix Experience. Jason is no cheap plastic copy of the real man, however.

A true-born eccentric, Jason is often to be seen wearing a top hat, wild jackets - often with chain mail shoulder-pieces, in case of a last-minute issuing of a knighthood! - purple trousers with winkle-picker boots and a whole treasure trove of turquoise and silver jewellery. To cap this all off, his sartorial ensemble is often completed by his bare chest showing from under his undone jacket. I think that some people who see someone dressed like this may well not like what they see, a few take outrageous fashion displays as a form of arrogance, but let me tell you, Jason Hendrix is one of the nicest people you could ever hope to meet. This guy has helped everyone from down-and-out friends to the Reading homeless. He has one of the biggest hearts in the whole of Reading.

I still think that I have not quite got across just how eccentric Jason Hendrix is, so let me enlighten you with a few more details. He has built a full-size Doctor Who Tardis in his flat, a handy guitar practice booth complete with 'Police' light box sign that lights up. He frequently plays guitar for up to eight hours a day and has been known to play guitar whilst naked! He decided to put an internal window into his bathroom for extra light, a window that looks through to the lounge area, but as you now know, Jason doesn't have too much of a problem with nudity! He is a very talented painter and decorator capable of exquisite marbling and wood effects, and is a very talented musician and songwriter to boot. He knows how to put on a show – his Hendrix-inspired gigs feature many arm gyrations, leg kicks and the Hendrixian pièce de resistance, playing the guitar remarkably well with his teeth. It's all really quite impressive.

Jason's flat is a treasure trove of music paraphernalia and memorabilia. The walls and bookshelves are a testament to many great bands back in the day when the guitar hero was a god. Thin Lizzy, Bob Dylan, Deep Purple, Led Zeppelin, The Who, you name it, it's all here. Toby walked about trance-like as he studied all the nostalgia around the living room. He had hardly said a word since we had arrived here, and then with some trepidation, he stepped up into the Tardis and closed the doors behind him. Jason and I shared a glance, and we both cracked up in hysterics at the thought of Toby being beamed off into space! As befitting a man with such looks, Jason has the colourful history to go with it.

A travelling troubadour of music who, for a while lived in a caravan overlooking Glastonbury Tor. He also used to run a cafe.

Naturally, the conversation moved onto Jimi Hendrix himself. It's not the screaming guitar solos or on-stage aerobatics that are the main draw, but the wondrous, beautifully crafted songs that are what makes Hendrix so exceptional. His catalogue of songs written in his short life before his death at that iconic age of 27 was testament to a masterful understanding of blues, rock, ballads, and funk.

Hendrix was one of a number of musicians to have died at 27, and the age has become so synonymous with musicians' deaths that those who have perished at this age are often referred to as the 27 Club, Forever 27 Club, Club 27 or the Curse of 27. Prominent musicians other than Hendrix who have died at this age include Kurt Cobain, Amy Winehouse, Jim Morrison, Janis Joplin, Robert Johnson, and Brian Jones.

Hendrix's blaze of creativity was made all the more alluring by his cheeky shyness. He was unique. Absolutely unique. Clapton watched him with awe from the sidelines. He was one of those magical people who helped shift the world forwards in a small way. We all move about on the surface of the world doing our everyday stuff, but some people manage to move the earth in a small way, and Hendrix was one of those individuals. We fell silent after our exuberant talk about our hero. Jason gave out a long 'yeeees' from his lungs as if to mourn his passing, but also to acknowledge some sort of external existence of the Hendrixian spirit.

It is never long before Jason picks up his guitar. Put him in a room with one, and it is never long before their paths collide. The metal slide buzzed up and down the guitar neck producing wondrous undulating tones that would resonate perfectly with a river setting. Toby looked close to dozing off in an armchair as I stepped up into the Tardis. Inside there were old reel-to-reel tape recording machines and all kinds of guitars, amplifiers, leads, and accessories. I think if Jimi Hendrix were to step into this machine he wouldn't be seen for days!

Suddenly the doors opened, and I was presented with the beaming smile of Jason's friend Mayya. Like Jason, Mayya has an excitable inner-child that looks for every opportunity to find reason to break free. I haven't seen Mayya since the last time I saw Jason. She pointed over to Toby who was now slumped like a world-weary old man in the armchair fast asleep. 'We've been on a long walk,' I told her. 'Really?' she replied. 'Come and tell me all about it.' We walked into the bedroom, and I began to unfold my story.

Mayya's face turned serious. She was remembering a night that she would rather forget. It was at the hotel next door to Jason's flat in 2005 that 16-year-old Mary Ann Leneghan was tortured before being stabbed to death in a horrific event that shocked the whole nation. Mary Ann's friend was also tortured in the hotel before being shot in the head. Miraculously the girl survived. A gang of six drug dealers had come to Reading from South West London to settle a feud with a rival drugs gang. The girls were kidnapped and used as bait in order to lure the rival drug gang into a confrontation. Mayya leaned forward. Her face seemed older, almost shamen-like. Her voice turning to a whisper: 'I could sense bad happenings that night,' she said. 'I wrote a dark poem that night. I never do that.'

Her eyes were intense, and I knew she was telling me the

truth. She was telling me exactly what she felt on that night. 'Bad happenings', she muttered again before turning to look out of the window. On returning to the living room where Jason was well into his songs, playing to a sleeping Toby, I went to the rear window and peered out. Sure enough, there were the low height hotel rooms next to the garden. The very rooms in which *it* happened. I glanced back at Mayya, whose gently nodding face confirmed that I was looking at the scene of the crime.

How horrific, I thought, that two ordinary young schoolgirls could be abducted off the streets of Britain, then raped and tortured with knives, boiling sugared water, a steel bar and cigarettes, before being stabbed and shot. Their only crime was to be in the wrong place at the wrong time. I fell asleep with a heavy heart. It hadn't crossed my mind at that point, but I would soon start thinking about a strange pattern of murders that have affected this particular region of Britain over a recent 12-year period.

At a little past 11 o'clock, Toby said his goodbyes and left Jason's flat. Having him as my walking companion from Wallingford had been great fun. I could barely make out Jason across the cigarette fug. I wondered if he would like to join me for the next leg of my journey, but he was far too busy with his decorating. A few more beers and Jason's own songs drifted past and, before I knew it, I was fast asleep in his armchair.

* * * * *

Named after an Anglo-Saxon tribe called the Readingas (Reada's people), Reading is today a large town that has an important story to tell. Reading Abbey was founded in 1121 by Henry I. The town then became a centre of pilgrimage, and by 1525 it was the largest town in Berkshire. In 1867, it replaced Abingdon to become the County Town of Berkshire. Thanks to Henry VIII's dissolution of the monasteries, Reading has only ruins where the abbey once stood. However, since 1971, Reading attracted another sort of pilgrimage when the now legendary Reading Rock Festival was established. This festival held on the August Bank Holiday of every year attracts well over 80,000 people down to the meadows by the Thames near the centre of Reading.

One thing that has always eluded Reading is the granting of city status. It has been the bookmaker's favourite on three occasions to be granted this status, but nothing has materialised. In the most recent bid, as part of the Queen's Diamond Jubilee celebrations, Reading missed out to Chelmsford, Perth, and St Asaph. Most people in this region believe that Reading is a city in all but name, and it seems that it can only be a matter of time before city status is granted.

Once important for cloth production and then ironworks in the 18th century, Reading retained its importance due to its ideal positioning on the confluence of the River Kennet and the River Thames, and its positioning on the major road route from London to Oxford and the West Country. The opening of the Kennet and Avon canal in 1810 made it possible to travel from Reading to the Bristol Channel by narrowboat. By the 19th century, Reading had become famous for a reputation that is often cited today: beer, biscuits, and bulbs, or the 'three B's' as it has come to be known.

In 1807, Suttons Seeds established itself in the town. This was followed in 1822 by the establishment of the famous biscuit manufacturers Huntley and Palmers and completed in 1875 by Simonds Brewery opening up. Unfortunately, none of these famous companies remain in the town today, but their legacy is part-preserved by the retention and refurbishment of part of the Victorian Huntley and Palmers factory that was saved from demolition, and an atmospheric pub beneath the Town Hall called the 3 B's.

As well as its pre-eminence as home to the Reading Music Festival, Reading has many more musical and stage connections. Well-known musicians from the town include Mike Oldfield, made famous by Tubular Bells and by being the guy who gave Richard Branson his first significant cash reserves with which to fund the beginnings of his global empire, and The Chemical Brothers, who attended Reading Blue Coat School. More recent Reading bands to have found fame include Sundara Karma, Pete and the Pirates, Morning Runner, The Cooper Temple Clause, OK Tokyo, Does it Offend You, Yeah? and My Luminaries.

Reading is also where jazz star Jamie Cullum cut his teeth performing in local pubs and clubs during his attendance at Reading University. In fact, Reading's eminent musical heritage is ancient. It was here in 1240 at Reading Abbey that 'Sumer is icumen' the first song ever recorded in Britain was noted down by a monk called John of Fornsete. Stars of the stage and entertainment from Reading include Sir Kenneth Branagh; Kate Winslet and her director ex-husband Sam Mendes; game show host Chris Tarrant, and actor Winston Ellis. Hyena-larynxed comedian Ricky Gervais also hails from the town, and much of his comedy references Reading and its environs.

HM Prison Reading was made famous by Oscar Wilde in his poem 'The Ballad of Reading Gaol.' Wilde was imprisoned at Reading Jail in from 1895 to 1897 on charges of homosexuality. He was known as prisoner C.3.3., and his terrible experiences of the prison were recorded in the poem. My favourite lines from the poem read, 'In Reading gaol by Reading town there is a pit of shame, and in it lies a wretched man eaten by teeth of flame, in a burning winding-sheet he lies, and his grave has got no name.' Other literary connections to Reading include the writers Jane Austen, who attended Reading Ladies Boarding School, and Mary Russell Mitford who lived in the town for a number of years.

Reading is a major town along the M4 corridor and makes up part of Britain's Silicone Valley that runs from West London to Bristol. The town is home to many technology companies that include Oracle, Cisco, Ericsson, Intec, Virgin Media, and Xerox. Reading University is ranked in the top one per cent of universities worldwide. On a more incidental note, it is worth pointing out that the Little Chef roadside restaurant chain was founded in the town in 1958, the same year Britain got its first motorway. I have enjoyed many 'Olympic' breakfasts over the years in Little Chefs!

In my opinion, Reading is also home to two kings. Both the kings that I refer to are regarded by Reading folk with great fondness. The first of these two is Sir John Madejski, who is often dubbed with the moniker the 'king of the Thames Valley'. The second man is well, ahem, a king for different reasons. He is the legend that is 'The Reading Elvis'. The Reading Elvis, or Dave Allen, to give him his unassuming real name, has become such a local legend around the town that he has a Facebook fan page set up by his 3000-odd followers. The page declares, 'This man brings joy to our town with his crazy-ass antics and his simple nature. God bless Reading Elvis for he is a true legend.'

Sir John Madejski is probably best known as the

Chairman of Reading Football Club and the driving force behind Reading's entry into The Premiership League in 2006, for the first time in their 135 year history. In 2012, the club was back in the Premiership and Madejski had at least secured the club for a while by selling the club to Anton Zingarevich, the son of Russian multi-billionnaire, Boris Zingarevich. He caught the attention of the national media in 2004 with gossipy stories about a romance with the late TV celebrity Cilla Black.

Many people local to the Reading area will know him more as the successful businessman who founded the *Thames Valley Autotrader*, later to become *Auto Trader*. Whilst on holiday in Florida in the mid-1970s, Madejski spotted a car sales magazine that included pictures of the cars for sale. Realising the potential of the idea, he launched his own version in the UK and the rest, as they say, is history.

Since selling his company Hurst Publishing in 1998 for £174 million, Madejski has made many numerous charitable donations including £500,000 to The Trustees of the Falkland Memorial Chapel Trust, and has contributed to the running of Thamesbridge College, Reading, which has opened under the new name of The John Madejski Academy. He has donated millions of pounds to various other causes and establishments including: Burlington House in London; The Henley Management College; The Victoria and Albert Museum; a lecture theatre at The University of Reading and The Museum of Reading. In regard of his considerable fortune and generosity, Madejski has said 'I'd like to enjoy it all before I kick the bucket.' Good on him, I say. In more recent times, Madejski has expressed an interest in an impressive and well-needed regeneration right in the heart of Reading.

After walking half the length of Broad Street, Reading's main shopping street, I turned down Union Street, or 'Smelly Alley', to give it its local nickname. It certainly manages to live up to its name as wafts from the fishmongers and butchers challenged my nose. This nickname was no doubt coined a long time ago when there were a lot more fishmongers here. It was announced in mid-2012 that Reading's 'Smelly Alley' was one of around 8,000 place nicknames in the UK that would now be considered by the Ordnance Survey for inclusion on their maps.

The inclusion of the local nicknames is designed to help emergency services. Other 'famous' nicknames being considered for inclusion include the 'Gateshead Flasher' (the Angel of the North), 'Spaghetti Junction' (the Gravelly Hill Interchange on the M6 in Birmingham) 'Terry Wogan's Lighthouse' (a disused tower built to test lifts in Northampton), 'Chip Alley' in Cardiff, and the 'Magic Roundabout' (that mind-boggling roundabout that I encountered back in Swindon).

About five minutes later, I found myself gazing at the world's largest statue of a lion. I was in Reading's Forbury Gardens. Work started on these scenic gardens in 1855, and the remit was to construct a botanical character. Forbury Gardens were given an extensive renovation in 2004, and I must say that they offer a most wonderful respite from the hustle and bustle of Reading's town centre, just outside. Some might be interested by the fact that Forbury, a suburb of the New Zealand city of Dunedin, was named after the gardens by William Henry Valpy, who was born in Reading.

The Maiwand Lion was erected in 1886 by the sculptor Blackall Simonds. It commemorates the loss of over 300 officers and men of the Royal Berkshire Regiment at the

Battle of Maiwand in Afghanistan, 1880. With the recent loss of so many British Soldiers in our more recent Afghan campaign, the presence of this mighty cenotaph is quite touching. Although not religious in any shape or form, I offer a few whispered words to the British soldiers who perished fighting in Afghanistan before walking round the monument and making my way towards the abbey ruins that are only a short distance away.

On my wanders through this seemingly affluent town, my thoughts turn to a *Reader's Digest* poll of 2007 that named Reading as the worst place in Britain to live with families. The poll looked at factors including crime rates, good local hospitals, and affordable housing. Reading came last in 408th place! Reading Council disputed the statistics used and pointed out that the survey was biased towards towns with a population of less than 40,000. Councillor Jo Lovelock defended the town saying to the BBC, 'Reading is the de facto capital of the Thames Valley and it is surrounded by beautiful countryside in the south of England. It also has excellent job prospects for the inhabitants and their children.' I'm sure that while there are some less than perfect aspects of Reading, it didn't deserve its title of 'Britain's worst town.'

The Sun newspaper attributed a surprising statistic to Reading in an article dated 9th February 2010. It claimed that, according to their research, Reading has more languages spoken than almost any town of a similar size in the world. The article reported that teachers in Reading were struggling to understand their pupils who spoke a staggering 127 different languages including Afrikaans, Uzbeki, Assamese, Chichewa, Kurdish, and four different kinds of Chinese. Whilst diversity is undoubtedly something to be championed, it is fair to point out how exactly do we expect teachers, the police, and various other authorities to cope with understanding all these different languages?

Expecting immigrants to have some understanding of English does not seem to me such an abstract idea when we live in a country which reputedly spends around £100 million annually just on translation fees. The Metropolitan Police in London spend nearly seven million pounds a year on interpreters for crime suspects.

On reaching the main road, I turned to my left reasoning that it is about time to start my journey back to the Thames. On my left stood the imposing walls of Reading Prison, a young offenders' institution and remand centre holding males aged 18 to 21. On my right was a large retail park, a sight that is so familiar in many British towns today. A short distance across the road from Reading Prison is the Reading branch of Toys R Us.

It was from this branch of Toys R Us that 'quiet and boring Paul' from Accounts managed to steal £3.6 million from the company before being noticed and sentenced to seven years imprisonment in 2009. 58-year-old Paul Hopes from nearby Woodley lavished money and gifts on five prostitutes and developed a cocaine habit (he doesn't seem so boring now, does he?). Paul's downfall came about as police suspected that the new found wealth of one of the prostitutes was a result of drugs dealings. Since this debacle, Toys R Us have said that they have made some changes to their accounting procedures. Let's hope that these procedures will work next time one of their employees starts fiddling them for millions of pounds.

I walked on, down past the railway station and over Caversham Bridge. When this bridge was opened in 1926, it was the longest concrete bridge in the world. Caversham Bridge is one of few crossings of the river here in this populated area, and that explains why it is so busy. For years now, there have been proposals to build another bridge across the river somewhere on this stretch of the Thames. As I wandered across, I remembered one point of interest about Reading that I forgot to mention.

Did you know that many of Reading's houses are built upon disused chalk mines that could collapse at any time? In January 2000, 30 houses in Reading's Field Road had to be evacuated after the land beneath them caved in into an abandoned mine. Some estimates have put the number of disused chalk mines in the town at 30. The council has spent millions of pounds on stabilisation projects in Field Road and other areas around the town. Most of the chalk mines were dug in the 18th and 19th centuries to provide chalk to the town's brickworks to improve the quality of the bricks. Not all of this region's chalk mines have been used for mining purposes only; in fact, some are far more intriguing, but I'll get to that a bit later on.

CHAPTER 10
300 Square Miles of Murder

Caversham hosts an eclectic mix of boutique shops and cafés. Other than a Waitrose and the ubiquitous Tesco, major trade names are mainly absent, no doubt because theycan be found not far away just over the bridge in Reading. You don't have to walk far from the crossroads in the centre of Caversham before you are climbing fairly steep roads - a reminder that Caversham is the gateway to the Chiltern Hills in this part of the world. Tucked away in lanes that run adjacent to the Thames and up on the hill in Caversham Heights sit the big, opulent houses. The house prices here are amongst the highest in the area.

Sitting atop the hill at Caversham near the villages of Emmer Green and Caversham Park Village lies Caversham Park House which was once home to William Cadogan, 1st Earl of Cadogan. The current house, which was built in 1850, is home to BBC Monitoring, a section of the BBC World Service that analyses news stories and information from around the world. It is also home to the BBC Written Archives Centre and BBC Radio Berkshire.

Caversham has had a few news stories of its own in recent years. In 2008, Mia Siadantan won the popular BBC television programme 'The Apprentice'. Siadantan helped her brother run the Myalacarte restaurant in central Caversham before leaving to work for the 'no-nonsense' businessman, Alan Sugar. She took maternity leave and never returned to Sugar's company. I also heard that Terry Lee Miall, drummer and fellow Ant for Eighties pop sensation Adam and the Ants is to be found holed up somewhere in Caversham.

As I walked through the Caversham streets to the sound of Adam Ant's 'Stand and Deliver' reverberating around my head, my thoughts turned to some strange occurrences in and around Caversham in recent times. Stranger than Adam and any of the Ants perhaps. Many of these strange occurrences concern the busy roundabout at the nearby hamlet of Playhatch. Over the years, various surreal items have been installed by a mysterious character that erstwhile appears to remain at large.

In October 2003, to the complete surprise of the morning commuters, a red front door complete with a pint of milk on the doorstep and a newspaper in the letterbox appeared on the small grass topped roundabout. *The Henley Standard* newspaper indicated that a prankster from Reading known as 'Impro Man' had claimed responsibility; his previous stunt had been to install a traffic island in the middle of a Thames backwater in Caversham!

A short while later, the prankster made a return to the Playhatch roundabout, this time to install four engraved tombstones, turning it into a surreal graveyard. Two of the engravings read 'The Dinner on the Roundabout' and 'Daisy Palmer'. Quite spooky, I suppose, if your name happens to be Daisy Palmer! In 2006, it was revealed that a 21-year-old conceptual artist called Dominic Downing from nearby Peppard Common had been caught in the early hours of January 3rd painting a wobbly zebra crossing across the King's Road in nearby Henley. Downing, a fine art student studying at Newcastle University, appeared before Oxford Magistrates where he pleaded guilty to three counts of criminal damage. He was ordered to pay £923 in court costs and compensation for cleaning the road. Asked if he would continue his painting escapades in Henley, he said 'I think I'll keep it legal from now on.'

Although Downing admitted to further pranks, he insisted that he was not behind the pranks at the Playhatch roundabout. The other pranks of his have included removing local place names from road signs and re-writing them with words such as 'Lust' and 'Love' and 'Heaven' and 'Hell'. He also admitted to erecting a mini Stonehenge at the Upper Thames Rowing Club at Henley, in a protest at the way 'modern society is killing our spirituality'.

In 2013, the 'Playhatch prankster' pulled off his biggest stunt yet: one which made the news around the world. He placed a postbox on the side of Sonning Bridge. Local Uri Geller, who was a Sonning resident at the time, commented that he had never seen anything like it anywhere around the world, and he suggested that a possible culprit was the 'ghost of a mischievous little girl' who had apparently been seen walking on the bridge. It looks like the mystery of the Playhatch prankster may remain unsolved.

Over one weekend in March 2017, a fake road sign appeared on the Playhatch roundabout. It had an arrow pointing towards Henley with the word 'Posh' written next to it and an arrow pointing towards Sonning with the words 'Even posher'. This sign caused quite a stir on social media and it was reported by the local press too. Shortly afterwards a statement was put out by an individual calling himself 'Dr Fisch'. He claimed to be behind this and many other pranks and said that there was 'much more to come…..on a grander scale.' Quite what Impro Man thinks of this we do not know, but we can be sure that with the emergence of this new prankster, the Playhatch roundabout and its local area are bound to keep people entertained for some time to come.

One person who could be blamed as the inspiration for many pranksters in Britain and around the world is the Bristol-born street artist Banksy. He became famous for his politically motivated stencils that appeared throughout London and some other parts of Britain in the 1990s and 2000s. Whilst many of his iconic works sell for hundreds of thousands of pounds today, and many have voiced the words 'sell out' in his direction, Banksy has remained, for years, the consummate urban graffiti guerrilla.

My own experience of Banksy relates to an 'installation' he made on the side of a building in a very prominent spot on the Chiswick flyover in West London. Banksy had written the words 'IT'S NOT A RACE' in large scruffy freehand paint. The building has now been demolished, but it did not fail to make an impact on me. In a world where we are constantly told how and how not to live, it is incredibly refreshing to see the insightful thoughts of a 'free man' scrawled for all to see, even if they are in crude graffiti. Banksy was well aware of the publicity and notoriety graffiti could garner. Much of his work features surrealism and humour too; there have been depictions of policemen kissing, anarchic rats, and cryptic messages.

I have always been fascinated as to what drives these guerrilla artists. The motivation can be political, artistic, humorous, and sometimes destructive. Sometimes, I suspect it is a mixture of all these. The guerrilla artist enjoys getting their message across in a fashion similar to mass-market advertising. They enjoy being unknown, they enjoy being talked about, being renegades, and being powerful. Perhaps the most common form of guerrilla artist is the hoaxer. For these, it is not so much about making a political statement, as it is the attention they receive and the alarm that they create. I believe that most guerrilla artists know that many people wonder who they are and what they are trying to say. People might identify with them and anticipate their next move with relish. The guerrilla then connects with people without ever meeting them.

Scientists have puzzled over why society is becoming seemingly more attracted to the hoaxer. They wonder whether it is because society has become more gullible. Others have pointed out that modern society has given the hoaxer more opportunities. The rise of democracy has made the individual far more important than ever before. The Internet has become the dream tool of the hoaxer who is now able to reach people in the most imaginative ways as never before. The lack of validation makes the Internet a perfect vehicle for the hoax. The public's love of gossip and conspiracy theories all add to the increasing acceptance of apparent 'fact', however suspect. We all know that life can sometimes be stranger than fiction, so we will often accept quite outrageous claims and feats as genuine.

For most of us, our main familiarity with the hoax is 1st April, April Fools' Day. Although the origins of this day remain obscure, the earliest association between April 1st and foolishness can be found in Chaucer's *Canterbury Tales* (1392). Popular throughout many countries of the world, big corporations as well as individuals get in on the April Fools' Day act. Many of us have probably fallen at one time or another for a clever and well-planned hoax in the press. In

Scotland, April Fools' Day is traditionally called Hunt-the-Gowk Day, a Gowk being Scottish for a foolish person. In today's world, we are often primed and ready to be hoaxed on 1st April every year; however, we remain more susceptible for the rest of the year. There have been some spectacular hoaxes over the years.

In 1912, an amateur palaeontologist called Charles Dawson claimed to have found part of a human skull that proved the missing link in the evolutionary relationship between man and apes. It wasn't until 1953 that a team of researchers proved the jawbone was from a modern orang-utan! Known as The Piltdown Man, this hoax would enter hoaxing legend.

In a similar echo of the Piltdown Man, and also in 1953, Cobb County police officer Sherley Brown stumbled across a strange creature on a highway near Austell, Georgia, USA. The two-foot-tall creature had the appearance of an alien, and three terrified-looking men at the scene claimed they had sighted a UFO. The 'alien' caused a media storm in the USA, and even representatives from the Air Force came along to see it. The whole thing was revealed as an elaborate hoax when anatomy experts identified the animal as a shaved Capuchin monkey with its tail cut off! The hoax turned out to be a bet with one man wagering his friends that he could get himself featured in the local paper within a week. He went one better than achieving this – he went into *Life* magazine too!

The emergence of widespread television after WWII gave the hoaxer a new and exciting platform. It was by using this new medium of television that the documentary programme *Panorama* broadcast what would become one of the most infamous hoaxes of all time on April 1, 1957. At the time, spaghetti was a relatively rare and exotic food in Britain, and the respected presenter Richard Dimbleby was shown reporting on the spaghetti harvest taking place in Southern Switzerland. People watched in bemusement as they saw a rural Swiss family pulling strands of spaghetti off spaghetti trees and collecting it in baskets. The BBC began receiving hundreds of calls from viewers. Some of them wanted to know if they could grow their own spaghetti, to which they were told to 'place a sprig of spaghetti in a tin of tomato sauce and hope for the best.' No doubt there were quite a few disappointed British spaghetti growers that year!

Many other hoaxes are notable for their imaginative feats and the considerable amount of time and effort involved in their creation. On April 1 1978, Dick Smith towed an iceberg into Sydney harbour, telling people he had towed it from Antarctica. A large number of the city's inhabitants turned out to see it arrive and only grew suspicious as rain washed away the firefighting and shaving foam to expose the white sheets beneath! On 31 March 1989, policemen were sent to investigate a flying saucer that had allegedly landed in Surrey, only to find a cleverly designed hot air balloon and a certain Richard Branson hiding inside an E.T. costume. Branson had originally planned to land in London's Hyde Park on April Fools' Day but had been blown down a day early into a Surrey field.

Perhaps the riskiest and most ambitious hoax to have ever been pulled off was that undertaken by a prankster called Porky Bickar of Sitka, Alaska. Porky had flown hundreds of old tyres into the crater of the local volcano, Mount Edgecumbe. He then set light to them before making a speedy escape. The residents of Sitka awoke one morning in 1974 to find their long dormant volcano belching out thick black smoke. Thousands of people were sent into a state of panic thinking that the volcano might soon explode with devastating consequences. Although a particularly elaborate and inventive hoax, it must be said that this particular one was quite cruel. I would imagine Porky kept a low profile around Sitka after pulling off this stunt!

* * * * *

As I walked back to Caversham Bridge, I thought about another hoax which is firmly rooted in the fields of Oxfordshire, perhaps some of the very ones that I had been walking through. Oxfordshire is home to one of the highest concentration of crop circles anywhere in the world. Although impressive to view from the air, I am sure that there can be very few people who seriously believe that these patterns, which range from the very simple to the impressively complex, are created by aliens. After all, that would be a serious amount of alien visits to Oxfordshire alone every year! Crop circles started to appear in Britain in the 1970s, and the earliest ones were claimed to have been the work of self-professed pranksters Doug Bower and Dave Chorley. After contacting the media with their claims in 1991, crop formations began to appear all over the world!

Joining the Thames Path again at Caversham Bridge, I set off to the east and aimed for the village of Wargrave. After picking up some provisions from a particularly convenient large Tesco, located just metres away from the Thames Path and accessible through a small clearing in the hedging, I was back on the trail. It wasn't far from the town that I started thinking about what had been troubling me earlier. Why on earth is Reading and its surrounding area home to so many murders?

Before I get started expounding on my hunch, it is worth pointing out that Reading was home to perhaps Britain's most prolific serial killer of all time: Amelia Dyer. Born in a small village near Bristol in 1838, Dyer had a love of literature and poetry, and she trained to become a nurse. She would later become a 'baby farmer' - a person who would take on babies from mothers who were unable to look after them themselves. Many of these babies had been born out of wedlock and were subsequently passed onto others to bring up. It was a lucrative industry, and evil Amelia Dyer realised that she could soon murder the babies after taking a payment from their desperate mothers.

After moving to Caversham and then onto Kensington Road, West Reading in 1895, she discarded the bodies of her victims in the Thames. A secluded spot near a weir at Caversham Lock was a place that she knew well. However, on 30 March 1896, a body was retrieved from the river at Reading by a bargeman. Dyer was hanged at Newgate Prison on 10 June 1896. It is unknown how many babies Dyer murdered; however, evidence points to many more than the three identified victims she was tried for. It has been speculated that she could be responsible for as many as 400 murders. It is quite possible that she could be Britain's most prolific serial murderer. Britain is already home to the person many acknowledge to be the world's most prolific murderer, Harold Shipman, who is believed to have been responsible for an estimated 250-plus murders. Some people have even suggested that Amelia Dyer was Jack the Ripper, who killed the prostitutes through botched abortions. There is, however, no evidence to connect the two.

The number of murders across the whole of Britain (as opposed to the England and Wales-only statistics, often quoted by the British press) has been declining in recent years, from well over 800 per year at the start of the millennium, to the current rate of between 600 and 700 per year. Several authorities, including the World Bank, put Britain's current murder rate at one per 100,000 people, and this seems about correct. Based on this, we would expect a town the size of Reading, with a population of 155,698 according to the 2011 census statistics, to have, on average, at least one murder per year.

In recent years, there have been a few high-profile murder cases in the town. The national media attention was mainly due to the fact that two of the murder victims from the town were teenage girls. As I mentioned in the previous chapter, 16-year-old Mary Ann Leneghan was tortured and then murdered in 2005. Then 18-year-old Asha Muneer was stabbed to death by her jealous ex-boyfriend, Gulamyr Akhter, in January 2010.

A much smaller town than Reading may only expect a murder every 10 or 20 years, and we could assume that most of Britain's villages would be unlikely to encounter a murder in 100 years. However, there has been an unprecedented surge of murders in this region of the Thames Valley over the 2004 to 2016 period. So many, in fact, that I propose that an area of no more than 300 square miles of the Thames Valley, centred roughly upon Henley-on-Thames, has made this quintessentially British town Britain's 'small town and village murder capital'. There have been at least 17 murders in this region in the 2004 to 2016 period. All of the murders have occurred within seven miles of the River Thames, most being much closer, and all correspond to a 63 mile stretch of the river from Abingdon in the west to Windsor in the east.

All of the small towns and villages associated with recent

murders that I am looking at have populations of 40,000 or less. Seven towns and four villages experienced murders or multiple murders during this 12-year period. What makes these findings all the more shocking is that there were three instances of multiple murders, and two of the towns were each the location of two completely separate murders. As I have mentioned, this is well above the murder rate one would expect for such a geographically tiny area consisting of small towns and villages and no city.

Here I have listed the murders in order of date and given their proximity to the 'murder capital' town of Henley-on-Thames, along the Abingdon to Windsor River Thames 'stretch of murder'. Murder statistics are notoriously difficult to get hold of in Britain and, as I have stated, the statistics occasionally quoted by the media usually only refer to England and Wales. This list has been methodically researched, but I accept that there may have been one or two murders that may have been accidentally missed when studying this geographical area over the last 12 years.

On 6 June 2004, disgruntled Stuart Horgan shot dead his 27-year-old estranged wife, Vicky Horgan and her 25-year-old sister Emma Walton in the small village of Highmoor Cross around four miles to the west of Henley-on-Thames. Horgan also shot their mother who survived. He committed suicide in prison shortly afterwards. Initially fearing that they were dealing with 'another Hungerford', the Berkshire town where gunman Michael Ryan shot dead 16 people before killing himself in 1987, the police were heavily criticised for their long delay in reaching the scene.

Little over a year on from the shocking murders at Highmoor, another multiple murder occurred at Wokingham, around 12 miles to the south-east of Henley.

On 14 October 2005, Thomas Palmer, a teenager who was obsessed with violent horror films, knifed to death two friends, Steven Bayliss, aged 16, and Twood Nadauld, aged 14, after claiming he had been teased by them. The particularly savage and brutal circumstances of the death of the two boys down a leafy lane in Wokingham stunned the nation. Palmer was found guilty of the murders, though it was indicated by his defence that he was in the first stages of schizophrenia.

The next murder occurred around seven miles to the south-east of Henley in the village of Winnersh. On 5 February 2006, Stephen Hunt, caretaker of the local Forest School, bludgeoned his wife to death after she admitted to sleeping with another man. Stephen then hid the body of his wife under one of the school minibuses. The following morning, as the children filed into the school, Hunt engaged in a charade pretending his wife was missing and searched for her around the school. He later admitted to the police that he was the murderer.

Moving on to Henley-on-Thames itself, we arrive at the scene of the next murder. Stephen Langford, a father of two and friend of the then local Tory MP Boris Johnson, was beaten to death in a drunken brawl with two youths outside a takeaway on 9 December 2006. It was reported as the first murder in the town of around 11,000 people for 60 years. The two youths - one of them a son of a millionaire music producer - were later cleared of the murder charges after pleading self-defence. This was believed to be the first 'murder' in Henley in over 60 years.

The next murder takes us to a sleepy hamlet down quiet Cherry Garden Lane near the village of Littlewick Green, around four miles to the south-east of Henley. Landscape gardener Daniel Quelch, 33, was stabbed 82 times by drug-abusing paranoid schizophrenic Benjamin Frankum, who had broken into his house. Miraculously, Frankum did not harm the children in the house, instead getting them cans of Coca-Cola and yogurt, telling them he was their 'new daddy'. Frankum's mental health issues were well-known by the authorities. He had been in various secure mental health units before being moved to a residential home. No alarm was raised as Frankum had disappeared off the radar; he had stopped taking his medication weeks before killing Daniel Quelch.

It has been estimated that up to 100 people a year are killed by mental health patients in Britain, but the Government appears to be very slow in addressing this worrying statistic. The prevalence of 'care in the community' schemes - as opposed to housing in secure institutions - has been blamed for many of the deaths. A lot of people in mental health services do not like to admit that the mentally ill can sometimes be violent for fear of causing a scandal. However, 100 deaths a year is a scandal for many people. Few of these disturbed murderers have any concise comprehension about what they are doing, their minds so tortured by voices, demons, and unbearable insecurities. It really must be about time for the authorities to realise they are the only people who can really do something to prevent the further needless loss of innocent lives on this scale.

In June 2009, Colin Scholey lost his temper and shook four-month-old Thomas Preece to death in Sonning Common, around four miles to the south-west of Henley.

On 30 June 2010, 50-year-old Stephen Rees slit his wife's throat with scissors at their home in the town of Woodley, around five miles to the south of Henley, after she admitted to having an affair. Ten minutes later, he threw himself under an InterCity train at nearby Twyford station, a well-known suicide spot.

The town of Didcot, around 19 miles to the north-west of Henley, has seen two separate instances of murder, including a multiple murder. Both incidents attracted national media attention. 17-year-old Jayden Parkinson was murdered by her obsessive and controlling ex-boyfriend Ben Blakeley on December 3rd 2013. Her body was found in an established grave at All Saints' churchyard in the town. In May 2015, 21-year-old Jed Allen, given the name 'the Wolverine killer' by some of the press, murdered his mother, her partner, and his half-sister before hanging himself in woodland in nearby Oxford.

On 28th July 2013, 24-year-old Sean Noctor was stabbed to death in Windsor, around 13 miles to the south-east of Henley, after being involved in a fight with a group of men.

The town of Abingdon, around 19 miles to the north-west of Henley, faced two murders in late 2015 in quick succession. On 3 November 2015, 26-year-old Kerry Reeves was shot in the head by two gunmen in her hometown. She died a short while later in hospital. On December 7 2015, 36-year-old Trevor Joyce stabbed pensioner Justin Skrewbowski to death in a Poundland store in the centre of Abingdon.

In November 2015, Josephine Williamson, 83, was murdered by her husband, Philip Williamson, in the town of Earley, around seven miles to the south of Henley.

Since the beginning of 2016, the list of murders in this small Thames Valley region has continued to grow. A murder investigation was launched when police officers were called to the Elmhurst Hotel in Earley on March 30th 2016, after a report of a man being assaulted by two men. The victim, Declan Walsh, died at the scene. 81-year-old Albertina Choules was murdered in her home in the village of Marlow Bottom on July 6th 2016. There have been serious incidents in recent years that have threatened to make the 300 square miles of murder list. In late 2015, two boys aged 15 and 17 were injured in a shooting incident in Burnham village. In another firearms incident, a man was blasted with a shotgun in a targeted attack in the village of Downley on the outskirts of High Wycombe on 27th Dec 2015. A man was shot and seriously injured at the Tea Party Festival held at Windsor Racecourse in August 2016.

So there we have it: proof that this serene stretch of the River Thames has gruesome stories to tell. Surely it is time that this small area of Britain gets a well-deserved respite from that most gruesome attribute of mankind: murder. Despite the relatively low murder rate in Britain, the chances of being murdered are actually higher than you may think. If you live to 80, then your lifetime chance of being murdered is just less than one in a thousand. Women are most likely to be murdered by their partners, and men are most likely to be murdered by their friends or acquaintances. Half of all murders are caused by quarrels or revenge, over half occur in the home, and the most common murder weapon is a knife.

* * * * *

Described by Jerome K Jerome in *Three Men in a Boat* as 'the most fairy-like little nook on the whole river', Sonning has long been regarded by many as the prettiest village on the Thames and, on that fine day, I could not disagree with that. Close to the lock here lies the appealing Sonning Bridge, constructed back in 1775. It has ten arches and is built of red brick. It would have been a shame to walk on past this jewel on the Thames, so I decided to take a quick look.

The main street soon winds up a steep hill, and the place was stacked up with traffic waiting to get over the single-file bridge. The backstreets and churchyard of Sonning are a joy to walk through, and a quick drink at The Bull pub just outside the churchyard provided me with suitable refreshment. The historical name of this village is actually Sunning, and older residents of the village may still refer to it in this way.

Notable people who live, or who have lived, in Sonning include Isabella of Valois, Queen of King Richard II of England; the dramatist Sir Terence Rattigan; U.S. General Dwight D. Eisenhower, who was stationed here before D-Day; guitarist Jimmy Page of Led Zeppelin; former footballer and football manager Glen Hoddle, and the 'mystifier' Uri Geller. It is reputed that the legendary highwayman Dick Turpin spent some time in Sonning, at his aunt's house which is now called Turpins. The churchyard here is the final resting place of two recipients of the Victoria Cross.

In 2015, Sonning gained who is arguably its most famous resident. To the joy of many a lady in the region, the US actor, George Clooney, arrived! To slightly lesser joy for his besotted legion of admirers, the long-time batchelor was moving into a house on an island in the River Thames with his new wife Amal. Locals have noticed a rise in the number of helicopters circling over the village as eager photographers swoop down, keeping an eye on the large renovation project that the Clooneys are undertaking.

The Great Western Railway passes through the Sonning Cutting about a half mile from the village. In 1841, it was the scene of one of the world's first railway disasters when a goods train ran into a landslip, killing nine passengers. Recent controversy has surrounded Sonning resident Ricky Gage who was one of the people behind an illegal sperm-broker website that was exposed in 2010. A lighter-hearted controversy was provided by local Vic Moszczynski who would decorate his large home with an incredible 22,000 fairy lights every Christmas until a few disgruntled locals opposed his annual garish festival display. The display has attracted many admirers over the years that drive up the exclusive road to see it, and donations to charity have topped £55,000. No doubt a few of the neighbours feel that the visiting hoards made the road a little less exclusive.

Behind the village of Sonning lies the village of Twyford. The village's name is Anglo-Saxon in origin and literally means 'double ford'. There are at least ten other Twyfords in Britain. Twyford, Berkshire, is situated on the busy Great Western Railway line and its proximity to local roads such as the A4 and M4 have made it a popular home for commuters. Twyford claims to have the oldest Badminton club in the country, and William Penn, the founder of Pennsylvania, spent the final years of his life in Ruscombe Fields, a house close to the village. Twyford was a finalist in the Great British High Street Awards 2015. The eventual winner was West Kilbride in Scotland.

The town of Woodley is located a short distance to the south-east of Sonning. Until the 1930s, Woodley was a very small village, but it underwent rapid expansion with the arrival of an airfield and the aircraft manufacturer Miles Aircraft Ltd. The famous aviator Douglas Bader lost his legs in an accident at the airfield here. Today, Woodley has grown to an extent that it merges into Reading at its south-western edges. Famous people from Woodley include the TV presenter Chris Tarrant and the vocalist Irwin Sparkes from the band The Hoosiers.

Once famous for brick-making, silk production, and bull-baiting, the town of Wokingham is situated only a little further from Sonning than Woodley. Wokingham is also famous for its two Molly's: Molly Millar was reputedly the town witch who lived by the wayside, and Molly Mogg, the daughter of the landlord and barmaid at the Rose Inn, was immortalised in the 1726 poem, 'Molly Mogg', or 'The Fair Maid of the Inn'. The ongoing notoriety of Wokingham is ensured as its local MP is one-time Conservative Party leader hopeful - and alleged Captain Spock lookalike - John Redwood.

Redwood is understandably not too impressed with his Star Trek nickname 'Vulcan', which all began when former Conservative MP-turned-political-sketch-writer Matthew Paris first noted similarities between the two. When he is not at home practising the Welsh national anthem, Redwood is performing his duties as the popular local MP who has been a Member of Parliament for Wokingham since 1987. The journalist and author Peter Hitchens has said that John Redwood is so bad at modern day telly politics because he is 'a genuine intellect'.

Other notable people from Wokingham include the writer Dick Francis and the actor Nicolas Hoult. Wokingham is home to one of 13 large sirens that are sounded in the event of an escape from nearby Broadmoor Hospital, a secure hospital which houses many dangerously disturbed patients including the notorious 'Yorkshire Ripper', Peter Sutcliffe. The sirens were introduced after the escape of child killer John Straffen in 1952. Straffen murdered five-year-old Linda Bowyer in the nearby village of Farley Hill on the day of his escape. Fortunately, he was captured shortly afterwards. Wokingham's notoriety is further enhanced by the fact that the level crossing on the railway line here has been the scene of fatalities in 2007, 2008, and 2010.

If all of these rather depressing Wokingham-related facts have left you somewhat down in the dumps, you could always try drowning your sorrows in one of the town's many pubs. Whilst it has been claimed that the city of York boasts the most pubs in Britain by area, Wokingham has been said to have the most by head of population. With the recent demise of the pub trade, it is debatable whether Wokingham still retains this 'title'. Further lightening of mood might be induced by the fact that Wokingham was ranked as the number one place to live in the United Kingdom by Halifax Estate Agents in 2007. It is also said to have the UK's highest amount per population of single mothers anywhere in Britain.

A short distance to the south of Wokingham is the village of Finchampstead. This village is situated amongst dense pine woods, much of which is owned by the National Trust. The large variety of finches in the area is what gave the village its name, and the local youth often refer to the village simply as 'Finch'. Sitting just to the north-east of Wokingham is the village of Binfield. The Stag and Hounds here was reportedly used as the hunting lodge by Henry VIII and Elizabeth I. The painter John Constable spent his honeymoon in the village in 1816 and sketched the local church. Bricks from Binfield were partly used in the construction of the Royal Albert Hall. The most famous resident of Binfield is undoubtedly the Sultan of Brunei who owns Binfield Manor, built in 1754 by Sir William Pitt. The Sultan is one of only two 'absolute ruler' sultans left in the world. The other one is the Sultan of Oman, who I will come across very shortly on my travels.

I rejoined the path after crossing the river at Sonning on a footbridge. Across the river, I saw the impressive 15 million pound white house which was home to Uri Geller for 35 years (the house was actually inspired by the White House in Washington). Uri moved back to Israel in late 2015. A large glass pyramid sits in the garden. Who knows what kinds of positive energies may reside in it? Uri Geller is a person who divides people's opinions. It seems that when it comes to this well-documented spoon-bender, people either love him or pass him off as a fake.

Whilst I would definitely class myself as a sceptic, I have long wondered whether some humans may possess certain 'paranormal' powers. My views on this subject were bolstered when a friend told me that Uri Geller had once bent one of their own spoons in front of their eyes, and they were convinced he hardly touched the thing. It's about time I looked into all this. Surely, if paranormal powers really did exist, it would have been proved beyond all doubt by now? But this is certainly not the case.

Uri Geller is perhaps the most famous paranormalist of them all. The Israeli shot to fame in the 1970s for his spoon bending and other supposed 'effects of the mind'. Whilst Geller used to refer to his abilities as psychic, he now prefers to refer to himself as a 'mystifier'. In the 1980s, Geller seemed to disappear from the public eye, only to re-emerge as a multi-millionaire living in a London mansion. He controversially stated that his new-found wealth had come from locating gold and oil for large companies. In more recent years, he has concentrated on producing television shows, being renowned for his friendship with the late pop icon Michael Jackson, who was best man when Geller renewed his wedding vows in 2001. Although Geller has his sceptics, no one has been able to demonstrate that he is a fraud. If Geller is simply an illusionist, then he must surely be one of the best in the world.

One of the most impressive things about Geller is that he can usually perform to order, hence many people have witnessed spoons bending 'before their eyes'. However, there have been occasions when he has been unable to summon his powers. The Nobel Prize-winning physicist Richard Feynman has commented that Geller was unable to bend a key for him and his son, and there have been people who have noticed distraction techniques being used before a bent spoon is produced. The most vocal critic of Geller must surely be the American stage magician James Randi who accuses Geller of passing off magic tricks as paranormal displays.

Randi has duplicated many of Geller's performances using stage magic techniques. One of Geller's supposed abilities that seem to let him down the most are his predictions. James Randi and *The Sun* newspaper have both pointed out that the teams and players he picks as winners actually most often lose. The 'curse of Uri Geller' was probably best exemplified when he placed 'energy-infused' crystals behind the goal of the Exeter City football team in an attempt to make them win. They lost the game 5-1! In 1992, Geller was asked to help in the investigation of the kidnapping of Hungarian model Helga Farkas. Geller predicted that she would be found alive and in good health, but she was tragically found to have been murdered by her kidnappers.

In 2007, James Randi and other sceptics pointed out that Geller appeared to have dropped his claims that he does not perform magic tricks, preferring to call himself an entertainer. Geller responded by saying that he has not stated that he does not have powers, just that he does not refer to them as supernatural. He said he prefers to be called a mystifier. Randi has discounted other claims for supernatural powers including people who claim to be 'human magnets', a phenomenon which allows people to fix sometimes incredible amounts of metallic objects to their bodies.

50-year-old Brenda Allison from Holloway, North London, is thought to have a much more powerful electromagnetic field than most people, and she blows light bulbs and shop tills as well as being able to stick numerous metal objects such as coins, safety pins, and spanners to her face and neck. Doctors have apparently told her that her increased magnetism is caused by stress. Others believe that she is accumulating static from her carpet. James Randi has demonstrated that many of these supposed magnetic effects no longer work when talcum powder is applied to the magnetic areas, insinuating that some people are applying some sort of glue to their bodies to make the items fix to them. Others have pointed out that people may be able to train their muscles to help hold onto objects.

The expert in electromagnetism, Kathy Geminiani, Director of the Bemer Health Centre Limited in Surrey, has said that lots of research has been conducted into the causes of increased human electromagnetism, but there is still no explanation for it other than we know it is not genetic. All humans have a small electromagnetic charge, but nothing nearly as much to make most of us have magnetic properties. Only iron and a few other metals can become magnetic, but the human body does not contain very much. Iron is the body's most plentiful metal, but each person has only the equivalent of two carpentry nails-worth.

Certainly, anyone with any genuine paranormal powers should contact James Randi as his foundation (The James Randi Educational Foundation) is offering a prize of one million dollars to anyone who can demonstrate evidence of any paranormal, supernatural, or occult power or event, under test conditions agreed by both parties. This prize remains unclaimed.

One paranormal power: clairvoyance, the ability to see into distant locations and the past and future, seemingly pervades into our lives more than any other. Plenty of Britons attend evenings with psychics or visit clairvoyants. There have been many documented cases of remote viewing, where psychics can 'see' distant events and even make sketches of places that they have never visited before. Clairvoyants occasionally make their predictions in Britain's newspapers and on television. Whilst many people would laugh at the prospect of visiting a mystic - with or without a crystal ball - many people still adhere to mystical beliefs even if it tends to be in the form of horoscopes.

One of Britain's most successful clairvoyants, and someone whose services have been used by the police, is Nella Jones. Jones' visions have aided the police forces of Southern England on many occasions. In an interview with Yorkshire journalist Shirley Davenport, Jones revealed that she 'saw the killer' in a mental image after watching a news report about the Yorkshire Ripper murders in January 1980. She said the man was called Peter, he was a truck driver from Bradford and lived in a house atop a flight of stone steps with the number six on the door. All of Jones' predictions turned out to be true when the killer was apprehended a year later.

Unfortunately, the police had filed her information away with the visions of other clairvoyants on the case and had not acted upon it. One of the problems for the police is knowing which clairvoyants to take most seriously. In addition, information provided by clairvoyants is difficult to decipher into precise facts. The deciphering of information received is what most clairvoyants say is the most difficult thing they have to deal with. Rather than a precise location, a clairvoyant will usually receive an approximation of, say, the location of a body. Their vision may only reveal it to be 'near water' or in a town beginning with the letter 'M'.

What the public seldom realise is that the police are often swamped with requests from clairvoyants to help them with many cases. A huge amount of information is inaccurate, and the police are often very wary of a lot of clairvoyant advice. However, when leads are very limited, the police are often willing to work with any information they can get. Because the public only really gets to hear about the cases where clairvoyants have been successful, it may give out the false impression that clairvoyants are more accurate than they are in reality. However, examples of clairvoyancy such as that of Nella Jones in her identification of Peter Sutcliffe are so remarkable that it seems almost impossible that she could have arrived at her predictions by chance. Indeed, psychic detectives have to be careful that they might not pass under suspicion themselves when they appear to 'know too much'.

Dr Chris Roe, a parapsychologist based at the University of Northampton, believes that up to 85 per cent of people may possess some form of clairvoyance. An increasing amount of scientists are taking research into paranormal powers seriously. Many of the world's militaries have been taking psychic powers seriously for years including the British Ministry of Defence. Professor Jessica Utts, a statistician from the University of California, has concluded that remote viewers used in experiments were correct 34 per cent of the time, a figure way beyond what chance guessing would allow.

It seems that there is still a lot more research to be done in this field before the whole scientific community is convinced that clairvoyance is a genuine skill that some or even most of us have. Whilst many people seem to be sceptical of clairvoyance, we live in a world in which many people claim to have 'a hunch' about something. Most people who have hunches would not acknowledge their feelings as clairvoyant but, in reality, the feelings they have could be coming from the same source.

Albert Einstein suggested that we only use ten per cent of our brains, so perhaps if we could engage some of the other 90 per cent we might find ourselves more conducive to the paranormal. We live in a world with four dimensions; length, width, depth, and time. However, theoretical physicists believe that there may be ten or eleven dimensions. Perhaps the paranormal powers lie within these extra dimensions, and we are only just getting glimpses of them at the moment. To quote that old Sci-fi phrase: the truth is out there!

Whilst I am sceptical about images of UFOs and claims of human contact with aliens, I think it would be fair to say that, on balance, there have to be other life forms alive in the universe. There are over four billion planets in our galaxy, the Milky Way, alone. Our planet is located in the

'Goldilocks zone', a place where our position in relation to our sun allows life to flourish because it is neither too hot nor too cold. There must surely be scores of planets that also inhabit a position in relation to their suns that would allow the formation of life. It would also be perfectly reasonable to suggest that there may well be life forms that are far more advanced than ours. The conditions on their planets could be such that they developed much more quickly than us and already have the ability to travel at or near light-speed in spacecraft.

It could be that in a universe or multi-verse as huge and quite possibly infinite as ours, alien life forms simply haven't reached us yet. Even if they are aware of us, we may not interest them enough to warrant investigation. We assume in our own importance that we are at the centre of the universe; we are in reality just a miniscule part of the picture. It could well be that alien life forms exist in different dimensions and, therefore, we cannot see them. They could be surrounding us, even controlling us, but we cannot see them. One chilling scenario is that we could be part of an alien experiment, our origins contrived from the very beginning. Another scenario, and one which many human beings accept as fact is that our origins are due to a God.

According to the 2011 Census, 59.5 per cent of British people described themselves as Christian; 4.4 per cent as Muslim; 1.3 per cent as Hindu, and 1.9 per cent stated 'other religion'. 25.7 per cent described themselves as having no religion and 7.2 per cent did not state their religion. Recent surveys have shown that the proportion of people describing themselves as Christian is falling. A survey in 2007 by Tearfund found that 53 per cent of people in Britain identified themselves as Christian and only 7 per cent as practising Christians. A report in 2007 by Christian Research showed that Roman Catholicism had better-attended services than Anglican services. One of the problems with most surveys is that they do not reveal the intensity of religious belief or non-belief.

Like an increasing number of people in the world today, I identify myself as an atheist. This does not, however, mean that I feel like I am a 'non-believer'. On the contrary, I believe in science and the scientific way of describing how the world and the human race evolved. In many ways, I would describe myself as pseudo-religious; after all, the scientific explanation for the creation of the world and living beings is as miraculous as any religious explanation. For example, the moment when basic molecules combined to create a simple life form on earth for the very first time is an event that I would call miraculous. Undeniably beautiful and remarkable. I find the fact that every second many thousands of billions of neutrinos fly through our bodies quite amazing. The fact is that both religious and scientific explanations of the world tell remarkable feats about a remarkable people inhabiting a remarkable planet. It is the story of the human race and of the human endeavour.

Britain is world-renowned for its religious tolerance, and I have found the tolerance shown by the general public after many terrorist plots and attacks by extremist Islamist groups quite remarkable. Although the anti-Islamic group The English Defence League sprung up from the hotbed of Luton town in June 2009, it has failed to garner widespread public sympathy despite a common knowledge that there are many discontented and angry Muslims on the streets of Britain today. It was estimated by MI5 in early 2017 that there were over 3500 radicalised Muslim individuals living in

Britain who posed a direct threat to national security.

Without the organised gatherings of religious groups, atheism has always proved a relatively lonely path. However, in recent years one man has become more associated with the atheist 'movement' than any other. Having published a series of books including *The Selfish Gene, The Extended Phenotype* and *The Blind Watchmaker*, the British scientist Richard Dawkins became a prominent spokesperson for the atheist viewpoint. Dawkins' prominence was particularly boosted by the publication of his 2006 book *The God Delusion*.

Richard Dawkins has pointed out that atheists are far more numerous than many people think; they are certainly very numerous in intellectual circles, he postulates. Dawkins' biggest problem seems to be with the dispute between 'Intelligent Design' and Darwinism, a dispute that is undermining the teaching of science. He is concerned by America, where a 1999 Gallup poll revealed that only 49 per cent of the population would vote for an atheist. For me, one of the most important contributions from Dawkins is the way in which he redresses the gap between theists and atheists. In his book *The God Delusion*, Dawkins describes how, on being asked whether he is an atheist, he points out that religious people are also atheists when considering gods they do not believe in such as Zeus, Apollo, Amon Ra, Mithras, Baal, Thor, Wotan, the Golden Calf, and the Flying Spaghetti Monster. It's just that the atheist does not believe in that one last god that the religious do.

One question that atheists might get asked, particularly in Christian countries, is whether they believe that Jesus existed. My answer to this is that he probably did exist. Obviously, I do not believe that he was ordained by some supernatural force such as God; he was probably a man of great benevolence and extraordinary gift. He could have stunned people with paranormal powers or perhaps illusion just as people like Uri Geller do today. He may never have claimed to have a divine origin or supernatural connections – these could have been embellishments added on as the fable was passed down over the centuries. Like so many things in this world, there can be part truths to things. We are a people that like rumour and gossip. We sometimes embellish stories to make us feel more important.

Some atheists like Richard Dawkins feel a need to disprove the existence of God. As Europe has become more secularised, Dawkins worries about increasing religious fundamentalism in the Middle East and Middle America. He sees the persecution of women and gay people as a legacy of some religions. He wants to unite the atheists in the world and, to this end, he has been successful, with many atheist groups and alliances around the world citing him and his works as inspiration. For me, Dawkins brings a refreshing viewpoint to the table, even if I do not agree with all of his views and ideas.

We have heard the words and opinions of the powerful religious organisations around the world for many centuries, and now it is time to hear the other argument. It is time for children to be brought up knowing that they can form their own opinions about what to believe in. If a child wishes to embrace religion or atheism, then that is fine. Socialisation is the process by which children learn or inherit cultural norms, customs, and ideologies. We live in a world where hundreds of millions of children have been socialised into believing in something simply because their parents believe in it. This is why you will often know what religion somebody is simply by asking them what country they were born in.

Many commentators have remarked on how moral decline is a product of a less religious Britain. *The Daily Mail* is one newspaper in which this argument is often seen to appear. The argument instinctively assumes that morality can only go hand-in-hand with religious faith. We cannot take such a dim and pessimistic view as this. Morality is a virtue that almost certainly precedes all religions, and the precursors of human morality can be traced to the behaviours of many other animals. In my experience, such tales of moral decline are used more as a means to sell scare stories in papers than having any real basis in everyday life. Sure, I would agree that there are not so many friendly chats over the garden fence these days. I think that that is the result of globalisation and advancing capitalism as much as any moral decline.

However, it is worthy of note that we do not have the amount of large-scale wars, industrial disasters, and intolerance as there once was in the not too distant past. The 'good ole days' were not always as good as some people may recall. I do not doubt that religion has brought much happiness and even purpose to a good many people's lives. I would, though, urge the religious to be cautious in their opinions of others who do not share the same faith. As an atheist, I do not believe that atheism is the biggest threat to the many different religions of the world. A look back through history would soon show that the biggest threat to religion is time itself.

* * * * *

A few twists and turns of the towpath and past the considerably large river islands of Hallsmead Ait and The

Lynch and I found myself traversing a well-trimmed meadow beneath a steep ridge. Atop this ridge sits part of the village of Shiplake. Shiplake College, an independent school, can be seen on top of the ridge and some of the school's rowers were out and about on the river on the day I breezed past. Shiplake is a wealthy little place and has been home at various times to the singer Vince Hill; the author Simon Kendrick; the guitar hero and former Thin Lizzy member, Gary Moore, and Ian Paice, drummer of rock band Deep Purple. The poet Alfred, Lord Tennyson and Emily Sellwood were married in the village church.

Perhaps the most famous former resident of Shiplake is Eric Arthur Blair, known by his pen name, George Orwell. Blair's family moved to Shiplake before the First World War, and he became friends with a young girl called Jacintha. I mentioned their antics in the last chapter. Jacintha and Eric would read and write poetry together and dreamed of becoming famous writers.

CHAPTER 11
The Entertainers

Driving through the village centre at breakneck speed, they smashed windows with their whips and fired their pistols at inn signs. This was the work of a man called Hellgate and his brothers. Wargrave had become the chosen home of Richard, 7th Earl of Barrymore, and his antics were turning the village into something out of the Wild West before the myth of the American Wild West had barely begun. Fabulously wealthy, Barrymore had come to Wargrave as a boy and had now returned after an education at Eton. Despite his hooliganism, Barrymore gave generously to the poor of Wargrave and built a Thames-side theatre at his home, Barrymore House. Costing £300,000 and seating around 400 people, Lord Barrymore's theatre was the largest privately owned theatre in England.

Barrymore's wild ways came to an abrupt end in 1793 when he was shot dead by his own carelessly placed gun. He was only 24 years old. A year earlier, his theatre had been pulled down by debtors. Lord Barrymore is buried in Wargrave in an unmarked grave. As well as being called Hellgate, he was also known as the Rake of Rakes. Anarchy was to return to Wargrave in 1914 when Suffragettes burned down the church of St Mary which dates from the 12th century.

Since the days of Barrymore, Wargrave has built a solid

reputation as being the home of many people associated with entertainment. The list is quite impressive, and along with the aforementioned Lord Barrymore, it includes the likes of the comedian Dave Allen; the actors Sandra Dickinson, Angela Baddeley, Peter Davidson and Robert Morley; the television presenter Raymond Baxter; the singer Mary Hopkins and the late magician, Paul Daniels. Perhaps it is the spirit of the Earl of Barrymore which attracts these entertainers to the banks of the Thames in this tranquil Berkshire village.

The only thing that shatters the tranquillity of this picturesque village is the large amount of traffic which rumbles through the High Street. A local tells me that successive businesses have failed as the parking here is a nightmare, and I must say how devoid of pedestrians the centre of this large village is. If anyone wants to see what a real commuter village looks like, then come to Wargrave.

Wargrave is a curious place, and I decided to stay here for the night. Despite what the rather gloomy name suggests, the word 'Wargrave' is derived from 'Weir-Grove' rather from the literal meaning of 'War Grave'. My thirst for intrigue and adventure needed satiating, and I felt that Wargrave had more secrets to reveal. My first drink was in The Bull Hotel. This quaint low-beamed little place seemed to be populated with a few farmer types and is also rumoured to be home to a ghost. One day in 1934, a sobbing woman was reported to be visiting here. A former landlady of the inn, she had been banished from here after her husband had caught her with her lover. According to folklore, she died from a broken heart. She probably really died from the cold or suicide. Her ghost is reported to be heard sobbing, and her teardrops are said to have stained the wallpaper.

In recent times, Wargrave has been rumoured to be home to a group of ravenous swingers. Their antics made the national press over a decade ago. After plucking up courage, I tentatively enquired with one of the farmer types. 'It goes on in here', he whispered with a hint of a grin, 'I think it also goes on at some local golf clubs and possibly the village boat club too.' I slunk out of The Bull with my thirst for intrigue about this place already satiated. The man had told me to look out for the 'pampas grass'. He told me that he thought there was some up a road called Purfield Drive, not far from here.

The Greyhound is another low-beamed charming pub. However, the crowd is decidedly younger here, and the banter is about Facebook and such things. No young farmers here! A small brass plaque is nailed to the bar with the words 'Wally's stool'. A fellow drinker told me that Wally was a well-known pub frequenter during the 60s, and by all accounts, 'a bit of a character'. At the far end of the High Street lies The George and Dragon. Having changed hands a few times in recent years, this establishment is now more of a restaurant than a public house. There is a fantastic terrace where you can enjoy sipping your drinks in the sunshine. Occasionally, a mock steamboat from up Henley way makes its way past this spot providing a 'Tom Sawyer moment'. I made my way down to the river bank, drink in hand.

It was at this spot in January 1879 that the small ferry boat hit ice and capsized throwing all four occupants into the river. Tragically, Essex Thomas, the ferryman, lost his ten-year-old daughter. A sad reflection of our past is that because of their class, the tragedy of the girl's death was little reported, and it was only recently that the girl was identified as Mary Anne Thomas. There have long been reports of a sprite called Benji near the George and Dragon, who is said to lure people to their deaths in the river. He has been sighted on a set of steps on the Shiplake bank of the river that leads down to the water. Being surrounded by flat farmland and only the odd tree, these mist-shrouded steps must surely rank as one of the creepiest sets of steps anywhere to be found. There was no sign of Benji on the night of my visit.

The next morning was crisp and cold. I don't normally like getting frosty like this in the morning, but the wonderful British fry-up did its job. My veins were so full of fat that it wouldn't have come as a surprise to anybody had I spontaneously combusted! I was sad to be leaving Wargrave, but I remembered that a short while back in Reading I told you that I would reveal a bit more about the chalk caves that are to be found in abundance in this part of the country.

Blink, and you would miss it, but just before a sharp bend in the road on the outskirts of the nearby village of Warren Row sits the secluded entrance to a nuclear bunker. Known as RSGs (Regional Seats of Government), the nuclear bunker had the official designation of RSG-6. In the event of a nuclear war, these RSGs would serve as miniature governments by running each region, maintaining law and order, communicating with the surviving population and controlling the remaining resources.

RSG-6 had particular importance due to its proximity to London and the fact that it was almost certainly the bunker that the Royal Family would use. In the event of nuclear war, the small village of Warren Row could have become the most powerful place in Britain. In March 1963, a group of activists called Spies for Peace broke into RSG-6 and photographed and copied as many documents as they could.

The activists produced copies of their findings and distributed them. The secret was out. A short while afterwards, a demonstration was held outside RSG-6, and the activities of Spies for Peace were making front-page news. Other demonstrations were held at RSGs based in Cambridge and Edinburgh.

The matter was debated in Parliament and, with the RSGs no longer a secret, they were abandoned. At the time of the disclosure of their information by the Spies for Peace, people around Britain had no idea that the Government accepted nuclear war as a possibility and were carefully planning for it. Before being given its new role as a Cold War nuclear bunker, the Warren Row site was an underground chalk quarry well-known in the region for its production of chalk whiting, a material used in the paint trade. Kintbury and Warren Row were the regional centres for this trade. The quarry was then used as an aircraft components factory during the Second World War. In more recent times, it has been used as a store by the Science Museum and is now used as a document store and wine cellar.

The busy A4 London to Bath road runs close to Upper Wargrave. This stretch of the road has become known as the Floral Mile because of the significant number of plant nurseries and garden centres that have sprung up along it. Next to the large Wyevale Garden Centre was the administrative head office of the Mabey Group, a company that is probably best known for supplying permanent and temporary road bridges around the world. I say 'was the head office' because the Mabey sign has recently been taken down. The Mabey Group employs over 1000 people and has an annual turnover of around £100 million.

The company has been in the news in recent years for fraudulent practices. In 2011, David Mabey was sentenced to eight months imprisonment for paying kickbacks to Saddam Hussein's regime. Mabey was ordered to pay £125,000 costs but, being one of Britain's richest men, this shouldn't have been too hard for him to find. The Mabey Group has also been investigated for suspected 'dodgy dealings' in the Philippines, Ghana, and Jamaica.

On leaving Wargrave, one cannot fail to notice the presence of Wargrave Manor high up above the river. This impressive house was once owned by the property magnate Nigel Broackes and was nearly bought by Elton John in 1975. The deal fell through, however, at the last moment and Elton bought Woodside in Old Windsor instead. Today, Wargrave Manor is the occasional home of Sultan Qaboos of Oman. Qaboos is an absolute ruler who tolerates no dissent. Despite his absolute status - held since he overthrew his own father in a palace coup in 1970 - his lack of rights for his citizens - they cannot even hold a public meeting without government approval - and his questionable leadership - Oman has come close to bankruptcy over the years whilst military spending has remained massive - Qaboos is a good friend of Britain.

In fact, the relationship between Britain and Oman is a fascinating and murky one made increasingly stranger by Oman's status as one of the world's most secretive states. One gets the impression that turning over a few stones in this odd relationship is enough to set the alarm bells ringing. When the journalist John Beasant wrote his book *Oman: The True-Life Drama And Intrigue Of An Arab State*, he was offered a substantial bribe not to publish it. When he refused, he was escorted to the airport and expelled from the country. The book is officially banned in Oman.

The story of how Sultan Qaboos came to depose his father is intertwined with the story of a shadowy former SAS brigadier called Timothy Landon or the 'White Sultan' as he came to be known. Having graduated at Sandhurst in 1962, Landon was seconded to Muscat, the Omani capital, to help with the British and Omani effort to repel a Communist insurgency trained and armed by Russia. The communists were successfully kept at bay. The British were becoming worried by the ultra-conservative ruler Sa'id Taimur who was showing a 'worrying independent streak', and they began to conspire with Taimur's son, Qaboos, to depose his father. British oil companies were anxious to capitalise on Oman's newly discovered oil reserves, and the British Government was only too happy to help them.

A bloodless coup occurred on 23 July 1970, and Qaboos was installed as the new leader. Sa'id Taimur died two years later in his suite on the top floor of London's Dorchester Hotel where he had been living. Asked about what his greatest regret was shortly before his death, he replied: 'Not having Landon shot.' Landon became a trusted personal advisor to Qaboos, advising him on all sorts of government issues. As Oman's oil revenues rapidly increased, so did its monumental arms spending. In 1980, £400 million was spent on defence in the country which had a population of just over two million people.

Around this time, Landon allegedly helped one oil company break oil sanctions to Rhodesia and South Africa. Qaboos rewarded Landon handsomely for his advice, and it was alleged that he sent Landon cheques for £1 million every birthday right up to Landon's death in 2007. By the time of his death, Landon had become one of Britain's wealthiest men with a fortune of around £500 million. In the early 1980s, Landon moved back to Britain but was shrouded in secrecy. He lived in a mansion in the remote hamlet of Faccombe, Hampshire, and owned the hamlet too. The locals remain tight-lipped about the 'White Sultan'. When Tim Landon died, his fortune was passed over to his son, Arthur Landon. At 34 years old, Landon has, been reported as being Britain's most eligible bachelor with a fortune estimated at around £200 million. He is a close friend of both Prince Harry and Prince William and is often seen accompanying the royal princes on various social events.

Britain remains a close friend of Qaboos, who has no doubt felt indebted for Britain's help with repelling the communists and then his father. For the most part, the Omani people seem to be happy with their leader, although, in a nation which severely restricts the media and allows no criticism of him, it is problematic getting an accurate picture of the real situation. Even today, the British government remain tight-lipped about much of its foreign policy and privatised commercial interests in Oman. Since the Arab Spring, there have been demonstrations against Qaboos, particularly in Oman's second city, Sohar, where the demonstrations turned violent, and several protesters were reported to have been killed. Qaboos responded to the unrest by replacing six cabinet members and boosting the minimum wage by more than 40 per cent. As Oman's oil reserves dwindle, it needs to rapidly diversify its economy.

Many Omanis were said to have grown frustrated with the involvement of people like Landon in their country. Even the Duke of Edinburgh has reportedly voiced 'distaste' at Landon's affairs in Oman. With the British having a military presence in Oman, and the geopolitical importance of Oman at the forefront again in the fight with Islamic extremists, it would seem that it is both in Britain's and Oman's interest to cooperate closely for the near future at least.

* * * * *

A short but pleasant walk brought me within range of Henley-on-Thames. High up along a ridge over on the other side of the river is the stunningly rustic and rocky Conway's Bridge. This bridge was built in 1783 by Humphrey Gainsborough, and it carries the main road from Wargrave to Henley. Humphrey Gainsborough was the brother of painter Thomas Gainsborough, and he has been described as one of Britain's greatest geniuses, even though very few people have heard of him.

As well as Conway's Bridge, Gainsborough constructed many locks on the River Thames, invented the most accurate sundial ever and developed the drill plough, advancing the ideas of Jethro Tull. He also designed a steam engine which he showed to James Watt. Watt patented his own design in 1769. It is likely that Gainsborough invented the steam engine, but he remains obscure today. He lived and died in Henley. I will raise a glass to him the next time I have one in my hand; I hope you will too.

Gainsborough's Conway's Bridge is built on the perimeter of the extensive grounds of one of Britain's most exclusive homes, Park Place. Up until September 2012, this house had held the title of being the most expensive in Britain; it was surpassed by a palatial 45 bedroom mansion in London's Knightsbridge with a whopping £300 million price tag! Park Place is a large French Renaissance-style house that was built in 1719 for the Duke of Hamilton.

Since then, the house has been in the possession of Frederick, Prince of Wales and the eccentric General Henry Seymour Conway. Conway made various bizarre alterations to the grounds including the additions of caverns, tunnels, an amphitheatre, and a Druid's Temple, made from a prehistoric stone circle consisting of 45 stones transported over from Jersey, where he was Governor. At one point, Queen Victoria had visited Park Place with an eye to buying it.

In recent years, a consortium wanted to purchase Park Place to turn it into an exclusive country club, but the proposal was turned down by Wokingham Council. The house was used in the filming of the outside scenes of the 2007 film, *St Trinian's*. It was recently developed by Michael Spink, who bought the house for £42 million in 2007. In 2011, Park Place was sold for £140 million to the Russian Billionaire Andrey Borodin. Despite the fact that Spink had spent over £100 million restoring the main house and gardens, in what is, I'm sure, a shrewd move, he has retained 300 acres of the estate for development. In mid-2016, a Moscow court ordered the seizure of Park Place as an indemnity for hundreds of millions of pounds it says Mr Borodin stole from the Bank of Moscow, which he once owned.

An impressive elevated wooden walkway over the Thames took me past the lock and weir and into more meadows populated by an increasing amount of runners, dog walkers, and dog mess. My eyes greeted the odd boat owner on the occasions that I could prise them away from scanning the pathway for horrific canine creations. Most of the boat owners were friendly, even the ones atop the gin palaces. I passed the River and Rowing Museum, opened by The

Queen in 1998. I passed by a bandstand, a group of students surrounded by pigeons, some more dog mess, and Hobbs' boatyard.

I was now in Henley-on-Thames, perhaps best known for its annual regatta held here since 1839. A must for any self-respecting socialite's calendar, the Henley Royal Regatta is a bevy of frenzied sporting activity and society hobnobbing. The regatta here is probably the most famous of its kind anywhere in the world and it is frequently visited by members of Britain's Royal Family. Henley has a way of managing to keep cropping up in popular culture, time and time again. The town has become associated with many television personalities and musicians, and the presence of the world-famous regatta has brought it much attention.

Perhaps the most famous Henley resident was the ex-Beatle George Harrison who lived in the eccentric Friar Park. As if in an attempt to outshine the 'bonkers-ness' that had been going on at nearby Park Place, Friar Park has underground waterways, waterfalls, and lakes. It has various skeleton-filled caverns, and there is a rock garden built in the shape of the Matterhorn, which features a piece of rock from the real thing on top. These creations were installed by the eccentric lawyer Sir Frank Crisp who lived at Friar Park from 1895 until 1919. It was at Friar Park in 1999 that an intruder managed to break in, despite the extensive security. He attacked and badly injured the former Beatle before being felled by Harrison's wife Olivia armed with a poker. George Harrison died in 2001.

The actor and former star of *The Likely Lads*, Rodney Bewes, has taken on Friar Park over its extensive use of razor wire for extra security. In November 2012, it was announced that Olivia Harrison had failed to get planning permission for the razor wire after objections from Rodney Bewes. Bewes has claimed that his cat, Maurice, had been injured three times by the razor wire at a cost of £1500 in vet bills. Martin Akehurst of Henley Town Council commented 'Razor wire has no place in Henley.' I can understand Mrs Harrison wanting the extra security measures after undergoing such an horrific attack on her and her husband in her own home. It was such a terrible injustice that an attack should happen to a peace-loving 'hippie' like George Harrison. It was Harrison who once said that 'If everybody who had a gun just shot themselves, there wouldn't be a problem.'

The second most famous Henley music star must surely be soul supremo Dusty Springfield who died in 1999 and is buried in the grounds of St Mary the Virgin Parish Church in central Henley. The former Blue singer Lee Ryan lives in Henley, and Liam Gallagher of Oasis reportedly once lived in the nearby hamlet of Satwell with his wife, Nicole Appleton of girl-group All Saints. A little further afield in the Chiltern Hills lived Carol Decker, formerly of the pop group T'Pau. Decker and her partner ran The Cherry Tree pub in Stoke Row until recently.

From the television world, the small Chiltern village of Stonor can boast the likes of razor-tongued inquisitor Jeremy Paxman. Softer-tongued inquirer Philip Schofield lives in the nearby Chiltern village of Fawley. Other Henley residents include the mathematician Marcus du Sautoy and Hollywood star Orlando Bloom, who has a second home in the town. So the message is loud and clear – if you want to bump into a celeb, come and take a trip over to Henley. But mind to keep a beady eye out for that dog mess!

Former Henley constituency MPs have been the

publishing tycoon and onetime Prime Minister candidate, Tarzan, er sorry, I meant Michael Hestletine and the loveable, if somewhat eccentric, Boris Johnson. After Britain voted to leave the EU, Johnson was tipped to become Prime Minister, but he declared he would not campaign for leadership following the surprise launch of a campaign by previous key ally, Michael Gove. John Redwood, the aforementioned MP for Wokingham, is a familiar face in Henley and got a fair amount of attention a few years back for dating a woman who lives in the town and who was an employee of dodgy dealing firm Mabey and Johnson, back near Wargrave.

Henley was once the stomping ground for one of Britain's most controversial police officers; Ali Dizaei. Dizaei has been the focus of much controversy and corruption allegations that saw him labelled 'The most dangerous man in the Met'. Dizaei joined the Thames Valley Police in 1986 and rose to the position of Chief Inspector. He was then transferred to the Metropolitan Police Service on promotion to Superintendent in 1999.

Other famous people who live, or who have lived, in Henley include George Orwell, Formula One baron Ross Brawn, Sir Ninian Stephen (Governer-General of Australia, 1982-1989) and the remarkable stuntman Gary Connery, who stunned the world in May 2012 by being the first person ever to jump from a height of 2400 feet and safely land without using a parachute. Connery jumped from a helicopter and used a wing-suit for the flight before plunging head first into an area containing 18,600 cardboard boxes. The incredible footage was seen by millions around the world.

Connery has performed stunts in films including *The*

Beach, Indiana Jones, and *Johnny English Reborn*. He has performed 450 base jumps including jumps from Nelson's Column, The London Eye, The Eiffel Tower, and The Hilton Hotel on Park Lane. He was the stunt double for The Queen when he jumped out of a helicopter in a dress at the opening ceremony of the 2012 London Olympics.

The financier Sir Martyn Arbib based his hugely successful Perpetual Fund in Henley. Arbib sold Perpetual to fund manager AMVESCAP in 2001 for more than £1 billion. After this, the company became known as Invesco Perpetual.

I have visited the Henley Regatta before. I always hear of people saying that they avoid Henley during regatta because of all the snobs. However, for me, it is their very presence that makes it all the more fun! I like observing the snobs – it feels kind of strange suddenly being in the minority. All of a sudden they seem populous and mundane! The regatta is fun. I once overheard a young brother and sister drunkenly discussing how they would divvy up their parents 'boring £10 million business.' They acted with surprise when I somewhat rudely interjected that they 'could always hand it over to me!'

In the late 1980s, Class War came to visit Henley Regatta. Their Marxist leader, Ian Bone, brought his motley crew of anarchists bearing the slogan 'Bash the Rich'. Bone is the publisher of the Class War newspaper and has been labelled 'Britain's most dangerous man.' For people intending to 'bash' some rich people, the Henley Regatta must surely be a good place to start.

I got on my way. I crossed the wonderfully arched Henley Bridge built in 1786 by William Hayward, walked past The Leander Club, the world's most famous rowing club, and was well on my way into a stretch of the Thames regarded by many as the loveliest. The Chiltern Hills roll away from the valley sides, and wooded hills peek out tantalising with their mysterious canopies. This stretch of the river north of Henley was chosen for the regatta because it is the longest naturally straight stretch of river in Britain. Since 1967, the regatta course has been one mile and 550 yards long.

Fawley Court is an impressive pile that winked at me from across the opposite bank of the river. A house on this site has been occupied since Norman times and has passed through many hands including a Parliamentarian and a plantation merchant. Iranian heiress Aida Hersham purchased the house in 2010 and has pledged to restore it fully to its original splendour. The original asking price for the house was £22 million. It had previously been owned by the Congregation of Marian Fathers and was used as a school for Polish boys.

To my immediate right were farm buildings which up until recently had been used as the venue of the 'Barn Bar', a popular drinking den during the Henley Regatta. It was here that I observed many drunken toff calamities, and that I sometimes thoughtfully interjected my thoughts into their conversations. Today, the buildings used for the Barn Bar have been redeveloped into offices and, during the regatta the 'Barn Bar' is located in fields right next door.

The buildings here are owned by the Copas Partnership, a firm based in Cookham which produces Britain's most expensive Christmas turkeys. Copas turkeys were the first in the UK to cost over £100. The premium organic range turkeys here are as pampered as any demanding diva. They are fed on a strictly monitored organic corn diet, and they listen to jazz and musicals on Radio Two to get them used to the human voice. They are also given their own mini-firework demonstration to get them prepared for all the whizzes and bangs on bonfire night!

With the gently rolling hills behind it, Temple Island is a marvel to look at. This well-sized river island marks the start of the regatta course and is unmistakeable due to the presence of an ornate fishing lodge for Fawley Court built upon its southern end in 1771. Henley Business School sits on a bend in the river, occupying what was once a stately home called Greenlands. Greenlands became the home of William Henry Smith, a newsagent who opened the first railway bookstall at Euston Station. The business was a great success and is now widely known under the abbreviated name W. H. Smith. Jerome K. Jerome rather amusingly summed up this grand house as 'the rather uninteresting looking residence of my newsagent.'

A short distance behind this spot lies the village of Fawley. This affluent little place is home to Sir William McAlpine, a former director of the construction company Sir Robert McAlpine. Born at the family-owned Dorchester Hotel in London, McAlpine was always going to have an advantage in the world of business. These days McAlpine likes to spend his time playing with his train set. When I say train set, I mean it in the most literal sense. McAlpine built Fawley Hill Railway, a private railway with over a mile of track. He has various steam locomotives, signal boxes and station features installed, and it is open by invitation only on select days usually in the summer period.

McAlpine even got married to his second wife on his private railway, so he could be close to his toys! He owns an interesting selection of animals including wallabies and llamas which led me to think that he may also be in on the competition with Friar Park and Park Place for the title of owning the most eccentric home. Some of these exotic animals have escaped from the estate over the years, and many locals now believe that there is a growing wild wallaby colony around Henley!

McAlpine is a generous man who has donated considerable amounts to charity, as well as being well known for his efforts in saving a small part of Britain's steam locomotive heritage. Not everyone has looked fondly upon the McAlpine name. From the 1930s onwards, the McAlpine family business employed large numbers of Irish who had come to England looking for work. The harsh ways in which the McAlpine management treated their labourers inspired the song 'McAlpine's Fusiliers'. The song, written by Dominic Behan, was made famous by The Dubliners, and the story has entered into Irish emigrant folklore. The McAlpine name was unfairly besmirched in November 2012 when unfounded allegations were made that William's brother, Alistair, was implicated in a North Wales child abuse scandal.

The river continues on its wide curve, and I was soon walking past the imposing white-painted Hambleden Mill. This large mill house remained in use until 1955 and has now been converted into luxury apartments. A short distance from the mill, still on the opposite bank of the river, sits a splendid six-bedroom thatched riverside mansion which has been recently bought for over £3 million by comedian and 'revolutionary' Russell Brand. It is reputed that the anti-capitalist is undertaking a £1 million refurbishment which includes the addition of a swimming pool and a cinema.

I walked by a small path that led down from the village

of Aston, and I was soon passing one of the most stunning properties to be found anywhere on the river. Culham Court was built in 1770 and is owned today by the Swiss financier and friend of Prince Charles, Urs Swarzenbach. Swarzenbach was so keen on the property, which he bought in 2007, that he paid £35 million for it, £10 million above the original asking price. Culham Court has a strong association with the world of finance. Previous owners have included Felicity Behrens, wife of the banker Michael Behrens, and Martyn Arbib's daughter Annabel Nicoll.

Swarzenbach is undertaking extensive refurbishment and alterations to Culham Estate, such as the extension of the deer park, a new driveway, a helipad for 'his and hers' helicopters and a Roman Catholic chapel. As if all this wasn't enough, Swarzenbach also acquired nearby Hambleden village for £39 million in 2007. Hambleden will be familiar to many millions of British residents without them even necessarily realising. It is an extremely popular place for filming, and it has served as a location for various films over the years including *Chitty Chitty Bang Bang*, *Dance with A Stranger*, *The Avengers*, *Band of Brothers* and various television series and adverts. Swarzenbach is often to be seen buzzing back and forth from his estate in his helicopter.

A few minutes later I was walking past Medmenham Abbey, a distinctive building with chalky whitewashed walls. Although founded in 1201 for Cistercian Monks, much of the building dates from later than this period. The Abbey was owned by former Chancellor of the Exchequer Sir Francis Dashwood in the 18th century. Dashwood, whose antics I shall explore a bit further on in this chapter, travelled to Medmenham from his residence at West Wycombe Park. He founded the notorious Hellfire Club at West Wycombe and brought chaos and drunken revelry to the quiet streets of Medmenham. In one notorious incident, one of Dashwood's guests, Sir Henry Vansittart, the Governor of Bengal, brought along his pet baboon which was dressed up as the Devil and proceeded to jump onto the back of a terrified Earl of Sandwich! Today, Medmenham Abbey is a private residence.

A little further on is the Victorian Tudor mansion that is Danesfield House. Danesfield got its name from a Danish settlement that once protected the river crossing at this spot. The mansion was designed in 1899 for Robert William Hudson, the son of Robert Hudson, the inventor of soap powder. Robert Hudson was the first person to ever use mass advertising for the promotion of a product. Danesfield was once owned by the Air Ministry and then the Carnation Milk Company before becoming a luxury hotel in 1991.

It was well into early evening, and I was just entering Hurley village. The quiet High Street appears to go on for an eternity, certainly much further than my sore feet were willing to carry me on that day. I walked as far as the Ye Olde Bell, which is claimed to be England's oldest Inn. It certainly felt very quaint and quite expensive too. I didn't feel that I completely fitted in there, to be honest, but I stopped for a sit down and a drink anyway. I was well worn, and my mind was racing ahead. I had told myself that I would be spending the night in Marlow.

The weir at Hurley Lock is considered to be the best spot in Britain for freestyle kayaking and that explained the assortment of vans and cars with odd-looking roof-rack contraptions affixed to them. A couple of kayakers almost knocked me off my feet as they brusquely rounded the corner of the narrow pathway, wearing their upturned kayaks on their heads like bizarre, ostentatious hats.

A brief chat I had earlier on with a hiker on the trail had revealed the presence of a 'large house somewhere behind Hurley'. The hiker expressed particular distaste to the owner of this house: 'They drive round in off-road vehicles and stare at you from the windows with binoculars. This is England for heaven's sake!' The distaste that this solitary walker exhibited stayed with me. I found out that the house in question is called Channy Grove. There is not much information about this mysterious house anywhere, but a local tells me that Channy Grove backs onto Juddmonte Farms, and the owner is none other than Prince Khalid bin Abdullah Al Saud, a member of the Saudi Arabian Royal Family.

Prince Khalid's family business is the massive conglomerate Mawared and his personal fortune has been estimated at over one billion dollars. The prince set up Juddmonte Farms in 1977, which comprises three farms in England, two in Ireland, and three in Kentucky, USA. Juddmonte Farms has had many notable successes, but a particular highlight was the unbeaten record of Frankel which became the highest-rated racehorse in the world a little over a year before his retirement in late 2012. It has been reported that Frankel might earn his owner over £100 million for his efforts in siring future champions. With such valuable racehorses on their farms, I wouldn't expect the prying binoculars of Channy Grove to be put away anytime soon!

I started out on the short ramble over to Marlow. Positioned close to Hurley Lock is Freebody's Boatyard, a family boatyard and the largest surviving builder of wooden boats in England. A long attractive wooden bridge took me over to the other bank of the river. Temple Bridge is the longest hardwood bridge in Britain and mightily attractive it is too, with its great sweeping arch. Up past Temple Lock, Bisham Abbey came into view. This historic building once belonged to the Knights Templar who extended the building in 1260. Bisham Abbey is also home to the National Sports Centre and headquarters of the England football team.

Bisham's All Saints Church offers an equally serene view from across the river. In August 1831, the people of Bisham were surprised by the sight of a man in a top hat walking around with a small boy with an unsightly skin disorder. The man was John Richardson, a freak show impresario from Marlow. Richardson claimed to have acquired the boy from the West Indies, and it was reported that he was heartbroken when the boy died. He was just five years old.

For anyone who has ever been to Budapest, as have I, a visit to Marlow might begin to inspire a sense of familiarity. Marlow Bridge was the inspiration for the much bigger Szechenyl Chain Bridge which crosses the Danube to link Buda with Pest. When it was built in 1849, the Szechenyl Chain Bridge was the longest suspension bridge in the world. Marlow Bridge is a stunningly attractive endeavour much like its Hungarian big brother. It was built in 1832 by William Tierney Clark and is the only suspension bridge across the non-tidal Thames.

A walk through a small park scattered with some friendly faces is a pleasant introduction to Marlow, and there doesn't seem to be the dog poo minefields that were so successfully deployed back in Henley! Marlow High Street was a welcome sight. 'Chelsea tractors' buzzed to and fro, and the occasional mum breezed past me with school kids in tow. This place feels quite young and cosmopolitan. Marlow is a vibrant and friendly place.

Marlow is famous for being the one-time home of poet Percy Bysshe Shelley and his second wife, Frankenstein author Mary Shelley; the poet T.S.Elliot, and the already much talked about author, Jerome K Jerome. The pop star and superego Robbie Williams has bought a house on the river at Bisham. Michelin Star chef Heston Blumenthal and TV presenter Paul Ross also live in Marlow. Quintuple Olympic gold medallist Sir Steve Redgrave lives in Marlow Bottom, a village that lies on the outskirts of the town.

Other sports stars that live, or have lived, in Marlow include former England goalkeeper David Seaman; the England cricket captain Andrew Strauss, and former Formula One racing driver Takuma Sato. Dr William Battie, an eminent 18th century physician who specialised in mental illness, lived in Marlow, and this is where the word 'batty' is said to originate from. Sir Miles Hobart, MP for Marlow, started the tradition of shutting the door in Black Rod's face in Parliament when he was Speaker of the House of Commons in 1628. The tradition of Black Rod continues in Parliament today and is no doubt attributed the word 'batty' by many who have seen it!

For me, at that very moment, Marlow was most famous for the amazing burger and chips that I was wolfing down at the Slug and Lettuce on the High Street! As it got dark, the pub started to fill up slowly. I had some time to kill before I felt ready to go to the B&B I had booked earlier. I did some window shopping up the High Street and then a bit of real shopping in the convenience store.

My intrigue took me down some poorly-lit back streets. On one deserted street, I found the curious premises of a company called Urenco; this firm turns out to be one of the world's biggest suppliers of enriched uranium, and their worldwide headquarters is based right here in genteel Marlow! As my imagination ran away with me, I pictured these premises being controlled by some sort of James Bond villain. 'Ah, Mr Bond, you will never get your hands on our enriched uranium supplies mwa ha ha ha.' It was time to retire to bed. Bed for that night was a rather comfortable B&B with an even more comfortable fry-up to look forward to in the morning.

The following morning, I was pleased as punch for having gotten up and away particularly early. I realise that I have forgotten to mention about a brilliant British eccentric who hails from Marlow Bottom. Lyndon Yorke is well-known in these parts for bizarre inventions. This bespectacled gent gets around in a number of homemade contraptions which include a wickerwork car, a floating bath chair and an Edwardian tricycle converted to 'sail' on the river. His tricycle called 'Tritanic' was built for the Henley Regatta and garnered much attention, as you can imagine!

In a 2001 televised competition by Kellogg's Fruit 'n' Fibre, Lyndon was chosen as the Number One British Eccentric and was presented this accolade by none other than the great 'funny-boned' comedian Sir Norman Wisdom (On the subject of Norman Wisdom has anybody else noted a fleeting resemblance between the late comic and the rather flamboyant Marlow resident and superego, singer Robbie Williams?). Lyndon also had the honour of being the first member to join the Eccentric Club of London when it was resurrected in 2008. As if to complement its most famous eccentric resident, Marlow Bottom also has the eccentric accolade of being the place where the fungus used to develop the strange meat substitute Quorn was discovered.

Quorn is still manufactured by a company called Marlow Foods.

When it comes to elaborate contraptions, it would seem that this is something that runs in the blood of the good people of Marlow. When the owners of Marlow's Beehive Treats store noticed that money was being stolen from their shop at night in the summer of 2011, they decided to set an elaborate plan to catch the thief. They laid in wait dressed in black and set an assortment of booby traps to tell them where the thief was and what he was up to. The thief was revealed to be their 20-year-old employee Oliver Longstaff, a hard-up local drama student who had built up a gambling debt. Longstaff pleaded guilty to theft at Wycombe Magistrates' Court and was handed a 12-month supervision order.

Longstaff was reported to have been given the 'shock of a lifetime' by his bosses and faced the added indignity of the nationwide press attention his apprehending had brought. Whilst we all know that kids and adults love sweets, it is worthy of note that the creator of the popular children's social networking site Moshi Monsters, Michael Acton Smith, lives in Marlow. Acton Smith is a true Web entrepreneur having developed the online retailer Firebox when he left university and going on to set up his company Mind Candy which launched alternate reality game Perplex City before making his fortune with Moshi Monsters.

One of the reasons that I had decided to haul myself up so early on that morning is so that I could take a hike up to High Wycombe. It's only about two miles north of Marlow, and it would seem a shame to miss out on this large thriving Chiltern town. High Wycombe urban area has a population of around 118,000 people according to the 2001 census. I used the busy A404 road as my guide. Even as this road, that is as straight as a die, dived out of sight, I could still hear its brutal roar. The A404 links the M4 motorway to the south near Maidenhead with the M40 to the north near High Wycombe in a stretch of dual carriageway about ten miles or so long.

I took the exit marked on my map and began walking through the noisy outskirts of the town. Soon the road led down a dramatic incline which brought me to a moot point: the first thing that you notice as you walk towards the centre of this town, located in an undeniably impressive setting on the southern tip of the Chilterns, is that much of High Wycombe is not very high at all. In fact, the town centre itself is very low. Low Wycombe would be a far more suitable name to me! It seemed to have taken me an age to get to the bottom of the hill.

The first thing that the visitor to High Wycombe is confronted with is a confusing array of roundabouts which seem to divert cars off in all directions away from Wycombe as soon as they arrive. Ominously, one of the first buildings that I saw was the police station, and High Wycombe definitely gets its fair share of problems. Apart from pitched battles between feuding families and the occasional shooting, High Wycombe made the news in 2006 as raids across the town by police were made to capture the suspects involved in the transatlantic passenger plane plot. Islamic fundamentalists planned to detonate homemade bombs concealed in drinks containers to bring down many passenger planes over the Atlantic Ocean. Searches for bomb-making equipment in local woodlands carried on long after the arrests of the plotters. High Wycombe crops up rather a lot in talk of countering home-grown Islamic fundamentalist terrorism in Britain.

The High Street revealed itself from behind a protective shield of buildings. The first thing that caught my eye was the Old Town Hall. Elevated above the High Street on spindly columns, this red brick leviathan assumes a commanding position over the town centre. I have always liked elevated buildings such as these as they lend a sense of imagination and ambition as well as a handy place to shelter from rainy weather. The one back at Abingdon is particularly grand. In recent years, High Wycombe has undergone a major facelift. A town-centre regeneration project has seen the development of some impressive architecture. All this is a far cry from when High Wycombe was a thriving furniture-making centre.

The town was famous for its bodgers - craftsmen who would turn out chair parts using traditional pole lathes. Bodgers were highly skilled wood-turners working in the beech woods of the Chiltern Hills, and they were very fast. Unfortunately today, the word bodger is often used to describe very shoddy workmanship. The bodging trade died out in the 1960s as fully mechanised mass production techniques took over. Interest in the work and lifestyle of the bodger lives on, however; indeed, a resurgence in traditional means of production, much like that favoured by William Morris of Kelmscott, is, I feel, perhaps just around the corner.

Like many of the towns and villages in the Thames Valley, High Wycombe boasts a significant contribution to the world of entertainment. Rock legend Ian Dury; soul legend Dusty Springfield, and singer-songwriter Howard Jones all hail from the town. The actors Colin Baker and James Corden come from High Wycombe, and celebrity chef

Heston Blumenthal and the acerbic comic Jimmy Carr both attended grammar schools in the town. The former British Prime Minister Benjamin Disraeli was a resident of Hughenden Manor just outside the town for three decades.

An eminent High Wycombe resident was the world-renowned philosopher Karl Popper. Popper is widely regarded as one of the greatest philosophers of science of the 20th century. Born in Vienna in 1902, Karl Popper could often be heard referring to his hometown 'Havvercomb' in his heavily accented English. The rugby player Matt Dawson and footballer Simon Church are from High Wycombe as is the hurdler and sprinter Nicola Sanders.

The person from High Wycombe who fascinates me the most, however, was a musician who you have almost certainly never heard of. This man has probably played more gigs than anyone else in the UK, in fact well over 6000. He wrote a song for David Bowie, graced our TV screens alongside the likes of Kylie Minogue (Minogue described him as 'inspirational' on TV-AM in October 1991); he was featured on TV adverts, signed to major record labels, awarded a Harp Beat rock plaque, and was highly respected amongst the musical community. He wrote countless brilliant songs. 'I've Got To Rock and Roll' was described by Nicky Horne of Capital Radio as being one of the greatest rock and roll songs of all time. His name was Les Payne. Les Who? I hear you ask.

Having spent much of the 1960s and 1970s playing support slots for the likes of Genesis and David Essex, Les would find that his progress in the world of music would become obstructed by nothing less than pure bad luck. His first single, 'I Can't Cry for You', released by RCA, became Radio 2 Jonnie Walkers' Record of the Week, but a vinyl shortage prevented the massively in-demand record from hitting the shelves of the shops in sufficient numbers. In 1982, another song, the anti-war 'Who Will Be the Winner', was released to great acclaim. However, within weeks, the Falklands War had begun, and as a result, the record was pulled from airplay. Kenny Everett was the only DJ to carry on promoting the song.

Les was not, however, one to give up easily, and the 1980s and 1990s saw him continue gigging at a legendary rate. The Harp Beat rock plaque award is normally given to musicians who have 'made it', but it was awarded to Les in recognition of his persistence in the music industry, and for being an inspiration to all musicians. The award attracted media attention from all over the world, and Les appeared on television news bulletins from Germany to Australia.

Tragically, Les passed away in early May 2017, before the release of his latest album and a book he was working on. He continued to gig and remained incredibly passionate about his music and the music of local musicians, right up to his passing at 73 years old. Despite being frequently labelled as 'pop's biggest failure' he saw things differently - he said: 'I would only consider myself a failure if I was going on a train every day to work in a bank!'

Les was the epitome of the rock and roll spirit, and he continues to inspire all around him, including many young musicians. He ran Dreamcatcher studios from his home in High Wycombe and welcomed enquiries to do recordings for musicians of all abilities. He was a music legend known for his amiability, humour and extraordinary persistence in a notoriously fickle industry. He leaves his wife, Pennie, sons Crispin and Elliot, sister Val and brothers Mike and Graham, step-children Josh and Libbie and grandchildren Tiegan,

Jobey and Flynn. At the time of finishing this book, Les' friends and family were working on finishing the last album he was working on: *The Ultimate Compliment*. His remarkable legacy will live on.

* * * * *

Just to the east of High Wycombe is Hughenden Manor, one-time home of former British Prime Minister, Benjamin Disraeli. Disraeli was Prime Minister in 1868 and again from 1874-1880. Since 1974, Hughenden Manor has been in the care of the National Trust, and the house is decorated as it would have been at the time it was occupied by Disraeli. Disraeli was a colourful figure who set many precedents. He was the first British Prime Minister to be born to Jewish parents. He was also an unusual candidate for being Prime Minister as he did not come from landowning stock. He was the author of several literary works including the novel, *Vivian Grey*.

As well known for his social life as well as his political one, Disraeli was Queen Victoria's favourite Prime Minister. Disraeli had a razor-sharp wit, and many of his observations and thoughts are remembered with a similar relish as those of another noted British Prime Minister and wit: Winston Churchill. Probably the most famous quote from Disraeli is: 'There are three kinds of lies. Lies, damned lies, and statistics.' However, my favourite Disraeli quote is one he made about travel: 'Like all great travellers, I have seen more than I remember, and remember more than I have seen.'

If Disraeli was known for his statesman-like public image and literary life, that might not be so much the case of fellow High Wycombe politician and one-time Chancellor of the Exchequer Sir Francis Dashwood who set up his

'Hellfire Club' around a century before. Whilst there were several Hellfire Clubs in 18th century Britain, Dashwood's club would become the most notorious. It was often referred to as the Order of Knights of West Wycombe and, like all the Hellfire Clubs, it was established as a meeting place for drunken, carnal revelry and orgy for rakish gentlemen of disrepute. Pagan rituals would often feature, and aristocrats and statesmen numbered significantly in its membership. Whilst few records about the West Wycombe Hellfire Clubs remain, it is generally believed that its members included John Montagu, 4th Earl of Sandwich; Juror Robert Vansittart; the renowned painter William Hogarth, plus occasional visits by Benjamin Franklin.

The club is believed to have had over 12 members at its peak. The location of Dashwood's club was in the West Wycombe Caves. Further revelries occurred just a few miles away at Medmenham Abbey along the banks of the Thames.

The Dashwood Estate at West Wycombe includes an imposing mausoleum high up on a hill, a complex system of tunnels which include a banqueting hall, a huge flint structure that resembles a fortress, and St Lawrence's Church which has a large golden sphere on top. This sphere, which can allegedly hold two people sitting inside it, is known locally as the Golden Ball and, along with Dashwood's other bizarre creations atop the hill, make for quite a surreal and mystical setting for people driving out west from High Wycombe. The estate was used in the Hammer Horror film of 1976 *To the Devil a Daughter*. Debauchery and penchant for the surreal never held Dashwood back from becoming Chancellor of the Exchequer!

I rejoined the Thames on the other side of the busy

A404. This is a particularly stunning spot as the river bends and houses climb the steep slope of the valley side on the opposite bank of the river. It is also a particularly wealthy spot, and the sophisticated bolt-hole of Cookham Dean village lies atop the valley side. A regal feel is lent to the Thames Path here as large trees line up along a neat lawn making it feel as though you are walking on the main drive up to a fine country manor. My eyes remained transfixed upon the opulent properties on the other side of the river. Lutyens Castle, a house built in the style of a castle, painted a particular fairytale scene. The houses here seem to sit on ridges cut into the slope of the hillside, and sweeping lawns run down to their river frontages and boat houses. What a wonderful place to live.

Tranquility returned to the riverbanks, and the main riparian inhabitants are once again cows. 'How far to Bourne End?' I enquire to a passer-by. 'Oh, only about 25 minutes or so,' came the friendly reply. I wasn't really that bothered about how long it would take as the scenery around there is simply sublime. Winter Hill came into view on the opposite bank. This is a well-known beauty spot. Quarry Wood shrouds the banks around Winter Hill. This is the 'Wild Wood' of Kenneth Grahame's *The Wind in the Willows*. Grahame grew up in Cookham Dean and would later return there and write the bedtime stories for his son, Alastair, that would become *The Wind in the Willows*. Another notable Cookham Dean resident was Dame Nellie Melba, an Australian opera star, whose legend would live on in the popular drink Peach Melba and the popular food Melba toast. Soon the steep bank of Winter Hill melted away, and the landscape became plate flat. This is Cock Marsh, an area which is home to rare species of flowers and birds. It is

The Entertainers

looked after by the National Trust.

My arrival in Bourne End took me down a long fenced pathway. Wooden chalets in various stages of dilapidation sit behind the fences, and the amount of timber frames lend this area a hint of the Mississippi. Some of the chalets on the river are well kept with neat little gardens. I caught tentative glimpses of an old Thames sailing barge through some openings. I walked past the sailing club, and within minutes I was in the centre of this affluent village. According to *The Daily Telegraph* in 2011, Bourne End is England's 14th richest village. It seems to manage to keep much of its wealth well hidden from its bustling centre, tucked down side streets and along the banks of the Thames.

The village sits near to the confluence of the River Wye and the Thames. It was once a popular place for water-powered mills and was popularly known as 'Bone End' before the mispronunciation was reversed by the vicar of Wooburn in 1858. In the 1920s, Bourne End became the home of two literary heavyweights: the children's writer, Enid Blyton, and the crime writer, Edgar Wallace. Other notable residents of Bourne End have included Louis Bleriot, the first man to fly across the English Channel; the playwright Sir Tom Stoppard, and *Carry On* films actor Kenneth Connor.

The shopping parade at Bourne End kept me well supplied with provisions, and I took a bit of time to peruse some other shops of interest. Just a short distance behind Bourne End sits the similarly-sized village of Flackwell Heath. This large village was made up of four original villages. The furniture industry once thrived here, as it did in nearby High Wycombe. The M40 motorway roars through Fennel Woods just to the north of the village. This wood made the news in 2006 when suspicious items were found relating to the High Wycombe transatlantic aircraft terrorist bomb plot. Notable residents of Flackwell Heath include the British paralympian Matt Sealy and the MP for Oxford West and Abingdon, Nicola Blackwood.

The villages of Wooburn and Wooburn Green lie just a short distance to the east of Flackwell Heath. The large village green at Wooburn Green is fringed by trees, cottages and the odd pub. The Chiltern Hills rising from behind the houses here make for a fantastic setting. Wooburn sits a short distance to the south near Bourne End. The name 'Wooburn' is derived from the Old English 'walled stream'. It was once a place of significant importance with its manor house being a palace of the Bishops of Lincoln.

The road from Wooburn travels under the M40 and into Loudwater, a 'hamlet' which now merges into the urban sprawl of High Wycombe. The M40 sweeps over Loudwater via an eye-catching elevated section. It is a popular spot for retail and industry with Loudwater being home to the world's largest envelope supplier, Madison Commercial. The name 'Loudwater' literally means 'noisy water' and it refers to the River Wye nearby. With the proximity of the elevated and inescapable M40 motorway, this area might as well be called 'Loudtraffic'!

To the east of High Wycombe there is a remarkable stretch of affluence marching towards London. This area is within the London commuter belt, and the house prices are vertiginous, to say the least. The pretty village of Penn sits high up in the Chilterns and was named as Britain's 6th richest village by *The Daily Telegraph* in 2011. Penn is the burial place of the British spy Donald Maclean and was once home to the actor and singer Stanley Holloway. The village is frequently used for filming. Further to the east lies the hamlet of Knotty Green; a famous one-time resident being Val Doonican.

The leafy affluence of Penn and Knotty Green soon give way to the sophisticated affluence of North Beaconsfield. The average house price here is very high. Beaconsfield was proclaimed the most expensive town in Britain by *The Daily Telegraph* in 2008, and was the first coach stopping place on the road between London and Oxford. Former Prime Minister Tony Blair famously contested the seat here in the 1982 by-election, but the good people of Beaconsfield weren't having any of that! Beaconsfield was the birthplace of popular author, Terry Pratchett. Other notable residents past and present include actor James Cordon; the musician Barry Gibb; the politician Airey Neave, and the well-known *Dragon's Den* businessman Peter Jones. The author G.K. Chesterton and the poet Edmund Waller are buried in Beaconsfield. The town is home to Bekonscot model village, the first model village in the world.

The remarkable affluence of this area is further reinforced by the nearby villages of Chalfont St Giles and Chalfont St Peter, and the town of Gerrards Cross. The name 'Chalfont' means 'chalk spring', and it has entered cockney rhyming slang legend due to the fact that Giles rhymes with piles, hence someone complaining about their 'Chalfonts' is usually referring to their hemorrhoids! The poet John Milton retired to Chalfont St Giles during the Great Plague of London in 1665, and completed his poem *Paradise Lost* here. Like Beaconsfield, the Chalfonts are popular for filming, not only due to their pleasant appeal but also due to their close proximity to the film studios at Pinewood.

Chalfont St Peter is the largest of the Chalfont villages;

in fact, it is one of the largest villages in the UK. Of course, the title of the largest village in Britain is claimed by Kidlington, which I passed close to earlier on in my travels. Assessing which village is the largest in Britain is actually quite difficult as there is no standard definition of what a village and its boundaries actually are. The population of Chalfont St Peter rocketed with the arrival of the railway at nearby Gerrards Cross. In 1901, there were around 1700 inhabitants; today there are around 13,000.

The Daily Telegraph put Chalfont St Peter as 4th in its list of Britain's richest villages in 2011. Reasons for the extreme house prices here were given as its accessibility to London and Heathrow, and that it allows people to get a bit of 'real England' without having to move way out into the countryside. The Chalfonts and Gerrards Cross are apparently popular with people moving out from Notting Hill and the 'international crowd'. Notable past or present residents of the Chalfonts include Noel Gallagher, John Laurie, and Mike Oldfield. The hell-raising rocker Ozzy Osbourne owns a home in Jordans, a village close by.

The pleasantness of Gerrards Cross is only slightly dampened by the fact that this town has one of Britain's largest landfill sites situated next door to it. The gas produced here is used to generate over ten megawatts of electricity which is supplied to the local power grid. Gerrards Cross came 2nd in *The Daily Telegraph*'s list of Britain's richest towns in 2008 and it is frequently referred to as 'Britain's Hollywood' due to its celebrity residents. However, in recent years the town has lost out to Beaconsfield in the desirability stakes as changes to the catchment areas for local schools have been made.

Tesco started construction of a supermarket in Gerrards

Cross in 2005, but got more than they bargained for when a rail tunnel being built below the construction site partially collapsed. Fortunately, nobody was injured, but the supermarket giant had to shell out more than £8 million in compensation. Construction of the tunnel began again in January 2009. Gerrards Cross can also boast yet another construction-related 'claim to fame'. Many of the houses built in the town in the 1950s had defective tiles which led to a change in the law that stated that 'A person who contracts to do work and supply materials warrants that the materials will be fit for purpose, even if the purchaser specifies the materials to be used.'

I bid farewell to Bourne End and crossed over to the other side of the river along the railway ridge and travelled the short distance to Cookham. Cookham actually comprises three villages. There is Cookham Village, situated on the banks of the Thames; Cookham Rise, a village that grew up alongside the village's railway station, and Cookham Dean, a rural village mostly sitting on top of the river valley side, parts of which were visible from the Thames Path a couple of miles or so back on my journey.

The painter Sir Stanley Spencer was born in Cookham on 30th June 1891. He remains the village's most famous son, and there is a gallery in the village dedicated to his life and works. The Stanley Spencer Gallery was first opened in 1962, just three years after the artist's death. It was opened by the friends of the artist, and it is still run exclusively by volunteers.

Many of Spencer's works were based on village life in Cookham, and he often used the village as a backdrop to his paintings of biblical scenes such as The Crucifixion and The Resurrection. Stanley Spencer referred to Cookham as his 'village in Heaven' and walking down the winding streets of this place, I could see what he meant. Naturally, Cookham has attracted many notable people to settle there over the years. In addition to Kenneth Grahame and Sir Stanley Spencer, past and present residents include wireless radio pioneer Guglielmo Marconi; Simon Alleyn, the 16th-century Vicar of Bray; the singer Chris Rea; Queen bassist John Deacon; TV presenters Ulrika Jonsson, Jim Rosenthal, and Timmy Mallett; the comedians Chris Barrie and Tim Brooke-Taylor, and the businessman Gerald Ratner. The John Lewis Partnership and The Chartered Institute of Marketing both have establishments in Cookham.

Walking away from Cookham and towards Maidenhead, the river enters Cookham Reach, a stretch of the Thames that has been described as the most stunning on the entire river. The steep beech tree-clad bank here allows the magnificent Cliveden House to perch high above the river in a commanding position. Jerome K Jerome described Cliveden Reach as 'perhaps the sweetest stretch of all the river' and Stanley Spencer enthused 'You can't walk by the river at Cliveden Reach and not believe in God.' Cliveden House was built in 1666 for George Villiers, later the second Duke of Buckingham. The house has a marvellous history of bizarre occurrences and scandal. George Villiers is reported to have killed a love rival in a dual and then made love with his conquest in his dead love rival's blood.

The house was later leased to Frederick, Prince of Wales, who owned Park Place, near Henley. It was during a party thrown at Cliveden House in 1941 that 'Rule Britannia' was performed for the very first time. It was also at Cliveden some time later that the Prince became the first person to be killed by a cricket ball. The house went through a period where it burned down twice before being rebuilt in its present Italianate style by Charles Barry, the same architect who designed the Houses of Parliament.

In 1893, Cliveden passed into the possession of the hugely wealthy Astor family. In 1919, Nancy Astor became the first woman to become a member of Parliament. It was during the Astor's tenure of Cliveden that the Profumo Affair occurred. This was one of the most scandalous debacles to have ever hit British politics. I walked past Spring Cottage on the other side of the river. In the early 1960s, this cottage was hired out by Lord Astor to the society osteopath Dr Stephen Ward, who used it as a party pad for his rich and famous friends. One particular couple who met here was a young attractive 19-year-old girl called Christine Keeler and John Profumo, the Secretary of State for War.

Keeler was also sleeping with a naval attaché, Yevgeny Ivanov, at the Soviet Embassy, so, once made public, it is pretty obvious why Profumo was given the boot. The scandal was so poisonous that it ultimately led to the downfall of Harold Macmillan's government. Spring Cottage is available as a holiday let today, and due to its scandalous past, it is no doubt a desirable place to stay. Today, Cliveden is in the hands of the National Trust, and it is leased out to a five-star luxury hotel brand. Trust members can wander through the grounds and take in the stunning views over the River Thames and the Thames Valley. A walk through the woods and down the steep bank to Spring Cottage is also well advised. Cliveden House is perfectly aligned with the Thames, and the view of it from the Thames Path here is breathtaking.

Cliveden Reach is where the Windsor, Maidenhead, and

Eton Flood Alleviation Scheme begins. A channel cut into the side of the river here can divert huge quantities of water into the Jubilee River, a seven-mile long manmade river which is the largest to have ever been constructed in Britain. It was completed in 2002 at a cost of £110 million and was put into action in January 2003 to alleviate a major flood.

Cliveden Reach terminates at Boulter's Lock, an iconic Thames lock that was made famous by Edward Gregory's lively painting *Boulter's Lock – Sunday Afternoon 1895*. This lock was hugely popular among Victorian and Edwardian families who would pack the banks to see society figures such as the Prince of Wales and Oscar Wilde glide past. I'm sure it must have made for quite a beguiling scene with the daring girls and their exposed ankles and young men with their monocles! It's quite amazing to think that there was a time when a young lady's exposed ankles would raise eyebrows. Today, nobody seems to raise an eyebrow at the scores of young girls who go out for an evening wearing little more than a couple of strands of thread!

CHAPTER 12

The Vicar of Bray

The river through Maidenhead splits past several islands. A stone's throw over on the right hand bank is the village of Taplow. Nearby Taplow Court is the site of an early Iron Age hill fort. Taplow Court was once home to William Grenfell, 1st Baron Desborough. The village was also home to the inventor Joseph Hinks who helped modernise lamps in the 19th century. Hinks patented the Duplex burner and extinguisher lever in 1865. His innovation revolutionised oil lamps and was exported all over the world. Taplow is also home to SGI-UK, a Buddhist retreat.

Sitting a short distance behind Taplow is the large village of Burnham. This was once a very important place due to the fact that the London to Bath road once ran through it; however, this all changed with the construction of Maidenhead Bridge which diverted the road to the south. Burnham High Street is a bustling centre with plenty of shops and fine old pubs. Notable people associated with Burnham include the writer Armando Iannucci; comedian, Tracy Ullman; the golfer Charles Whitcombe, and the billionaire businessman Mike Ashley.

Little is known about Mike Ashley other than the fact he owns Newcastle United and his wealth has recently been estimated to be in the region of £1.7 billion. He grew up in Burnham and attended Burnham Grammar School. He opened his first sports shop in Maidenhead in the 1980s and quickly expanded, opening dozens more. Much of his wealth has been accumulated through the acquisition of sports brands including Donnay, Dunlop, Slazenger, Kangol, and Lonsdale.

A wonderful interruption to my journey was made by the whistle of a large steamboat travelling past me on the Thames. Some of the billowing steam wafted across which had the most magnificent heady smell. I passed over Maidenhead Bridge. Built in 1770 from Portland Stone, this bridge reminds me a bit of Henley Bridge. Looking downstream from the top of the bridge, I took in the fantastic view of Isambard Kingdom Brunel's Sounding Arch railway bridge. This bridge carries the Great Western Railway over the Thames and was the subject of J.M.W. Turner's famous painting *Rain, Speed and Steam* that now hangs in The National Gallery. The most remarkable thing about this bridge is that it had the widest and flattest brick arches in the world on completion in 1838. It is quite incredible how the bricks in the two middle sections remain in place. It really has to be seen to be believed.

Looking upstream, I surveyed the dilapidated affair that was the Skindles Hotel. Once a racy nightspot, back in the days when Maidenhead was a mecca for the 'in-crowd', the hotel was demolished in 2015, and the site is awaiting redevelopment. Past guests of Skindles have included Winston Churchill and bon viveur, Princess Margaret. The site has been earmarked for a development of several hundred houses and flats. In the 1960s and 1970s, Skindles was a well-known music venue attracting the likes of bands such as The Beatles, The Rolling Stones, and The Strawbs. Maidenhead's reputation was so racy that in the late 19th century the phrase 'Are you married or do you live in Maidenhead?' was commonly used!

Since the demise of Skindles, famous rockers have continued to visit Maidenhead, but many have been heading towards Oldfield, a Thames-side mansion owned by Colin Johnson, former manager of Status Quo, Rod Stewart, and The Stranglers. Johnson and his wife converted their £3.5 million home into a boutique hotel that has put up the odd rock star including Jimmy Page and Chris Rea as well as lucky guests with bookings at Heston Blumenthal's Fat Duck or Michel Roux's Waterside Inn at nearby Bray.

Today, Maidenhead may well have lost much of the glamour that garnered its reputation as the jewel of the Thames during Edwardian times. However, it remains an affluent town with many redeeming characteristics, though few may be found in its narrow pedestrianised town centre. Additional dreariness might be added by the fact that, since 1901, Maidenhead has maintained the record as having the highest 60-minute rainfall of anywhere in the UK (92mm). Situated well within the M4 corridor, Maidenhead is home to many hi-tech firms. The town centre has been earmarked for a major new renovation plan. Research by the New Economic Foundation rated Maidenhead as an example of a clone town with a proliferation of chain shops.

One of the most notable additions to Britain's high streets in recent years has been the rise of the coffee shop. Maidenhead is by no means an exception to this phenomenon. Chains such as Costa Coffee, Starbucks, and Caffè Nero have sprung up in their thousands. Costa Coffee alone has over 1700 shops in Britain. These coffee shop chains have found their way into many of Britain's village high streets. Like pubs, independent coffee shops and tea rooms have been forced out of business throughout the nation.

One town that has put up a remarkable fight is Totnes in Devon. In 2012, 5700 people signed a petition and protested against the opening of a Costa Coffee in the picturesque town. The town's residents reasoned that Totnes has a long and proud history of independent retailers and that it has one of the lowest percentages of branded stores of any town of its size in the UK. To many people's surprise, Costa took note of the local population's views and backed down.

Famous one-time residents of Maidenhead have included the actress Diana Dors, the broadcaster Richard Dimbleby, and the author Hugh Lofting. The novelist Nick Hornby, *Dragon's Den* star Peter Jones, and children's presenter Toby Anstis were all educated at Maidenhead Grammar School. The Spice Girls shared a house in the town shortly before their rise to global domination. Perhaps Maidenhead's most eccentric current resident has to be the motor specialist Ed China. Not content with just making eccentric vehicles such as motorised double beds, sheds, and office desks, China also holds the Guinness World Record for the 'fastest furniture' after he constructed an armchair car which he then thrashed along a racing track at a scary 92 miles per hour! In 1992, China set up his company, Cummfy Banana Limited, which designs and manufactures unique vehicles for corporate and special occasions, and for promotional purposes. So if you see a piece of household furniture come flying past you next time you are driving along this region's roads, you have probably just witnessed one of Ed's wacky creations. Either that or it might be time for a trip to the psychiatrist!

There was a time when Maidenhead was famous for its

highwaymen. Maidenhead Thicket and Hounslow Heath became the most dangerous places along the Bath Road. The Thicket, an area of woodland to the west of the town, became so infested with highwaymen that it could make the violence in some of the the inner cities of today's Britain pale in comparison. In 1742, a Reading stagecoach travelling between Henley and Oxford was robbed by two highwaymen. In 1748, John Williams was sentenced to death at Abingdon for highway robbery on Maidenhead Thicket.

In 1781, George and Joseph Weston robbed the Royal Mail at the Thicket. After removing a post boy at gunpoint, the brothers rode the cart to a field near Lot's Farm close to Twyford. They had got away with £10,000 of money, roughly equivalent to £3 million today. It would be the Maidenhead mail robbery that made the brothers famous. They had carried out robberies throughout England, and their careers were finally ended when they were hanged at Newgate Prison in 1782. The brothers had made their final attempt to escape the prison two days earlier. In 1793, Lord Elgin was attacked by footpads in the Thicket but managed to escape. In 1740, John Clark was sentenced to death for robbing the Duke of Marlborough's coach between Reading and Maidenhead and for carrying out a further 23 highway robberies.

The grounds of Hall Place at nearby Burchett's Green are said to be haunted by the ghost of Claude Duval, one of the most famous highwaymen in Britain. Local legend has it that Dick Turpin, the most famous highwayman of them all once carried out robberies along this stretch of the Bath Road but, as Turpin operated mainly in his native county of Essex, these stories may well be unfounded.

Highway robbery began to die out in the late 18th and

early 19th centuries as modern banking systems with less need for money in transit and early police forces such as the Bow Street Runners were established. In recent years, Maidenhead Thicket has become known as a meet-up place for gay men and for 'dogging'. It looks like this thicket is set to remain a place of surprises and curious goings on for some time yet!

Moving away from the road and rail bridges at Maidenhead and towards the famous village of Bray, I passed a wonderful collection of waterside mansions and villas with perfectly manicured lawns that make up Maidenhead's 'Millionaire's Row'. One passer-by caught me gazing in awe at some of the houses and presented me with an elaborate story about how many of these homes are owned by Arabs who 'keep them well-lit under spotlight at night because their owners are afraid of the dark!' I've never heard that Arabs are any more afraid of the dark than anyone else and took the vaguely racist comment with a pinch of salt!

Situated on a bend in the river, Bray's most famous past resident is undoubtedly Simon Alleyn, the infamous Vicar of Bray. Alleyn managed to hold onto his job by converting repeatedly between Catholicism and Protestantism during the reigns of Henry VIII and his three children. His famous words decree, 'And this is law, I will maintain, unto my dying day, Sir. That whatsoever King shall reign, I will be the Vicar of Bray, Sir!' Bray's most famous living resident must surely be the gastronomic alchemist Heston Blumenthal. The chef has his Michelin 3-star restaurant The Fat Duck in the village along with two other restaurants: The Hind's Head and The Crown Inn. The village has been named Britain's 'Gastronomic Capital' as it is also home to Michel Roux's

Waterside Inn, another Michelin 3-star restaurant.

Not all the locals are happy, however, with their village's status as Britain's 'gastronomic capital'. In fact, several neighbours of The Fat Duck have complained to the local council, citing the dishevelled appearance of the rear preparation area of the restaurant, and the rowdy nature of its many employees. Blumenthal has applied for planning permission to extend his kitchen, and many of the problems cited are typical of any enterprise that becomes remarkably successful. Famous Bray residents have included Michael Parkinson; the disgraced Rolf Harris, and Gerald Ratner.

The path soon led me under the roaring M4 motorway and past the village of Dorney. My travels took me past the Grade I listed mansion, Dorney Court, the site of the first pineapple to ever be grown in Britain. The local public house is named The Pineapple in tribute. A cornfield near the village is where a lone gunman, James Hanratty, abducted Valerie Storie and Michael Gregsten in 1961. He forced them to drive to a lay-by on the A6 in Bedfordshire before he shot and killed Gregsten and raped Storie before shooting her five times. She survived but was left paralysed. Hanratty was one of the last people to be executed in Britain before capital punishment was effectively abolished.

I passed Monkey Island with its luxury hotel. This is an intriguing place. Once owned by the monks of Merton Abbey near Bray (hence, Monk-ey Island), the island was purchased by the keen angler the 3rd Duke of Marlborough in 1738. In the mid-1800s, a luxury hotel was established, and guests have included Edward VII and Queen Alexandra, Dames Clara Butt and Nellie Melba (of Melba toast and Peach Melba fame). Sir Edward Elgar, George Bernard Shaw, Walter Sickert and Siegfried Sassoon all stayed in a creative retreat called The Hut which overlooks Monkey Island. The Hut was then purchased by the Moss family whose son, Stirling, would go on to become a legendary racing driver.

Bray Studios cast an imposing presence along the opposite bank of the river, sitting alongside Down Place. Hammer Film Productions bought the derelict country pile Down Place in 1951 and built a studio in the grounds of the house. Films such as *The Curse of Frankenstein* and *Horror of Dracula* were filmed here. Bray Studios continues to be used as a film studio despite funding difficulties in more recent years. There has been rumour that the current owner of the studio is trying to get permission to redevelop the site into residential housing.

Not far from here lies the affluent village of Holyport. This village is somewhat overshadowed by its showy neighbour, Bray. It does, however, have a few claims to fame. I am told by a local that the veteran BBC TV presenter Frank Bough lives in the village and it is also home to one of the world's few real tennis courts. The rules of real tennis are similar to lawn tennis, though it is more complex and the game still uses a cork-based ball. Holyport is now perhaps a little more famous as Eton College sponsors a free school that is built in the village. The secondary school has around 500 pupils and is based upon many of the principles of Eton College itself. A fifth of places are reserved for pupils from poor homes. Eton College designs the curriculum and offers a host of other services, including the use of its extensive sports facilities. The school opened in September 2014.

This particular stretch of the Thames snakes past the Dorney Rowing Lake, an eight-lane, 2.2 kilometre long behemoth completed in 2016 and used as a 2012 London

Olympics venue. The river weaves its way past Windsor Racecourse and dives under the Windsor and Eton Relief Road. Just before the bridge, there is a sharp bend in the river, which is quickly preceded by White Lilies Island. The Mill House here has been home to the guitarist Jimmy Page, actor Sir Michael Caine, and the singer Natalie Imbruglia. I'm not sure who the present lucky residents are. In 1980, the legendary Led Zeppelin drummer John Bonham died at the house after a drinking binge, aged 32.

Up ahead of me, I could see the awesome hulk of Windsor Castle sat in its commanding position overlooking the Thames. This is the largest inhabited castle in the world, and it is said to be the Queen's favourite royal residence. I quickly got lost in all the excitement exuded by the throngs of American and Japanese tourists. I've been to Windsor a few times before, and I remember well that night in November 1992 when I saw the castle on fire on the news. The first castle at Windsor was built by William the Conqueror in 1070 to protect the western approaches to London. The castle was rebuilt in stone by Henry II in 1170, and the poet Geoffrey Chaucer was the 'Clerk of Works' at Windsor Castle in 1391.

After a period of decline following the Reformation, life was brought back to Windsor once again when George III moved there. The royal presence rejuvenated the town, and it received a particular boost with Queen Victoria's residence in the castle from 1840. The railway came to town shortly afterwards. Windsor is unusual in that it has two railway stations. Both stations were constructed around the same time as two competing train companies wanted the accolade of carrying Queen Victoria to Windsor. I walked over Windsor Bridge, built in 1822, which led me into Eton.

Right on time, my old buddy Toby walked up to me at the Gourmet Burger Bar. He is one of the few people that I know who never turns up late. He's not a procrastinator like me, though he probably wouldn't undertake such a crazy feat as walking the length of the River Thames. 'So how's the walk down the river going?' Toby launched at me. 'Yeah, not bad', I hastily replied with one eye on the kitchen, letting him know that getting fed was my number one priority. I was feeling quite worn down, and I still had a lot of ground to cover before finding somewhere to stay for the night.

Eton High Street is a pleasant affair with lots of upmarket boutiques and antique shops. It is also home to the oldest Victorian pillar box still in use in the world. The one thing that Eton is most famous for is, of course, Eton College, the most famous public school in the world. Founded in 1440 by Henry VI for poor boys, Eton is now a much bigger school, being home to over 1300 pupils as opposed to just around 300 in the late 18th century. The Duke of Wellington is often misquoted as saying that 'The Battle of Waterloo was won on the playing-fields of Eton' when what he really did say, according to the historian Sir Edward Creasey, was 'There grows the stuff that won Waterloo', a comment he made as he passed an Eton cricket match. It has been said of Eton that, 'no other school can claim to have sent forth such a cohort of distinguished figures to make their mark on the world.'

Indeed, the list of distinguished former pupils is a long one. David Cameron is the 19th British Prime Minister to have attended Eton. Other notable Old Etonians include George Orwell, Percy Bysshe Shelley, Ian Fleming, John Maynard Keynes, Sir Ranulph Fiennes, Damian Lewis, Hugh Laurie, and Dominic West. West has commented unenthusiastically about his Old Etonian status, saying, 'It is a stigma that is slightly above 'paedophile' in the media gallery of infamy.' No doubt a major factor in the creating of this 'stigma' is the elitism with which Eton has become synonymous. No school in Britain has come to symbolise the split in social inequality as much as Eton. People like former Prime Minister David Cameron are only too aware of how an education at Eton can wield potential damage to their careers and they tread carefully around the issue.

Social inequality has become a persistent issue in Britain, and one that was barely addressed by the 13-year-long 1997-2010 Labour government. A study by Professor John Mills of the London School of Economics, published in January 2011, showed an increasingly divided Britain where the richest ten per cent of the population are more than 100 times richer than the poorest ten per cent of society. All across Britain, emerald enclaves of wealth lay just a stones-throw from impoverished areas. Inequality pervades into almost every area of people's lives. A recent study into health inequality in Britain has shown that despite spending increases on the NHS, the poorest not only die sooner but become ill younger, to the extent that Britain's wealthier residents are likely to have 17 years more of disability-free life than the poorer ones.

A report on social mobility by former cabinet minister Alan Milburn found that wealth, private education, and access to university remains key to well-paid professionals. The report found that while only seven per cent of the population attended independent schools, 75 per cent of judges, 70 per cent of finance directors, 45 per cent of senior civil servants and 32 per cent of MPs were privately educated. In an amusing episode in 2008, David Cameron named 'The Eton Rifles', a song by The Jam, as one of his favourites. The song recounts the difficulties faced by the unemployed and lower paid working classes in protesting against a system loaded against them. Paul Weller from The Jam issued the scathing rejection 'Which part of it didn't he get? It wasn't intended as a jolly drinking song for the cadet corps.' I hummed the song as I made my way back past the red brick and yellow stone college buildings.

Back on the Windsor side of the river, I treated myself to a sumptuous dinner at Browns. 'I might as well eat like a king in Windsor!' I thought as I merrily munched my way through an oversized burger and chips. After my meal I set off on foot for my next Windsor attraction. Measuring nearly three miles in length, the Long Walk sits in the 20 square kilometres of Windsor Great Park. It runs right from the castle gates and up to The Copper Horse, a statue of King George III atop Snow Hill. The walk is well worth it as the views from The Copper Horse are magical.

Amongst the happy tourists at the foot of the monument, I opened my rucksack and pulled out my compact binoculars. The first thing I scanned over was the castle itself, and it wasn't long before I spotted a giant pair of binoculars staring straight back at me from atop the castle! Fortunately, there was nobody behind them, but it served as a timely reminder about how seriously security around the royals and their residences is taken. Just over the crowns of the trees to my right, I caught tantalising glimpses of London through the haze. Raising the binoculars to my eyes once again, I could see The Houses of Parliament, The London Eye, and Millbank Tower. Soon, I would be walking past these as I neared the end of my journey.

Windsor has many other notable attributes. The town

was home to William Shakespeare during his writing of *The Merry Wives of Windsor*. The comedians Freddie Starr and Billy Connolly, the actress Anna Friel and actor Kris Marshall once lived in the town. The adventurer Ranulph Fiennes and Dhani Harrison, son of ex-Beatle George Harrison, were both born in Windsor. Sir Sydney Camp, who invented the Hawker Hurricane and other WWII fighter aircraft, was also a onetime Windsor resident.

Other eccentric though lesser known characters associated with Windsor include the stand-up comic and UK Uncut activist, Jonnie Marbles, famous for trying to attack Rupert Murdoch with a custard pie during a Parliamentary Committee in 2011. Windsor is also reputedly home to an elaborate busker called Mark Handley who is known for his 'nimble dancing feet'!

If Windsor and Eton are known for their pomp and opulence, then what lied a short distance to the north of me might as well be regarded as the polar opposite: Slough is one of the larger towns that lie close to the Thames, and it is quite a famous place, if only for perhaps, the wrong reasons. To many people, Slough may well be summed up by just a few things: a giant industrial estate - the place where Wernham Hogg, the fictional office from the hit TV show *The Office* starring Ricky Gervais was set - and a place unto which the poet Sir John Betjeman implored friendly German Bombs to fall. 'Come, friendly bombs, and fall on Slough! It isn't fit for humans now' are the opening lines of his famous poem 'Slough', first published in 1937. Despite how it sounds, the poem isn't specifically about Slough itself but has more to do with the spread of industrialisation throughout Britain's towns and cities in general. Betjeman's daughter, Candida Lycett-Green has said her father regretted writing it.

Slough Trading Estate occupies former agricultural land that was used to store and repair a very large number of vehicles coming back from the battlefields of World War I. The government sold the site in 1920 to Slough Trading Co. Ltd. In 1925, the company was allowed to establish an industrial estate and the rest, as they say, is history. In 1906, James Horlick opened a huge factory next to Slough Railway Station to produce his malted milk product. This impressive red-brick structure along with its giant brick chimney greets all rail visitors to Slough and remains testament to the industrial might of the town.

The UK headquarters of Mars, Inc. is based in Slough. The Mars Bar was developed at this factory over 70 years ago. In recent years, Mars have moved much of their production to the Czech Republic. Citroen manufactured cars here until 1966. Another manufacturing giant with their production plant in the estate is Dulux.

In more recent years, there has been a major shift away from manufacturing towards an information-based commerce. Tech companies to have UK or European headquarters in Slough include Research in Motion, Compusys, and O2. Other UK company headquarters include Sara Lee and Furniture Village. Gerry Anderson produced many films on Slough Trading Estate including *Thunderbirds*. Sadly, Anderson passed away in December 2012.

Crossbow House, the building on Slough Trading Estate that was the supposed HQ of Wernham Hogg in *The Office*, was demolished in 2013 to much sadness from people including Ricky Gervais. The building featured in the opening sequences of the show.

Whilst many people may turn their nose up at having a

trading estate in the middle of their town, there are many for whom it is very attractive for employment. I personally love Slough and love the estate. For me, too many towns have become focused on the dreary 'over-domestication' of people, the only relief from endless residential developments being huge retail parks. We seem to have forgotten the functional purposes of most urban areas in the first place: they are places of making and places of work. I would much rather see towns like Slough that have functioning industries alive and breathing within them, as opposed to ones where every vestige of commerce and industry has been eradicated and filled in with residential buildings sitting cheek by jowl.

One thing that is certainly evident to anyone venturing into Slough is that it has a vibrant multicultural population. With the establishment of the trading estate, Slough began attracting vast numbers of people. These people travelled to Slough from all over the UK and particularly from Wales. Large housing estates were developed after WWII to house people who had migrated from war-damaged London. In the post-war years, significant numbers of immigrants from Commonwealth countries such as India, Pakistan, Antigua, and Barbuda have settled in Slough. In recent years, Slough has received an influx of Polish workers, although immigration from Poland is not such a recent phenomenon in Slough as many people might think it is. The town and surroundings had a number of Polish refugee camps in the early 1950s, and few of these people relished returning to a Poland that was now in the Soviet Bloc.

When you look at it, it is clear that Slough has many positives. Having the trading estate has meant that the town has been better protected against economic slow-downs than many others across the UK. Slough has plentiful quantities of cheap housing that, coupled to excellent transport links, have made it an attractive town for young professionals and families. Windsor, the Thames, the Chilterns, and London are all in close proximity. In short, there is plenty to do with families and friends. Slough is also one of the sunniest inland areas of the UK, and rainfall is low compared to the rest of the UK. In recent years, Slough has become quite a 'hip' place to be associated with.

Travelling out just to the north of Slough, one will stumble upon an area of affluence which includes the villages of Farnham Royal, Farnham Common, and Stoke Poges. Fuzzy-Felt was invented by Lois Allen in her cottage in Farnham Common during WWII. The painter Sir Edwin Landseer was a frequent visitor to Stoke Poges Manor House, and his most famous painting *Monarch of the Glen* is rumoured to have been created there, using the deer in the park as models. The poet Thomas Gray's *Elegy Written in a Country Churchyard* is believed to have been written in the churchyard of the St Giles church at Stoke Poges; indeed Gray is buried there. Stoke Park Club is a famous upmarket hotel and golf course. The hotel and its grounds have appeared in many films including *Goldfinger, Bridget Jones' Diary, Wimbledon* and *Layer Cake*. Many of the movie stars filming at nearby Pinewood Studios stay at Stoke Park Club.

Pinewood is Britain's answer to Hollywood, and it was named as such because of the number of huge pine trees growing there. Pinewood Studios was built on the estate of Heatherden Hall, a large Victorian house. The estate was transformed in 1935 by the flour magnate J. Arthur Rank and Charles Boot. The studio owners devised a system whereby several films could be filmed simultaneously, and Pinewood soon achieved the highest output of any studio in the world.

The 1950s saw the birth of the hugely successful *Carry On* films. The 1960s saw the launch of Pinewood's most famous enterprise, the *James Bond* franchise. The *Superman* franchise almost certainly saved the film studios from financial ruin in the 1970s. Unfavourable UK tax laws in the 1990s ushered in some of Pinewood's and the British film industry's darkest days. Pinewood has extensive water filming facilities and is home to the world's most famous stage: the 007 Stage.

Datchet Bridge is the only bridge to have been built across the Thames and completely removed. What a sight it must have been too! Built one half in timber and the other half in iron, this bizarre bridge was the product of a dispute between Berkshire and Buckinghamshire, who could not agree on who should pay for it. Having a bridge at Datchet might have seemed more pertinent than ever, as the village was once home to the Honourable Evelyn Ellis (1843-1913), the first person in Britain to own a motor car. Ellis went on to found the RAC and her Panhard-Levassor car is on exhibition at the Science Museum in South Kensington. Another motoring pioneer to be associated with Datchet is Lord Montagu who once owned a car manufacturing workshop here.

Once known as 'Black Datchet' because of the large number of shady characters who lived here, Datchet is, or has, been home to notable people such as Sir Donald Pleasance, Daniella Westbrook, Barry Davies, Billy Cotton, and Billie Whitelaw. Joan Collins now owns the house where her father used to live, though it is not one of her main residences.

The river winds its way past Man Friday's Island, so called because when looked at on a map, the island looks like

Man Friday's footprint. The forensic scientist Dr Julius Grant once lived on this island. Grant proved in 1984 that the infamous Hitler Diaries were an elaborate forgery. The forgery had been given authenticity by Hugh Trevor-Roper, who had managed to get them published in *The Sunday Times*.

The link with forgery and this part of the Thames only became stronger as I strolled past Old Windsor. For this was the home of Paul Bint, Britain's most notorious conman. Bint, or 'King Con' as he is frequently referred to by the British press, has over 150 convictions for deception and is known for posing as a plastic surgeon, a barrister, an aristocrat, a property magnate, a police officer, an army officer, a doctor (who shockingly conned his way into hospitals and managed to perform minor procedures and write prescriptions for people), a ballet dancer, and even the Earl of Arundel. He was known to be residing in Manor Lodge bail hostel in the village. Bint claims to have had an Eton education and to be a pal of Elton John. In 2011, Bint said that he had swindled £2 million from his victims, and had slept with 2500 women.

Britain has seen many elaborate con artists at work over the years including builder Graham Tumbler, who convinced Dover council in 2008 that he was Francis Rossi from Status Quo in order to get VIP treatment for a year. In 2009, Roger Day from Leicestershire was exposed as a bogus SAS hero who had turned up to a Remembrance Day parade clad in a vast array of medals. Day fled from the proceedings when a real SAS veteran grilled him about his 'impossible' 21 medals.

In one of the most audacious cases of deception, solicitor Conn Farrell, retired contracts manager Patrick Dolan, and lorry driver Anthony Lee, duped two businessmen into handing over a one-million pound advance after the fraudsters had tricked them into thinking that they had bought the Ritz Hotel in London for £250 million, a price well below the estimated market value of £450-600 million. Anthony Lee was sentenced to five years in jail for being at the heart of the scam.

Archaelogical evidence suggests royal connections have been established in Old Windsor since the 9th century at least, and this large village was the site of an important palace of the Saxon kings. The palace was superseded by the Norman castle at 'New Windsor'. Windsor Great Park is largely within the bounds of Old Windsor, and rock superstar Sir Elton John and golfing star Nick Faldo live in close proximity to some of the royal residences.

Soon I was walking past a pair of Lutyens' gatehouses and onto the fine hallowed meadows of Runnymede. Having raised exorbitant taxes and subjected his people to abject misrule, King John of England was forced to stamp his royal seal on the Magna Carta, a document underpinning basic human rights, on the 15th day of June in the year 1215. To this day, Runnymede is known as the place where human rights were 'born', and it remains the first recorded attempt to establish basic human rights. Instrumental in their efforts to force the King to agree was the brilliant Stephen Langton, Archbishop of Canterbury.

Today, the historic Magna Carta agreement is marked by the small but elegant memorial on the slopes of Coopers Hill. This memorial was presented to Britain by the American Bar Association in 1957. Although the exact position where the Magna Carta was sealed at Runnymede is not known, it is believed to have taken place next to the ancient Ankerwyke Yew tree. The legendary Ankerwyke is thought to be up to 2000 years old, and the changes to Britain it must have witnessed during its long life are quite extraordinary. Higher up on the slopes of Cooper's Hill is the Kennedy Memorial, given to the people of America in 1965 in tribute to President John F. Kennedy. The Commonwealth Air Forces Memorial sits on the top of the hill and is dedicated to the 20,456 airmen who have no known grave.

There can be few finer places than Wraysbury to spend a night by the river, and I am fortunate enough to have family friends who live in this village. We spent the evening chatting over several glasses of wine and the sort of food that makes you feel slightly uncomfortable that your hosts have gone to such lengths to prepare just for you. The next morning started with a brief exploration of the village. There is evidence of human activity from Neolithic times in Wraysbury, and the land was used as hunting grounds when the Saxons resided at Old Windsor.

Lying to the south of here is the town of Egham and the large village of Englefield Green. Egham is home to a large Proctor & Gamble research centre and various other research and hi-tech firms. Englefield Green is an affluent village which is home to Royal Holloway College, part of The University of London. The College's world-famous Founder's Building can be seen along the A30.

A mile or so even further to the south lies the village of Virginia Water. The village name comes from the lake at nearby Windsor Great Park. The world-famous Wentworth Estate is here. The estate is favoured by many well-known celebrities and business people. Past and present residents include Bruce Forsyth, Boris Berezovsky, Diana Dors, Russ Abbot, the Sultan of Brunei, Gary Numan, Ron Dennis,

Elton John, and Cliff Richard. The estate gained notoriety in 1998 when former Chilean president General Augusto Pinochet was kept under house arrest pending an attempt to extradite him to face trial in Spain. The area's significant affluence is continued a short distance to the west into the village of Sunningdale and the small town of Ascot.

It may sound a bit melodramatic, but the next bridge that I walked under brought about a watershed moment for me. Walking under the roaring M25 motorway was a significant milestone in my journey. I truly felt that I was walking within the outer bounds of London, and the M25 does indeed contain nearly all of Greater London within its arduous grip. The nice thing about this bridge is that they have managed to keep the original stone fascia of Sir Edward Lutyens' old bridge intact.

Completed in 1986, the 117-mile M25 motorway, or London Orbital motorway as it is also known, is one of Europe's busiest roads. Traffic levels exceeded maximum designed capacity shortly after opening, and the M25 has been widened in many areas since. The excessive traffic jams, exacerbated by frequent road works have led to the M25 being labelled 'the world's largest car park'. The road inspired Chris Rea's song 'The Road to Hell'. It has not always been hated, however. The M25 was popular amongst the rave scene as it helped get the rave crowd out to parties that took place on the outskirts of London. It was this use of the M25 for raves that inspired the name of the electro band Orbital.

Staines is the location of the London Stone, installed in 1285. This stone marks the dividing point between the upper and lower Thames, and the name 'Staines' comes from the word 'Stana' which means stones. It is thought it refers to a group of nine ancient stones that were mentioned in a 12th-century charter of Chertsey Abbey. Staines was the home of the world's first linoleum factory and also the home of the Lagonda car factory. Linoleum is widely considered to be the first product name to become a generic term, but has now largely been replaced by PVC flooring. Lagonda was established in 1906 and has been owned by Aston Martin since 1947.

Staines is associated with certain people and events that many people may well believe have well, um, stained its character (so sorry!). Nearby Laleham House was the home of the Lucan Family. The disappearance of the 7th Lord Lucan after allegedly killing his children's nanny in 1974 has become one of the world's most enduring murder mysteries. Another character associated with Staines is the fictional character Ali G (of the Staines Massiv), created by comic mastermind Sacha Baron Cohen.

In December 2011, the local borough council voted to change the name of Staines to Staines-upon-Thames in an attempt to give the town more appeal. Much media coverage was created as a result of speculation that the town was carrying out the name change in an attempt to discourage association with Ali G. Things have gone remarkably well for Baron Cohen himself since his early successes with his 'rude-boy' comedy character. On a more serious note, Staines was the site of England's worst air disaster when British European Airways Flight 548 crashed in 1972, killing all 118 people on board.

CHAPTER 13

Metropolis

Chertsey is one of Britain's oldest towns and the site of St Erkenwald's Great Benedictine Abbey. The Abbey's fate was sealed like so many others by Henry VIII. Once famous for metal working and a prosperous bell foundry, Chertsey is today a London commuter belt town. Nearby, people whizz around the fun attractions at Thorpe Park. Near to Shepperton Lock, the river is joined by the River Wey.

I decided to indulge myself in a spot of luxury by booking into the rather plush Warren Lodge Hotel in Shepperton. After various nights spent sleeping in everything from a disused military bunker through to friend's floors and creepy woods, I thought I rather deserved it! The proximity of the world-famous Shepperton Studios meant that this area was once referred to as the 'Hollywood of Great Britain'. Many famous actors have stayed or dined at the hotel, including Laurence Olivier and Kirk Douglas. Whole, or parts of, films made here include Ridley Scott's *Alien*, Harry Enfiled's *Kevin and Perry Go Large* and John Huston's *Lawrence of Arabia*. Notable past and present residents of Shepperton include the film director, John Boorman; the singers Tom Jones, Ray Dorset, and Tom Rush, and the author Lynne Reid Banks. *Empire of the Sun* author JG Ballard lived in a modest house here from 1956 until his death in 2009.

I was soon passing under Walton Bridge. Completed in

1750, the first Walton Bridge has been described as the 'most beautiful wooden arch bridge in the world.' Appearing in the *Domesday Book* of 1086 as 'Waletona', Walton-on-Thames is mostly of modern construction. The town was heavily bombed by the Luftwaffe in World War II, owing to the proximity of important aircraft factories at nearby Brooklands. Past and present notable people associated with Walton-on-Thames include: the actress and singer, Dame Julie Andrews; the singer-songwriter, Nick Lowe; the actress Fay Ripley, and the aircraft designer John Carver Meadows, who first pioneered supersonic British experimental aircraft. Walton is also famous for the Walton Hop, reported to have been the first disco in Britain.

From the river at Sunbury-on-Thames, the unusual cupola of St Mary's Church can be seen. It was under a yew tree in this graveyard that Oliver Twist and Bill Sykes slept before going onto the robbery in Shepperton, in Charles Dickens' famous novel, *Oliver Twist*.

I walked past some magnificent Georgian houses, and I was soon walking beside Hampton Village, home to one of Britain's most illustrious homes: Hampton Court Palace. I walked past a houseboat called The Astoria, built in 1913 for the entrepreneur Fred Karno. Karno made his fortune from comedy music hall. It was he who discovered Charlie Chaplin and invented the now famous 'custard pie in the face gag'. Although he went bankrupt in 1926, Karno's name lives on in the term 'Karno's army' which is used to describe a chaotic group or organisation. The Astoria was acquired by the music hall star Vesta Victoria, and in 1986 it was purchased by David Gilmour of Pink Floyd. He turned the boat into a recording studio, and his 2006 album *On an island* was recorded there. Other notable people associated with

Hampton or its surrounds include the actor David Garrick and the Queen guitarist, more latterly known as saviour of Britain's badgers, Brian May.

I passed Tagg's Island, the biggest island on this stretch of the Thames. It was named after the boat builder Thomas Tagg who built a hotel on the island which attracted the rich and famous. Bushey Park came as a welcome break from this built-up stretch of the Thames. Most of the rules of modern field hockey were devised here. It is home to the world's oldest surviving hockey club: Teddington Hockey Club. Soon Hampton Court itself came into view - a red brick sprawling monolith, featuring the greatest array of chimneys I have ever seen on any single building.

Hampton Court Palace was once the largest royal residence in Britain. It actually comprises two palaces: the Tudor palace of Henry VIII and an additional one built for King William III and Queen Mary II. Henry VIII confiscated Hampton Court from Cardinal Wolsey, and it became his favourite residence. I vaguely remembered visiting here when I was around seven or eight years old. The palace is steeped in British history. In 1603-4, William Shakespeare and his company performed for James I in the great hall. Wolsey's Royal Tennis Court dating from 1526 is the greatest surviving real tennis court in England. George II was the last monarch to reside at Hampton Court, and the palace was opened to the public in 1838 by Queen Victoria.

I walked past the large inhabited island at Thames Ditton. This village appears in the *Domesday Book* under two names: 'Ditone' and 'Ditune'. It is interesting that these names have the words 'tone' and 'tune' in them, as the village of Thames Ditton is where the renowned speaker manufacturer Celestion was once located. AC Cars had a factory in the village from 1911 until 1984. Notable people associated with Thames Ditton include Dick Emery and Ronan Keating.

A short walk further on brought me to Surbiton. There are many fine examples of Art Deco architecture here. It's imposing Grade II listed Art Deco railway station is a fine example, and it resembles a power station more than a transport hub. Surbiton will always be associated with suburbia in many people's minds, as it was the supposed setting of the classic British TV series, *The Good Life*.

Kingston Bridge is a fine five-arched construction made from Portland Stone. Literally meaning 'Kings town', seven Saxon Kings were crowned at Kingston including Eadweard the Elder, Edmund I, and Ethelred the Unready. Kingston was as good a place as any to stop, rest my feet and stock up on some provisions. I sat down with a refreshing drink and watched as the Kingston crowds glided past me. Groups of capped streetwise young men shunted along, some with their earphones pumping out music demonically loud. Notable people from Kingston include the legendary water and land speed record holder, Donald Campbell, and the cinema photography pioneer, Eadweard Muybridge.

Toby managed to find the Kingston University Student Union a bit before me. A long and exhausting walk brought me up to it. He was inside, in his element amongst the beer, bands, and girls, and I can't say that I didn't have a great evening too. He told me that we would be allowed in, despite not being students, and he was right. That night, we slept in his car. We hadn't managed to get lucky with anyone, but we had drunk for Britain, seen some good live bands, and generally had a great time all round. The following morning, Toby drove me back down the hill to the riverbank. I was pleased that he had ventured out so far to visit me one last time.

Teddington Lock is an impressive sight and, at 650 feet in length, it is the longest lock system on the Thames. It was from here that the fleet of Thames-based 'Little Ships' assembled before taking part in the Dunkirk Evacuation. Buried in the graveyard at St Mary's in Teddington is Dr Stephen Hales (1677-1761) known as the father of plant physiology. Hales was also the first person to study blood pressure in humans and animals.

The association between Teddington and innovation doesn't end there. The 'bouncing bomb' used in World War II was developed here along with the first accurate atomic clock. Many of television's most popular comedy programs were made at Teddington Studios, including *The Benny Hill Show, The Office,* and Harry Hill's *TV Burp.* The actor, Sir Noel Coward and the comedian Julian Clary were born in Teddington. A magnificent couple wouldn't they have made, don't you think?! The comedian Benny Hill lived for a while in Teddington and died alone in his riverside apartment here in 1992. Interestingly, Michael Jackson once described Benny Hill as 'the funniest comedian in the world, my all-time hero.'

Eel Pie Island may have an unusual name but, according to many, this is where the swinging sixties got started. Originally attracting the likes of jazz legend George Melly and Kenny Ball in the 1950s, by the 1960s the concert venue of Eel Pie Island had become a regular gig for The Rolling Stones; John Mayall's Bluesbreakers, featuring Eric Clapton; The Who; Pink Floyd, and Genesis. In 1964, David Jones played his first gig on the island. Jones would later change his name to David Bowie. The music scene on the island was pretty much finished off when Eel Pie Island Hotel burned down in 1971. However, recent years have seen a rekindled interest in its musical past. Trevor Bayliss, the inventor of the wind-up radio, is a resident of the island. Another ingenious invention of his is electric shoes, which charge a small battery when they are walked in.

Upon reaching Twickenham, I was well within range of central London. Although today mostly associated with rugby - Twickenham is home to Rugby Football Union, and Twickenham Rugby Stadium is the world's largest rugby stadium - Twickenham was once home to industrial-scale gunpowder manufacture. Production started here in the 15th century and explosions, many of them involving fatalities, were frequent. One explosion on 11th March 1758 was so powerful it was felt way back up river at Reading.

Today, the scene is one of peace and tranquillity, and my walk was interrupted only by the occasional sightings of great houses, such as York House, Orleans House, Marble Hill House, and Ham House, where a statue of Father Thames sits at the front of the garden. Notable past and present residents of Twickenham include the tea merchant Thomas Twining, and the author Henry Fielding, who wrote *Tom Jones* whilst living in Pembroke Lodge. Pembroke Lodge was also the childhood home of the philosopher, logician, and social critic Bertrand Russell. Twickenham was also home to Gerald Holtom, who designed the now famous Campaign for Nuclear Disarmament (CND) logo.

From atop Richmond Hill, I surveyed one of the most famous views over the River Thames. The view of the river from here has been immortalised by several poets and painters, most notably J.M.W Turner's painting: *England: Richmond Hill on the Prince Regent's Birthday*. The view from

Richmond Hill is the only view in England to be protected by an act of Parliament. There are some fine houses here as one would only expect, and past and present residents of Richmond Hill include Mick Jagger and Jerry Hall; the Naturalist Sir David Attenborough; the actor John Mills, and the actress and writer, Mary Hayley Bell. The biggest residence here, by a long way, is the Royal Star and Garter Home; once a home for disabled ex-servicemen, it is now being developed into apartments.

I headed down to leafy Richmond to stock up on provisions. There is a wonderful green in the centre of town, which provided welcome respite away from the oppressive vehicular aggression. I made my way back to the river frontage which is, to say at the least, rather spectacular. Somewhat disappointingly, this fine Georgian slab of riverfront architecture was not constructed in the Georgian period, but rather it was created in this style by the architect Quinlan Terry in the 1980s. A fine job he has done too.

Richmond was first used as a royal residence by Edward I in 1299. Henry VIII was born at Richmond, and modern technology had an interesting first here when Elizabeth I had the world's first flushing loo installed at the Richmond Palace. After Charles I's reign, the Palace was left to decay and all that remains today are just a few surviving parts, such as the gatehouse and the trumpeter's house. Notable people past and present from Richmond include the film director and actor, Sir Richard Attenborough, and Leonard and Virginia Woolf who lived at Hogarth House and founded the Hogarth Press there. Many residents of Richmond, Virginia, would probably be aware that their city is so named because their founder, William Byro II, regarded the view of The James River similar to the view of The Thames from Richmond Hill.

Brentford may be in no way as salubrious as Richmond, but there is something very honest and hardworking about the place. It is so named because of the river Brent which joins the River Thames here. The town marks the start of the M4 corridor and travellers into London along this route are carried above on a long elevated section of the M4 motorway which breezes past many office blocks including the sparkling global HQ of GlaxoSmithKline.

I got some great views across into Kew Gardens. The Royal Botanical Gardens at Kew were initially laid out in 1759 for Princess Augusta, the grieving widow of Friederick, Prince of Wales (who was killed by a cricket ball upriver at Cliveden). It is now world famous as a World Heritage Site that is home to the largest collection of living plants in the world. The greenhouses at Kew are famous in their own right. The Palm House, completed in 1848, was the first large-scale building in the world to be made from wrought iron, and the Temperate House, completed in 1899, is the world's largest Victorian glasshouse.

My journey took me past The National Archives and up past Chiswick Bridge. Mortlake is home to The Stage, London's largest brewery. The distinctive church of St Mary's, Mortlake, soon came into view. Buried here is Dr John Dee (1527-1608), a controversial astrologer and advisor to Elizabeth I. He was one of the first people to use research and analysis to build a scientific understanding of the world around him. His ideas would be taken up by Isaac Newton many years later. Dee was the first person to coin the terms 'British Isles' and 'British Empire' in a work of 1576.

It was not long before Chiswick came well into view. I had heard a lot about this place over the years and was looking forward to a good ramble through the town.

Chiswick, or 'cheese farm' to give it its literal translation, started life as a fishing village. The western end of Chiswick High Road is truncated by the busy A4 London to Bath road which buzzed with near-constant activity. I dashed across the A4, making note of one of Chiswick's most famous residents, the Chiswick Tramp, who has decided to live beneath the flyover itself. No such quiet life, I suspect. The Chiswick Tramp has become a folk legend in these parts, no doubt due to the slogans written on pieces of cardboard that he displays outside of his grimy cardboard home. Past messages have included 'A vile and brutal country England' and 'Sum of cash stolen by English scum £5'. He seems to have it in for the English!

Chiswick High Road has a pleasant mix of charming cafés and boutiques. There is definitely affluence here. As I walked the High Road, I kept a beady eye out for another of Chiswick's folk heroes: a Polish street sweeper who has become nicknamed Ziggy Dust. He became a YouTube sensation after footage of him picking up litter from the street whilst executing some pretty flash dance moves emerged.

On 8 September 1944, the first V2 rocket to hit London fell on Staveley Road in Chiswick, demolishing six houses and killing three people. Plenty of famous people have been born in Chiswick including the comedian Mel Smith; the actress Dame Helen Mirren; the athlete Sebastian Coe; the engineer Edward Thornycroft; the singer Kim Wilde, and both Pete Townshend and John Entwistle from *The Who*.

I met up with my old mate Davo, who has a flat in Chiswick and knew that I would be popping down. He eagerly showed me his local haunts before we retired to his flat in a fantastically solid Victorian terrace. He loves living in Chiswick, even though it means putting up with his neighbour's erratic parking! After a comfortable night's sleep on Davo's couch, I made my way back down to the river.

I could see Kelmscott House on the other side of the river. William Morris lived here from 1879 until his death in 1896. Morris named the house after Kelmscott Manor, his home back upriver in Oxfordshire. As previously mentioned, Morris was a well-known socialist and the Hammersmith branch of the Socialist Party would often meet at Kelmscott House.

Hammersmith Bridge beamed resplendent with its green and gold paintwork. In what must surely be one of the most questionable forms of state-sponsored commercial advertising ever, the bridge was apparently painted to reflect the colours of Harrods, whose depository is situated at nearby Barnes. This wonderful cast iron suspension bridge was opened in 1887, and it must surely be one of the prettiest on the river. The IRA tried to blow it up on several occasions.

Hammersmith is one of London's key transport hubs and seems to me to be comprised of one giant built-upon roundabout sat just to the north of the A4 flyover. Little remains of the old Hammersmith village, and I found myself wandering through a giant soulless shopping centre right in the centre to find some food. Feeling uninspired, I decided that the best thing to perk me up in this situation would be a MacDonald's. I normally try to find something a little more authentic or independent, but all the walking had kind of got the better of me. Anyone visiting Hammersmith might be forgiven for thinking that this London district is much closer to the Thames than it actually is, due to the looming presence of a grand ship-shaped office block called The Ark, completed in 1992. I quite like it, but I suspect that it is not to all tastes.

Notable past and present residents of Hammersmith include the stonemason George Wimpey (1855-1913), and the scholar Edward Johnston (1872-1944). Hammersmith is popular with actors - Alan Rickman, Hugh Grant, and Mischa Barton have been one-time residents. There must be something funny in the air in Hammersmith as it has been home at one time or another to three of Britain's funniest comedians: Bill Bailey, Lee Mack, and Sacha Baron Cohen.

As I walked between Hammersmith and Putney Bridge, I could see the London Wetland Centre whose bullrushes and reeds gave me a reminder of what the river was like back before I hit the big urban metropolis. Fulham Palace, county home of the Bishops of London since the 11th century, lies on this stretch of the river. The Bishops vacated the Palace in 1973, and it is now a museum and café. Over the years, the various bishops introduced new species of trees into England. The tamarisk, the acacia, the American magnolia and the maple all made their first appearance here.

The current Putney Bridge was designed by Sir Joseph Bazalgette and opened in 1886. Bazalgette is most renowned for creating central London's sewer network. The civil engineer also created the Thames Embankment, giving the city a significant part of its character that it retains to this day. The white stone Putney Bridge strides across the river and is unusual in that it is the only major bridge in Britain to have a church at both ends, in this case All Saints and St Mary's, Putney. All Saints Church is the burial place of ten Bishops of London. St Mary's Church was where the historical Putney Debates took place between Oliver Cromwell and the Levellers in 1647. Ideas such as 'one man one vote' and Parliamentary constituencies being defined by population rather than wealth were discussed here for the first time. These ideals would go on to influence The American Constitution written over 100 years later.

Londoners have flocked to Putney for centuries to enjoy its open spaces and clean air. Putney Heath was a well-known rendezvous for highwaymen. The district has been the starting point for the annual University Boat Race since 1845, and it is known as one of the most significant centres for rowing in Britain with over twenty rowing clubs based along the embankment. Notable past and present residents of Putney include the former British Prime Minister Clemente Atlee; the entrepreneur Sir Richard Branson; Queen bassist John Deacon; the author Nigel Williams, and former decathlete Daley Thompson.

I was soon passing through the district of Wandsworth, which grew up around the mouth of the River Wandle, the largest tributary of the Thames in London. In addition to being well-known for being London's oldest industrial area, Wandsworth is also famous for being the home of The Ram Brewery, which, until it closed in 2006, was the oldest continuously working brewery in Britain, having started operation way back in 1581.

Just visible from across the river from Wandsworth is Hurlingham House. Built by Dr William Cadogan in 1760, the house is where polo was first introduced into England in 1874. The governing body of the sport is known as the Hurlingham Polo Association. I was now entering the Borough of Battersea. St Mary's Battersea is a delightful church that sits right upon the river nestled amongst several residential tower blocks, including the giant imposing ski ramp of the Montevetro building. In 1782, the poet and artist William Blake married Catherine Boucher here at St Mary's.

Prior to the Industrial Revolution, Battersea was mostly farmland, providing food for the City of London. In 1929, construction began on Battersea Power Station which was completed in 1939. It would soon become one of the capital's most identifiable landmarks, resembling, as it does, a giant upturned table. It became famous worldwide when it was featured on the cover of Pink Floyd's 1977 album *Animals*.

More recently, plans for a major redevelopment scheme at Battersea Power Station have been approved, and it is being turned into a huge mixed-use complex. Notable people who live or who have lived in Battersea are G.K Chesterton, Harry Hill, Rich Hall, Vivienne Westwood, Rick Parfitt, Bob Geldof, Simon Le Bon, chef Gordon Ramsay, and the anti-slavery campaigner William Wilberforce. Battersea is also home to the famous Dogs and Cats Home.

I had decided it was time to do a bit of exploring into Chelsea, just north of the river. The Chelsea Design Centre is certainly an upscale place, and only the well-heeled are likely to be able to afford the wonderful products and interior design services on offer here. Many of Britain's top interior design and fittings companies are here: interior specialists Colefax and Fowler; Nicholas Haslam; Porta Romana, and Zoffany, plus some wonderful bathroom equipment manufacturers including luxurious free-standing baths from Victoria and Albert and brassware from Samuel Heath, one of Britain's few remaining tap manufacturers.

The whole place was eerily quiet on the day of my visit. Apart from the occasional well-dressed individual who darted from store to store, I felt as though I was walking through a museum. However, despite the lack of custom, the mirror-polished obsidian black Rolls Royce complete with chauffeur that was parked up right outside the main entrance gave me the impression that this place doesn't actually need that many customers to survive!

The word 'Chelsea' originates from the old English term for a landing place on the river for chalk or limestone. Chelsea is well-known for the affluence of its inhabitants. No doubt helped by recent reality shows such as *Made in Chelsea*, the Chelsea set are often referred to as 'Sloanes' or even 'Sloane Rangers' after Sloane Square in the borough. The term 'Chelsea tractor' was coined as a reflection of the amount of (mostly unnecessary) four-wheel drive vehicles that predominate in the borough. Chelsea is home to one of the largest communities of Americans living outside of the USA, with over six per cent of Chelsea residents having been born in the USA. The list of notable people who live, or have lived, in Chelsea, is very long indeed, with just a few being: Charles Cadogan, 8th Earl of Cadogan; J.M.W. Turner; Oscar Wilde; John Betjeman; Eric Clapton; Mick Jagger, and Mark Twain. One of the wittiest comments I have ever come across was made in a conversation between Mick Jagger and George Melly. On being told by Jagger that his wrinkles were laughter lines, Melly retorted; 'surely nothing can be *that* funny!'

The King's Road played an important part in Swinging Sixties' London. Much of its legendary status is in its association with the British punk movement as much as the Sloane movement. Malcolm McLaren opened his punk clothing 'Sex' shop here.

It was a hot day, and many of the pubs along the road had thrown open all the doors and windows that they possibly could. The excited, high-pitched voices of a couple of precocious Sloane girls pierced my left ear as I walked past the window of one pub. Soon I had exited the hustle of the King's Road, and I was traipsing through Cadogan Square. I cut up past the magnificent red brick cylinder of the Albert Hall, and I threw myself into the welcome tranquil embrace of Hyde Park; a sea of tranquillity after the madness of the city. Soon, the diesel engines were just a distant hum as the grasses grew taller, and the park's trails began to undulate. I found a great spot to grab a bite to eat and lay sprawled out on the scented grass beneath the hot sky. A while later, I walked down the wider gravelly paths on the outer fringes of the park. Cyclists and joggers buzzed past me, and excited people congregated in small groups.

Park Lane is a magnificent boulevard flanked on one side by Hyde Park and on the other by grand buildings that include The Dorchester Hotel; the 101 metre tall Hilton Hotel, and some very exclusive car dealerships. However, all is not well in this part of the capital, and the media has made much recent comment on the Roma gypsies that congregate and sleep rough in the underpasses that cross under the busy road.

Whilst the vast majority of immigrants to Britain have no criminal intentions, the Roma in London have been associated (rightly or wrongly) with a sizeable chunk of the capital's crime. Crime in London reflects the extreme rich/poor polarity across modern Britain as a whole. Whilst some of the capital's crime is masterminded by the seemingly homeless Roma gypsies of Park Lane, much extortion, fraud, and all sorts of high-level corruption are organised from the salubrious flats and hotel rooms that tower over it. A sizeable portion of West London's prime real estate has been bought up by all sorts of shady characters. Bill Browder, the founder of the massively successful Russian Hermitage Capital investment fund, has claimed that Britain is a 'Brothel for dirty Russian money.' Browder, a fierce critic of Russia's Vladimir Putin, has claimed that the Belgravia and Knightsbridge economies are levitating on dirty money.

A good distance down Park Lane I turned off down Mount Street and disappeared into the exclusive warren of Mayfair streets. I breezed past Scott's restaurant which is frequented by many a well-heeled celebrity. Outside another restaurant, a posh black four-wheel drive screeched to a halt, practically abandoned in the middle of the street, and a flustered Gordon Ramsay, the craggy-faced celebrity chef du jour, hotfooted it into what was presumably one of his top notch eateries. I craned forward to peer through the windows, catching glimpses of his surprised and enamoured diners as he sashayed past. 'Give me Rick Stein any day!', I sarcastically muttered to myself as I motored on.

It seemed that in this part of the capital every other car is a black Bentley Continental (you soon grow tired of seeing them!) and that every other building is home to an asset management company. I caught a fleeting glimpse of a Damien Hirst butterfly painting in the lobby of one company.

Picadilly Circus is a panoply of lights and sounds, and it looked wonderful all lit up even before the sunlight had completely retreated. Tourists were standing around the famous Eros statue in a blaze of photograph flash bulbs, and it filled me with pride to be around so many people happy to be here in Britain. The frenetic streets of Soho are an assault on the senses. City slickers, rickshaw pedallers, beggars, and precocious fashion queens scoot along the streets crossing into restaurants, bars, cafés, and God-knows-what manner of seedy joints in this pulsating square mile of entertainment and pleasure.

Once dominated by the sex industry, Soho is now just as well-known for its media companies, restaurants, and upmarket clubs. This area was once grazing farmland until it was acquired by Henry VIII in 1536 as a Royal Park for the Palace of Whitehall. The name 'Soho' is believed to be derived from a former hunting cry. Having been at the centre of the Beatnik culture in London in the 1950s, Soho had become a serious music centre by the 1960s, being home to the legendary Marquee Club and Trident Studios.

Soho's last great dandy, Sebastian Horsley, died in June 2010 from an overdose. Horsley was an artist, writer, and bon viveur. His often eccentric artistic feats included travelling to the Philippines to undergo a genuine crucifixion, which he did without painkillers. I remember seeing an incredible documentary about this. Both fascinating and disturbing, Horsley's spirit will no doubt haunt the salacious streets of Soho for many years to come.

I took a walk down Denmark Street, known as Britain's Tin Pan Alley. Although not particularly long, this street was once crammed full of music shops, rehearsal rooms, and recording studios. Jimi Hendrix, Donovan, and The Rolling Stones are just a few of the bands that have recorded here. In a sad reflection of our times, much of Denmark Street is to be demolished in a major redevelopment of the area.

After another perusal and a few pints in Soho, I headed into Chinatown to find some food. After peering through quite a few windows, I found a very reasonable 'All you can eat' buffet. The place was quiet and relaxing. The presence of a member of staff napping on some chairs at the back of the eatery added to the serene feel of the place. I watched as the hectic Soho nightlife flittered past the window and left the restaurant full and light-headed after a few glasses of wine. That night, I checked into the pleasant but sprawling Travelodge in Covent Garden.

CHAPTER 14

Into The Sea

The following morning, I made my way through the throngs at Covent Garden which was once a fruit and vegetable market. The market relocated to Nine Elms in 1974 and, since then, the area has become associated with entertainment. I had to work my way through the streets a little in the upriver direction to rejoin the Thames at the Houses of Parliament.

Designed by Charles Barry in the mid-19th century, the present day Houses of Parliament were opened in 1867. They sit next to the River Thames, so as not to be surrounded completely by rebellious mobs. The river outside the Parliament building is the only restricted area on the navigable Thames, to help protect Parliament from acts of terror. However, the British people all know that the greatest act of attempted terrorism on their parliament came from underneath it, not from outside of it. On 5th November 1605, Guy Fawkes was caught attempting to blow up the Houses of Parliament in the famous Gunpowder Plot.

The Houses of Parliament are located in one of the most recognisable buildings in the world, and have certainly been the most powerful in the world for a long period in their history. The most famous part of the building is the 98-metre-tall clock tower, more popularly known as 'Big Ben'. The name 'Big Ben' actually only refers to the hour bell of the clock which chimed in the tower for the first time on 31 May 1859.

I spun round on my heels and continued my journey downriver along the Thames Embankment. Built in 1889 by Richard D'Oyly Carte, The Savoy Hotel was the first hotel in Britain to have electric lights. Its guest list is long and illustrious. Marilyn Monroe, Mae West, Greta Garbo, John Wayne, Noel Coward, and Errol Flynn are just a few of the celebrities who have stayed here. Vivienne Leigh met her husband Laurence Olivier in the foyer; George Gershwin played piano in the ballroom, and Elton John left a bath running whilst taking a phone call, causing a leak in the room below!

I walked along the Victoria Embankment, the construction of which was completed in 1870 under the direction of the civil engineer Joseph Bazalgette. Standing 60-foot-tall, next to the Thames, and just a stone's throw from the Savoy Hotel, is Cleopatra's Needle. The obelisk was presented to the British in 1819 by the Turkish Viceroy of Egypt, Mohammed Ali. Six lives were lost as men battled to save the needle when it was swept off its pontoon in a storm in the notorious Bay of Biscay. It was finally lifted into its present-day position on the Embankment in 1878.

This got me thinking that we rarely consider the price paid with people's lives in the construction of various monuments and structures around the world. It is all too easy to marvel at some wonders of the world without thinking about those who have toiled to build them. Five people were killed during the construction of the Empire State Building, ten people were killed during the construction of the Channel Tunnel; over 100 were killed during the construction of the Hoover Dam, some being rumoured to have fallen into the setting concrete and now entombed by the dam itself. Remarkably and thankfully, nobody died during the construction of the Eiffel Tower.

Walking further along the Victoria Embankment, I was surrounded by a panoply of famous landmarks. Next door to The Savoy is the imposing facade of Shell Mex House. Built in the 1930s, this was the original London headquarters of Shell Petroleum, and its huge art deco clock face, the biggest clock face in London, became known as 'Big Benzine'. Across the river, I got an impressive view of the London Eye which, when it opened in 2000, was the tallest observation wheel in the Western Hemisphere.

Much of London's South Bank was extensively redeveloped for the staging of the 1951 Festival of Britain. This event featured many visions of the future of Britain, and it proved a welcome boost to a nation still very much in the shadow of WWII. Festival Hall is the only remnant from the festival, and it was the first post-war building in England to become Grade I listed.

A short distance along the river's South Bank sits the Oxo Building, home to one of the canniest pieces of marketing ever. Advertising restrictions meant that the Liebig Extract of Meat Company could not erect advertising signs to publicise their product. To get around this they added a 67-metre tower to their packing and storage centre that spelled out 'OXO' in glazing bars on the windows on all four sides. Today, the OXO Building is home to apartments and shops. Beyond the OXO Tower, I could clearly see The Shard. Standing some 310 metres tall and completed in 2012, it is the fourth tallest building in Europe and the 104th tallest in the world.

My journey soon brought me to London's celebrated

Waterloo Bridge. The present bridge opened in 1945 and was built mostly by women as most of the men were away fighting. This fact has led it to being frequently referred to as 'The Ladies Bridge'. Due to its position at a bend in the river, the views from Waterloo Bridge are widely considered to be some of the finest in London, and I must say I would have to agree. The views from this bridge were the inspiration for the song *Waterloo Sunset* written in 1967 by Ray Davies of The Kinks. One individual whose memories of this bridge wouldn't have been so happy would undoubtedly have been those of the Bulgarian dissident Georgi Markov, who was stabbed by a poison-tipped umbrella whilst waiting for a bus on this bridge in 1978. He was injected with a fatal ricin-filled pellet by an agent of the Bulgarian secret police in an assassination assisted by the KGB.

Deciding that it was time for some more exploration of the Big Smoke, I turned away from the Embankment and pressed on towards the City. I turned right onto The Strand. The famous city landmarks just kept on coming. Somerset House was an impressive sight in the blazing sun. The Strand soon gave way to Fleet Street, home to Britain's thriving newspaper industry until much of it relocated to Wapping in the 1980s. Up ahead, I could see the dome of St Paul's Cathedral nestled just in front of a clutch of skyscrapers and mid-rise buildings. Many of the views of St Paul's are protected. It is only in the last ten years or so that many of these new towers have appeared. For over 20 years, the City of London only had one true skyscraper – The Natwest Tower, or Tower 42 as it is known today, built in 1981.

Not everyone is particularly enamoured by London's

latest clutch of skyscrapers, Prince Charles being one of them. I must say, however, how much I am a fan of the skyscraper if used in the right context. London, in my opinion, has so far got it right. I have always loved the contrast between the old and the new, the rustic beauty of old stone buildings juxtaposed with the monolithic glass and steel bastions of the new skyscrapers. I'm the sort of chap who would buy a quaint thatched cottage and fit it with a modern minimalist kitchen with ultra-thin stone worktops and brightly painted glass splashbacks, so I understand the way I see things may be very different from the traditionalist crew. However, I ask them to consider that why should we not use the best up-to-date building materials of our time to build or renovate structures? After all, the thatched cottage was likely to have been regarded as modern at some point. Everything is new at least once in its existence.

One of the things that makes London so fascinating to me is the way that it has developed two central business districts. The Canary Wharf development, just three miles or so to the east of the City, played an important role in the regeneration of East London. Work began in the late Eighties, but most of the skyscrapers here were not built until after the millennium. It is also important to note that the building of these skyscrapers has been less controversial than those in the City. Nevertheless, just as many skyscrapers seem to be going up in the City as have done in Canary Wharf, and London now boasts two gleaming clusters of 'scrapers'.

New York too has two clusters of skyscrapers – in Midtown and in the downtown financial district. However, in my opinion, the sheer abundance of skyscrapers in both these districts gives the skyline of New York a crowded and undefined appearance. Many more skyscrapers are under construction or planned for London in the next few years. A third cluster of skyscrapers is currently being developed in the Nine Elms region, next to the Thames.

London is classified by the Globalization and World Cities Research Network as being - along with New York - one of the two Alpha Plus Plus cities in the world. This makes them the leading two cities in the world; both being vastly more integrated within the global economy than any of the other world cities.

With a span of 37 metres, the dome of St Paul's is one of the largest church domes in the world. The present church dates from the late 17th Century and was designed by Sir Christopher Wren. It remained the tallest building in London from 1710 until 1962. Many people believe that the expression 'Robbing Peter to pay Paul' has its origins in the 16th century when part of the estate of St Peter's Cathedral in Westminster was taken to pay for the repairs to St Paul's Cathedral in the City.

Walking into the heart of the city with my backpack and hiking boots, I felt like a complete alien in amongst all the suited city slickers. I felt even more alien stopping to take the odd photograph. I don't know why there are so few tourists in this grand area. Maybe there are some unwritten rules for visitors to areas of 'extreme capitalism' that others are aware of but I am not! All around me, tall buildings reached for the heavens: 'The Gherkin'; 'The Cheesegrater', and one of the newest, 'The Walkie Talkie' building. During the construction of the latter, it was noted that the concave design of the building focused light onto the streets below, leading to temperatures that could damage cars and burn carpets. The press renamed the building 'The Walkie

Scorchie'. A permanent awning has now been installed to prevent this occurring.

These shiny new towers of trade must be truly inspiring places to work in, not least for the wonderful views across London that most workers must be afforded. However, it is not just Prince Charles and English Heritage that have shown a dislike to these. Some have speculated that these brand new towers are harbingers of economic doom as well as being 'blots on the landscape'.

Much like the hemlines of women's skirts, which are said to rise in times of increasing economic prosperity, so too are new skyscrapers believed to be symbolic of economic shifts. In a 2010 article for *Bloomberg*, Mark Gilbert commented on how skyscrapers in London have traditionally been the harbingers of doom. He speculated how the upcoming building of skyscrapers such as 'The Cheesegrater' and 'The Walkie Talkie' would in actual fact be the foundations of a double-dip recession. In fact, as it were, a double-dip recession was only narrowly avoided.

Gilbert pointed out how London's newest skyscrapers have always demonstrated this trend. The Post Office Tower (completed 1964), The Natwest Tower (completed 1980), and One Canada Square (completed 1991), were all indicators of recession in their day. This effect has also been demonstrated on a worldwide scale. Both The Empire State Building (completed 1931), and The Chrysler Building (completed 1930), were completed at the start of The Great Depression. A month after the completion of the one and a half billion dollar Burj Khalifa, Dubai needed a ten-billion dollar lifeline of funds to avoid defaulting in the worldwide recession of 2008.

There didn't seem to be any hint of recession as I strode

into The Royal Exchange, once the heart of the City's markets, now an uber high-end shopping mall. If I felt out of place with my rucksack and hiking boots on the streets of the City before, I sure felt it then. The girl at the desk in the plush art gallery honed into the plastic carrier bag dangling from my hand with laser eyes. I have to admit that I was deliberately holding a carrier bag to attract attention to myself and throw a two-fingered salute to the ubiquitous wealthy 'in-crowd' that I was becoming rather tired of. 'Still', I resolved to myself, 'you will be in the East End soon'. I got the impression that she took pity on me as she struck up a conversation. But then, with my confidence growing, I realised that maybe she thought my downtrodden downmarket appearance might just be a ruse to hide my vast wealth. Wealth possibly accumulated working for some nondescript wealth management firm squirrelled away in one of the nearby winding side streets!

We whiled away the time talking about art, and the attractive young lady handed me some brochures. From what she was saying, she has sold art to many a well-heeled aristocrat. Whilst I cannot say I am a great fan of the British aristocracy and their privileged lives, I must say that I am a fan of the way the 'old money' crowd mostly seem to have no desire to demonstrate their wealth. A lot of them seem contented to drive battered old vehicles, wear generations-old clothes and live in some of the scruffiest old piles imaginable. The multi-billionaire Tetra-pack founder, Hans Rausing, comes to mind. After accumulating a vast fortune from inventing the square card milk carton (an invention that quite a few people might claim makes their lives more difficult than dealing with the original bottle containers that it replaces), Rausing, now into his 90's, insists on driving the same old beaten up Lada car.

The girl in the art gallery was becoming more and more animated. She told me about how she once closed a sale for a £450,000 painting at her previous gallery. She told me how she could find me almost any painting by nearly any notable artist in the world through her 'extended network of contacts', and I was sure she was right. If this hadn't been an art gallery situated right at the heart of the City of London, I would probably have thought she had entered into a fantasy world long ago. This livewire young lady then enthusiastically presented me with her business card. It was time to leave. I slipped back onto the streets of London, dreaming about the young lady I had just met. I imagined for one moment that I existed in her wonderful champagne glass-chinking, business hob-nobbing, giddy networking world of art and aestheticism.

Using my nose for navigation, I soon found myself enjoying the welcoming open space of Tower Hill, a large expanse of cobbled grounds sweeping down to the river with the towering architecture of the City as a backdrop. The White Tower was built by William the Conqueror in 1078. In 2007, Moira Cameron became the first-ever female Yeoman Warder at The Tower. Commonly known as Beefeaters, they were originally prison guards and have been around since 1485. The Beefeaters now conduct a largely ceremonial role, and there are 35 of them resident at the Tower.

From the pier down on the river I was afforded impressive views over Tower Bridge, the Armadillo-esque City Hall, and Southwark beyond. Sitting in the water, just moored off the opposite bank, is the light cruiser HMS Belfast. She was launched on St Patrick's Day, 17th March 1938, and is now a museum ship operated by the Imperial

War Museum. It has been calculated that if the six-inch guns in both the forward turrets were to fire, the shell salvo would hit Scratchwood Services located on the M1 some 11.7 miles away!

Just a few streets eastward away from The Tower of London, the opulence of the City begins to fade. However, there are enclaves sprouting up that hint at the 'money crew' taking over in the East End. Aldgate is bursting with new developments. Upscale blocks of new apartments jostle for position as the huge billboards outside boast of wonderful views over the City. I wondered how long it would be before this newfound wealth had marched all the way up through Whitechapel and overtaken Bethnal Green. I was quietly pleased with myself to have navigated my way from The Tower of London to Brick Lane just using my nose. I like to think that years of inquisitive exploration have left me with a well-honed sense of direction.

An ornate iron arch welcomed me to Brick Lane. I dropped all of my gear onto the floor of my cheap accommodation. My hotel was basic but clean, and the friendly receptionist was far happier to accept cash rather than my card. My rumbling stomach led me to a curry house I had walked past earlier. The promo guy out on the street had told me about a 'curry for a tenner'. After a large bottle of Cobra beer and a generous tikka massala and rice, I wondered if ten quid was the real price. It turned out it was. Wow! This is incredible, I thought as I floated my bloated belly through the front door. Brick Lane is famous as the 'curry capital' of the UK, and I wasn't about to dispute this. You may well be aware of this already, but the vast majority of Britain's Indian restaurants are not run by Indians at all but by Bangladeshis, and a large number of these come from the city of Sylhet.

I set off up the road to explore some more of Brick Lane and Bethnal Green. For centuries, the East End has been the first port of call for many of Britain's immigrant communities. I darted along busy Bethnal Green road for a couple of blocks before crossing back down to Whitechapel. The Blind Beggar would be just like any other traditional British pub if it weren't for playing witness to one of the most notorious events in Britain's gangland past. On 9th March 1966, Ronnie Kray shot and murdered George Cornell, an associate of rival mobsters the Richardsons, as he was sitting at the bar. The incident was portrayed in the classic 1991 film *The Krays*. With the sun crackling in my eyes, I couldn't make out a thing through the tinted windows.

With some trepidation, I pushed the entrance door, and it ground open. With such a reputation, and not being able to see in first, I wasn't quite sure what I was letting myself in for but, to my relief, the place was home to a jovial atmosphere. A lively middle-aged couple sat near the bar and, through the door to the garden, I could make out a hip young crowd with all kinds of facial piercings and roll-up cigarettes having a good time. I sat down on a secluded bench and enjoyed a couple of pints considering that fateful night when Ronnie Kray sent George Cornell to meet his maker just yards from where I was sat.

As I was relaxing with my cider, a stocky and slightly shifty-looking young chap breezed through the entrance doors. He walked right up to my table and stood right in front of me, looking past my head at the wall behind. 'Alwight?', he said in a vacant manner with a strong East-End accent. 'Y-es', I nervously replied wondering if history might be about to repeat itself (I have a knack for finding myself in the wrong place at the wrong time!). It transpired that, rather than deliberately trying to freak me out (which he had started to do quite successfully), he was reading the only placard in the pub dedicated to the Krays.

'There used to be much more memorabilia in here like this,' he began, 'but I don't think that they want it anymore.' 'That's a shame,' I replied, turning round to take a look at the placard myself. 'Are you local?' I enquired. 'Nah, I live in the West End, but my grandad comes from round 'ere. It's all changed, now though. It's more multicultural.' It's always good to hear the views of people even if they don't approve of things, I thought. Despite his gloom, I didn't feel that this chap held any particular bad feelings towards the local ethnic communities.

The East End of London has been an area of change for a long time. Few things demonstrate this better than the Jamme Masjid Mosque on Brick Lane which, prior to 1976, was a synagogue catering to a large local Jewish population. Immigration returned to play a big part in the May 2015 general election with the surprise outright majority win by the Conservative Party. Opinion tends to be split on the effect immigration has on existing local populations, particularly in inner city areas such as Bethnal Green. Some say 'white flight' occurs simply when immigrants move in, whereas others have stated that both whites and non-whites will move out of an area when they are economically able to do so. What is for sure is that the immigration argument is set to rumble on for years, and it certainly played a central role in Britain's momentous June 2016 'Brexit' EU Referendum decision to part company with the EU.

I exited The Blind Beggar and tumbled along the

monstrously busy Whitechapel Road with its smorgasbord of tumbledown market stalls and veiled women. I couldn't believe my ears as I squeezed past a line of three women in full body black burqas. The leading woman hollered words which I simply cannot put into print here. Let's just say that it was a much more colourful version of 'I should have slapped her'! Maybe I should not have been surprised at the similarities they displayed to many Western women; I just didn't expect such a terse opinion to be issued loudly from somebody dressed so conservatively! The burqa may well effectively cover up how a woman appears, but it certainly cannot cover up her opinions!

One of the joys of walking amongst strangers on busy streets is picking up on these little snippets of conversations that are often surprising, if not arresting. A little further down the road, I overheard two bouncers on the door of what I could only describe as a 'strip pub' talking about how funny it would be if the punters could hear the sort of mundane things that the strippers spent their time talking about, such as how to repair a broken washing machine! The East End is truly a great place to hear the gossip. Maybe I won't be so critical next time I watch *EastEnders*! A lot of it really goes on down this way!

The following morning, I made my way along Commercial Road back to join the Thames. Canary Wharf is an imposing sight, and I once heard it described as a 'chunk of downtown Chicago that has been scooped up and dropped into East London.' I like that. It was well worth the nerve-wrenching, near suicidal runs across various busy roads and interchanges to get there. All around, the vertiginous monuments to capitalism raced up towards the open skies. Canary Wharf was originally constructed in 1937 to handle cargoes of fruit from the Canary Islands. The massive regeneration of the area occurred in the 1980s, and Canary Wharf is one of the largest commercial developments in the world. Standing at 235 metres tall, One Canada Square was Britain's tallest building from 1991 until 2012. This accolade now goes to the 310-metre-tall Shard.

Trekking south, I passed Canary Wharf and traversed the neighbourhood of Millwall on my way back to the bank of the Thames. Isambard Kingdom Brunel's great ship, Leviathan, was built at the John Russell shipyard in Millwall. Later renamed the SS Great Eastern, she would remain the world's largest ship for 40 years. The famous photograph of Brunel standing in front of huge iron chains was taken at this shipyard during the construction of Leviathan.

I was soon passing beneath the Thames in a wonderful tunnel constructed by another celebrated engineer - The Greenwich Foot Tunnel was designed by the civil engineer Sir Alexander Binnie and was opened on 4th of August 1902. The northern end of the tunnel was damaged by bombing during WWII, and a thick inner lining restricts the size of the tunnel at this end. It is quite a surreal feeling walking through this 370-metre long cast-iron and concrete tube that sags down lower in the middle before curving back up to the exit at the other end. As dismounted cyclists breezed past me pushing their buzzing bicycles, I cast my eyes up upon the roof and imagined the monstrous Thames and its sediments flowing just a few feet above. The spiral staircase at the southern end led me back up to street level and onto some fine views of the city and the docklands from the South Bank.

Built on the Clyde in 1869 for the Jock Willis Shipping Line, Cutty Sark was one of the fastest tea clippers to be built and also one of the last, as sailing ships gave way to steam propulsion vessels. These days, she sits resplendent atop a glass roof that resembles a wave. The nation looked on aghast in 2007 as images of this magnificent vessel on fire were beamed across our television screens. After initial suspicion of arson, the conclusion of an investigation into the blaze pointed towards the most likely cause being a vacuum cleaner that had been left switched on over the course of a weekend. After a restoration reported to have cost up to £50 million, she now basks in the sun in her South London glory all over again.

I was now ambling along the streets of Deptford. This area of Lewisham has quite a few claims to fame. In 1577, Francis Drake left Deptford to become the first Englishman to sail around the world. Deptford was also home to the first yacht to be built in Britain in 1661. The world's first artificial fertiliser was manufactured at Deptford Creek and, in 1889, the world's largest power station was designed and built here by the electrical engineer Sebastian De Ferranti. Deptford is where the band Dire Straits formed back in 1977, and it is also home to one of Britain's largest Buddhist communities.

The Royal Naval College at Greenwich stands on the site of the medieval Palace of Placentia. Henry VIII was born here in 1491, and Elizabeth I made Greenwich her favourite summer residence. Queen Mary II turned Greenwich into a naval hospital, and this remained so until 1869 when the Royal Naval College took over. Today, it is part of The University of Greenwich, and a real hive of activity with students blazing to and fro as I walked past the main entrance.

High up on the hill in Greenwich sits the Royal Observatory, the first observatory in England. In 1884, at the International Meridian Conference, it was voted that Greenwich should be the location of the Prime Meridian, partly to do with the observatory's pioneering work on calculating new ways of timekeeping. Ever since then, the world sets its clocks by Greenwich Mean Time. The Prime Meridian is used by ships as the reference measure on their charts and maps.

I was filled with anticipation as I trundled through the light industrial hinterland of the Greenwich Peninsula, very close now to my journey's end. There was a huge controversy about the £600 million cost of The Millennium Dome project. Few people knew it at the time, but The Dome itself had cost 'only' £43 million to build. The developers were forbidden from disclosing costs at the time, leading to much speculation as to how it cost £600 million 'just to build a big tent!' It is not until you get up close to the dome that you can fully appreciate the complexity and beauty of this building. The 100-metre-tall yellow support spindles are far bigger than they appear from even a short distance away. Giant steel cables whoosh out from concrete blocks in the ground and up onto the giant dome. Amazingly, the entire roof structure of The Dome weighs less than the air contained within the building!

Over my head the Thames cable car, or Emirates Air Line, to call it by its official name, elegantly airlifts people to and fro across the river. Emirates Air Line will certainly hope people call it by its official name after spending £36 million for it to bear its name for the next ten years. Transport for London had initially budgeted for a total cost of £25 million for the cable line service when it opened in June 2012. However, this soon spiralled to £60 million after they forgot to take into account such things as project management, land acquisition, and legal costs. Quite mandatory requirements one would think!

As I reached the end of the Thames Path, beside the Thames Barrier at Charlton, I reflected back on my journey. A journey along a river that runs like a silver thread through the history of Britain and, indeed, through a sizeable chunk of the history of the modern world. The Thames winds its way past hundreds of important historical sites such as Runnymede, where the Magna Carta was signed; Windsor, home to the world's largest occupied castle, and last but not least, London, once the most powerful city in the world, which is today, alongside New York, one of the world's two most powerful cities. World-renowned centres of innovation and learning are dotted along the river, such as the Culham Science Centre, the Rutherford Appleton Laboratory and the University of Oxford.

So much of Britain's industrial might and innovation has been provided from right across the nation, not just this small part of the kingdom that I have traversed. Without continued decentralisation, London will continue to remain an effective city-state, vastly more powerful and interconnected than any other British city. The British are an innovative and brilliant people, despite their appetite for occasional melancholy and reservedness. Britain's recent decision to withdraw from the EU will test our innovative capabilities to the maximum and, despite the predictions of the doomsayers, I think Britain will shine brightly in this brave new world.

Printed in Great Britain
by Amazon